GOLDEN GOALS, RUSTED REALITIES

Work and Aging in America

GOLDEN GOALS, RUSTED REALITIES

Work and Aging in America

Dr. Richard Mowsesian

NEW HORIZON PRESS
Far Hills, New Jersey

Distributed by
Macmillan Publishing Company, New York

Library of Congress Cataloging-in-Publication Data

Mowsesian, Richard.
  Golden goals, rusted realities.

  Bibliography: p.
  Includes index.
  1. Aged—Employment—United States. 2. Life span, Productive—United States. 3. Work—Psychological aspects. 4. Identity (Psychology). I Title.
HD6280.M68 1986   305.2'6'0973   86-21805
ISBN 0-88282-024-9

This book is dedicated to my wife, Ila, who with me strives to live the work and aging process gracefully. It is dedicated also to John, Nora, Satoor, and Varteni, significant others who have experienced the aging process while devoting the major portion of their lives to the work activity.

CONTENTS

PREFACE

Researching, writing, talking and thinking about the aged and aging can be traumatic. The emotions evoked affect all human beings similarly and yet differently: the old because others perceive them to be old; the young because there is a growing awareness that they too are aging.

Growing older is an experience we all live through, regardless of when we first realize it. In this respect, we are all alike. But this is where the similarity stops. Our activities, life experiences, and daily living are unique, making each of us special and different. The longer we experience the aging process, the more dissimilar we become. We are all born with the same set of "givens," comprised of genetic makeup, family group, time in history, and community; and while of the same order, are also individual in that no one of us experiences them in quite the same way. Yet it is because of these "givens" and our unique life experiences that we are so different from each other. As we live, grow, learn, work, interact and experience each of life's mercurial dimensions, our differences become highlighted. Such differences become more and more pronounced the longer we live.

This book is about people experiencing the aging process and how it relates to a principal life activity—work. Since living and experiencing the aging process as well as the activity of work is with us constantly, they affect every facet of our lives. Therefore, this book is also about those major dimensions of society and our social institutions which have direct impact on the aging process and the work activity. It is important to include society's dimensions in our analysis since it—through its social institutions—treats individuals as being homogeneous rather than addressing their uniqueness.

One cannot examine any aspect of the aging process and the work activity without getting involved in moral, ethical, social and personal issues. Complete objectivity is impossible. We are all caught up in the process since we each are personally

affected. We are talking about ourselves as well as those significant and not-so-significant others in our lives. For each of the
issues explored we will see ourselves or see others with whom
we are personally or intimately involved. The viewpoint expressed herein involves the need to be concerned about ourselves in our growing-older process. It is in this way that we can
also be concerned about others. The picture we will be present-
ing is not necessarily pleasant or happy, nor is it one with which
everyone will agree. We believe it to be representative. As a
result, we must ask, do I want this to happen to me? Is this how I
wish to be viewed by others? Is this how I want society to affect
me?

Much of the literature concerned with aging in America
treats the topic in a generally impersonal way. It is as if the older
population is an amorphous mass to be treated as one. Yet, the
evidence overwhelmingly supports the individuality of people
who make up the older population group. The impersonal
treatment of older people—more particularly the older worker
—has resulted from society and its institutions arbitrarily
defining who is and is not old. Such impersonality and definition of old is particularly noted in the political process which
has resulted in legislation which perpetuates it. It also is noted
in questionable labor market practices which are particularly
evident in the work environment.

Economists, sociologists, gerontologists, as well as
writers and researchers in other disciplines have, in effect—
whether intentionally or not—placed older people into "age
ghettoes." In an effort to break with such stereotypical views,
this volume examines aging and work by bringing together
offerings from history, economics, social and developmental
psychology, education, medicine, and politics. It is believed
that examining our topic from such a broad perspective emphasizes the importance of viewing aging as a uniquely individual process which society—through its institutions—has
chosen to ignore. Such a perspective portends the possibility of
increasing the options as to how one wishes to live his life
without being relegated to an age ghetto, the only exit being
death.

Certainly work, in its broadest definition, is an important
activity throughout the aging process. Most people will work

forty or more years for pay. Others will work many years for no pay. To be concerned about work is to be concerned about *all* people who engage in the activity, regardless of its form or associated rewards. America is being challenged with a new array of issues and problems having to do with the quality of life. It is older workers, perhaps, who are singularly the most disenfranchised group in choice of lifestyles and participation in helping to resolve problems emerging in the changing ethos. This is especially true in the work arena. And yet, it is this very same group who has contributed the major portion of their lives to the development of this country through their work who are arbitrarily rebuffed from continued participation upon reaching a socially-defined age. It has been their efforts in the work place that have contributed to the changes and the emoluments now enjoyed by the younger generation. Older workers suffer the ultimate in job discrimination. They are frequently denied employment even though they have demonstrated skills and exhibit no physical incapacities.

A fundamental thesis of this book is that older workers are a grossly overlooked human resource who have much to contribute to resolving the ever-changing problems with which society is confronted. We believe than an examination of issues and problems associated with the under-utilization of this human resource is merited.

It is hoped that this study will have particular interest for all those who are concerned with America's problems associated with an aging society. As a result, they may begin to perceive that—as human service workers—they can be more effective when they attempt to work *with* older people rather than focusing on what they can do *to* or *for* them, which has in the past been the focus of most support programs for older people.

ACKNOWLEDGMENTS _____ _____

No scholarly endeavor is the result of one person's effort. Certainly the errors and omissions as well as the strengths and weaknesses are the author's responsibility. This is no less true for this volume. Several individuals and groups, however, have had a profound effect on my views, my thinking, and in my completing this work. I would be derelict in not acknowledging their contributions to me as a person, my development as a professional, and to the completion of this work. First, the seeds for this volume were germinated while I was an advanced study fellow at the Advanced Study Center of the National Center for Research in Vocational Education at Ohio State University. The study center's contributions of time, money and support allowed me the freedom and resources to begin my basic explorations on this topic. The University of Texas at Austin, through the Department of Educational Psychology and the Institute of Human Development and Family Studies, has been generous and supportive in more ways that I can specify. My mentors and colleagues throughout my professional career have been instrumental in both my personal as well as my professional development. They have often been my sounding board, contributing their ideas, and causing me to reach beyond that which I thought I was capable. To them I owe a great personal debt. Those who have a particular impact are, in alphabetical order, Robert A. Divine, Royal B. Embree, Jr., Gail F. Farwell, Leo J. Goldmen, Earl Jennings, H. Paul Kelley, Guy J. Manaster, Robert H. Mathewson, Robert Peck, Jackson B. Reid, and John W. M. Rothney. Students in my seminars, classes, and in tutorials have also made a major contribution. They have uniformly been my sharpest critics. Through their penetrating questions they have helped shape my views and organize my thoughts. Sandy Dicus performed the yeoman task of typing the original drafts of the manuscript. The magnitude of her contributions can never be adequately acknowledged. Valerie Stephenson typed the final draft and suffered through the birth pangs of the author. Last, but perhaps the most important, is Blanche Debenport. It was her persistent editing, while she flew all over the country, that finally got this manuscript into some comprehensible form. To you all, my deepest and heartfelt thanks.

Richard Mowsesian

INTRODUCTION

American society has been expressing concern since World War II about the rights and values of the ever-increasing number of its older citizens, and is expected to continue the debate well into the next century. As the ranks of the aged grow, society must consider how best to cope with their specific problem—that to be old in a work-oriented industrial society such as the United States is to be relegated to being a non-person.

Regardless of the bases for a work ethic, man historically has survived because he was willing to work throughout his life. Industrialization of society, which was the result of man's inventiveness and intellectual genius, drastically altered his relationship to the work activity and the lifelong need to work.

To be old in a modern industrial work-oriented society is to be ejected, as Alex Comfort notes, ". . . from a citizenship traditionally based on work. In other words, it is a demeaning idleness, non-use, not being called upon any longer to contribute, and hence being put down as a spent person of no public account, instructed to run away and play until death comes out to call us to bed." To be denied access to the work ethic environment is to be denied recognition of one's ability to exercise his responsibilities as a citizen.

The modern-day model of old age as a depressive time of decline and frustration is a legacy inherited from the Industrial Revolution. In a prior era, to be old and still contributing to self and society was to be venerated and emulated by the younger generation. This was due to the visible manifestations of the years of accumulated wisdom and skill of the elders; and to the importance of a work ethic which called for demonstrating the material acquisitions resulting from lifelong work; usually land, house and animals forming the legacy to the younger generation. Through hard work, judicious decision-making, and a conservative, thrifty attitude, each generation added to the legacy of previous generations. In sum, the elders of a family group were, in a sense, the caretakers of the family wealth. In this model, aging was truly a gradual lifelong developmental process that had few points of ambiguity.

Industrialization and the modernization of society altered the work ethic and undermined the elder's role. Accumulation of wealth as a result of hard work became somewhat less visible, taking the form of less tangible assets such as those represented by bankbooks, stocks and bonds, rather than the family farm, ranch or plantation. Members of the younger generation witnessed individuals going to and from work rather than working at home or in the family environs. The value of the individual worker who had knowledge and skill associated with the diversity of a total work activity gave way to job fragmentation and the routinization of the assembly line. This tended to subordinate the individual to the institution. External organizations and agencies became the repositories of knowledge. It was these external groups rather than society's elders which transmitted skills and knowledge needed to be developed by youth. As the older person's roles were taken over by organizations and social institutions, the concept of retirement for all workers was introduced. The traditional work roles of older people were usurped by industrial technology, and were not replaced by any alternatives other than retirement.

The work ethic which held together pre-industrial generational groups was no longer valid. Changing work ethics, however, as with other cultural mores, lagged behind the rapid social changes. Elders, infirmed, women and minorities were the ones to suffer. Without work and a clearly-defined work ethic to sustain them, older citizens suffer the indignity of becoming non-persons. Technocrats "... replaced wise old men as repositors of knowledge: The aged no longer served as the medium by which skills were transmitted from one generation to another," R. B. Calhoun wrote in his book, *In Search of the New Old*.

THE SOCIAL CONTEXT

With urbanization and social advances, the importance of work and the aging process has become a social concern. In a more rural, agriculturally-oriented era, family constellations and small community groups assumed an interdependent relationship in sharing work and the care of older individuals. All work which was perceived to have value was rewarded and revered. As one aged in this milieu, he or she built up credits that were "cashed in" when his or her productive contributions were curtailed or reduced. All members of the family unit and small community groups assumed varying degrees of responsibility for the welfare of each other, regardless of age. These close-knit relationships began to erode when—as a result of industrialization—formations of large urban centers began. The previously close-knit family units and community groups began to assume modified relationships as well as geographical boundaries.

Due to restricted living space, urbanization gave rise to loosely-defined neighborhoods and altered family structures. As they reached young adulthood, people moved from the immediate family to form their own family units. They assumed new jobs being created by changing technology. As individuals aged they became more dependent upon social institutions for their own care and maintenance. Rather than older persons receiving their expected rewards for lifelong productivity from their internal social world, they became dependent upon their external social world for a more impersonal distribution of these rewards. Within this altering social context, growing older was a process one dreaded rather than looked forward to. To be old was to be obsolete, discarded, and forced to be dependent on the largess of an impersonal external society.

The work environment was perhaps more harsh in its treatment of people as they aged than were changing social conditions. Whereas the "one-life, one-career" concept was rewarded in early work environments, the rapid modernization of society made this concept obsolete. During the post-World War II era, the prevailing attitude in the United States was to continually make room in the work place for younger workers, an attitude which was similar to those prevailing during the 1930s. The economic prosperity experienced during the 1950s and 1960s was such that the cost of maintaining non-productive individuals (youth and elderly) was assumed to be affordable by society. Since the 1970s, however, this belief has been eroded to a point that policy makers, communities, and individuals have begun to reassess its validity. They are beginning to seek new alternatives to the care, maintenance, and continued productivity of older citizens.

At the same time, society's demands for consumable goods—especially during the decade immediately following World War II—was such that it was the youth to whom business and industry turned for the innovations and creative ideas needed to keep pace. Moreover, as the effects of modernization of society impacted upon older persons in society, they were shunted aside in favor of youth. The older work force who, in time of national emergency produced much of the goods to preserve a threatened United States society, were cast aside once this emergency ended, through traditional as well as newly-instituted early-retirement practices, ostensibly to lead the "good life" of ease and comfort. The "hype" of the marketeers achieved the objective of creating and perpetuating the myths of growing old as a leisure activity. It was the growing number of older people who began to rebel against these myths and sought to expose the reality of their plight. Changing demographics, brought on by the reduced birth rates of the late 1960s and through the 1970s, may alter our future perceptions of older people's value as continued participants in the labor force. These, as well as a new social awareness about growing old, may expose as false the traditional myths about aging in modern American society. Recent concerns related to the survival of the Social Security System, the introduction of lifelong learning concepts as being an important aspect of life, and programs such as Senior Community Programs seeking to place older people back into the work environment are examples of changing social perceptions and attitudes about aging in American society.

HUMAN IDENTITY

The importance of work as a means to identify who and what we are long has been an article of faith in the United States.

The value and worth of a society, as well as individuals within their society, has been evaluated throughout the ages on the basis of the work they perform and their productivity. Since World War I, the United States was perceived by others as the industrial nation to be emulated in terms of its productivity, industriousness and quality of its work force. It was during this same period that the United States became a youth-oriented society and developed social systems and institutions relegating older workers to a secondary status. It was also during this era that myths associated with the inability of older workers to continue their productivity began to gain acceptance, giving rise to sophisticated retirement plans and programs. Finally, it was the influence of these beliefs which perhaps brought about the broad theory of disengagement which assumed, in part, that gradual withdrawal from work and associated work activities, as well as withdrawal from continued active social participation, was a life stage to be associated with older people.

No one specific event or factor can be identified with the changing negative perceptions of older people as workers in a work-oriented society during the past fifty years. It was a combination of factors which denigrated age in relation to work. In essence, this forced older workers out of the labor force and into a position of dependence upon the largess of an external society over which they have little or no influence. Their identity as valued and important contributors to society is curtailed and denied. Society is saying that we no longer want older people to be independent and autonomous over their lives; instead we want them dependent upon society to make the decisions which will govern their remaining years. American society, through its benign neglect of older people, has relegated them to a human "scrap heap," to be stockpiled as outdated equipment, not to be recycled until they have rusted out (died) or a national emergency necessitates reactivating them for temporary duty. Such is the perceived identity of an older person, though few people will overtly admit to this concept. All social systems and programs designed to assist older people in maintaining themselves in this "human stockpile" are also designed to foster dependency upon the system, rather than independence *from* the system, though this was not the intent of the framers of existing systems and programs. Only those older people who had the foresight or were affluent enough to maintain economic independence are not dependent upon the "system." They, however, are few in number.

Denial of a continuous involvement in a work-oriented environment is a socially-imposed value designed to accommodate a rising youth population and a rapidly-changing industrial technology which is trying to keep pace with society's demands for goods and services. With these changes has come a devaluation of work as being important in and of itself. Where workers in the past enjoyed some of life's satisfactions in a "job well done" and were looked upon as good workers, enjoying the status of the transmitters of skills developed over a lifetime of effort, they are now basically operators who guide the machines which do the work. In many situations, computer technology has been employed to assume even this task, negating the need for the traditional worker. Work and its satisfactions are no longer seen as being as important as they once were. Movement toward more technology has resulted in an apparent surplus of workers, at least in some manufacturing areas. The worker—and more especially the older worker—has been, in a sense, rendered obsolete at a time when he is physically, psychologically, and socially more able to work for longer periods of time than ever before. Society's coping mechanism for these changes has been to introduce early retirement, thus denying older workers access to an environment in which their personal identities traditionally were defined. Apparently, we have yet to define alternative life activities which can substitute for the importance of work.

In our nation older people are living longer and many are now rebelling, asserting that they belong in the mainstream of American life, too young to be shunted off to the "scrap heap" of non-valued, non-productive human beings. They are not willing to continue to behave in the assumed traditional behavioral styles, and they refuse to suffer society's benign neglect. Many older people feel that the traditionally-assumed behaviors which society has defined for them are no longer appropriate. They want to assume their rightful place as responsible, important, and contributing members of society, in spite of society's systems of caretaking. L. Rukeyser has suggested that, as a result of changing demographics, the strain on past social systems designed to care for people in their old age is creating discontinuities between the young and the old. He further suggests that this could result in an "age war" in American society. Perhaps the early signs of non-traditional, non-conforming behavior by older people—those trying to retain or redefine their identity, worth and dignity as human beings— will further exacerbate these discontinuities. Today older people are trying to project a clearer, more optimistic picture of their rightful place in society, one which has been clouded and denied them during the past fifty to seventy years.

1

AGING AND WORK — ASSUMPTIONS

During the last decade, a national focus on the aging American population has been influenced by at least two factors. First, the plight of the older American as a socially-disenfranchised segment of society was the topic of the 1971 White House Conference on Aging. While one authority, H. J. Pratt, appeared to be pessimistic about this conference—calling it "Symbolic Politics"—there did emerge some positive outcomes as a result of recommendations forwarded to the President. These resulted in Congressional amendments to both the Older Americans Act, and the Age Discrimination in Employment Act, among others. Also, this resulted in both the establishment and expansion of social services to the aged, for example, nutritional programs to feed the frail elderly, funding to train professionals to work with the aged, increasing Social Security entitlements, and initiating and strengthening various advisory councils such as the Federal Council on Aging, and federal bureaus such as the Administration on Aging.

Government has become progressively more involved with older citizens' concerns. This is the result of an industrialization which highlights the dire poverty being experienced—especially by older persons—in growing metropolitan industrial centers. The onset of the 1930s Depression was a visible manifestation of this poverty and emphasized the need for some form of "insurance" to provide financial income upon retirement from the labor force. This need culminated in the enactment of the Social Security Act of 1935. Its intent was to solve extreme unemployment problems and prevent the collapse of the United States economy. The passage of this act effectively and arbitrarily defined who was or was not old and how an individual might or might not continue to function—at least as a worker in society—upon reaching that arbitrary age.

The number of persons initially affected by this action was relatively small. Society—concerned about large-scale suffering due to unemployment—was convinced this was a proper course of action for both the individual's and society's welfare. In fact, during a time when there was wide-scale despair, this act contributed to the development of attitudes and beliefs for a brighter, more assured future. In a Maslovian sense, people began to believe their basic needs could be met in their lifetime if they worked hard and aspired to the "good life." Less visible, though no less important, has been the progressive involvement of state and local governments. Private sector involvement with aging concerns has also escalated, for example, development and improvement of private pension plans, pre-retirement planning programs, and expansion of private nursing home facilities.

A broad base of public and private support for assisting older persons has emerged and has received a major stimulus from the conclusions and recommendations resulting from the 1971 White House Conference on Aging. Most such governmental and private actions have given rise to short-term intervention programs which have been modified or revised to meet older people's needs as they have been identified. Legislative action has a long way to go in recognizing the need to implement a long-term aging policy which takes into account the active participation and continued contribution of older citizens in a developing and expanding society.

The visible increase in the numbers of older persons has also contributed to society's rising awareness and concern with aging in America. Their sheer numbers, as well as increased costs associated with older citizens' care and maintenance, has made aging an issue of national significance. It is of special concern for those who have retired, those who are unable to work due to physical disabilities, and those whose sole means for financial independence is Social Security and the social welfare system. Thus, by association and changing attitudes during the last fifty years, those who are retired from the labor force for whatever reason are arbitrarily defined by society as "old," regardless of their retirement age.

In 1900, there were approximately three million people who were sixty-five years of age or older in the United States. By 1950 there were over twelve million, and by 1970, nearly twenty-three million. By the year 2000, over thirty million older persons will comprise the age group of sixty-five and older (20 percent of the population). Some authorities estimate that improved nutritional programs, generally-improved health, popularization of programs designed to encourage good health practices and physical fitness, and possibilities for medical advances which will cure deadly diseases will enlarge the ranks of our older citizenry.

Other estimates suggest that the combined financial outlay for old-age assistance, health care, medicare and disability compensation amounted to $135 billion in 1979, and will exceed $800 billion by the year 2000. The discrepancies seem to be due to differences in types of expenditures included in the estimates. However, regardless of the numerical discrepancies, the magnitude of these figures is sufficient to raise concerns regarding society's relationship to an aging society. For how long and to what extent will society be willing to support older Americans at an increasing level of funding? Finally, when the large wave of the World War II baby boom reaches retirement age, it will substantially increase the aging population of America and increase interest in that segment's concerns,

especially as these concerns are mirrored in labor force participation rates.

THE ISSUE

Researchers, practitioners, and policy-makers lack extensive and systematic examinations of the concerns of the
aging, though some recent efforts have been initiated. Such
examinations suggesting long-term directions as well as future
policy determinations associated with aging in America are
badly needed. Previously, the primary focus in dealing with
aging issues in the United States has been designed to suggest
programs and activities which assume doing *"to"* or *"for"* the
aging population. The national effort has been concentrated on
developing and maintaining a series of social welfare programs
for old people. Very little time or attention has been devoted to
designing policy strategies and programs which involve doing
"with" aging persons. Such helpful documents as the Federal
Council on Aging's *Annual Report* relate some efforts in this
direction and suggest some future possibilities. However, there
seem to be very few systematic examinations of issues surrounding the relationship of aging and work as an avenue to
helping resolve some of the current as well as future problems—
encouraging older Americans to participate in resolving their
own dilemma. One reason this issue has not been of major
concern in the past is the relatively recent observable increase
in the numbers of persons in the older age group, with the
attendant increase in the costs of maintaining them. Other
reasons for previous lack of concern have to do with defining
the group in clearer terms and coming to grips with the diversity it manifests, both within and without the labor force.

It would be erroneous to continue to assume that an
aging American population is a homogeneous group, even
though Federal legislation appears to assume so by virtue of
their chronological age. As people grow older it seems easier to
overlook the fact that they come from widely diverse backgrounds, experiences, and lifestyles. It is the combination of
these factors which determines the degree of their hetero-

geneity, and suggests that the aged—rather than becoming more similar as they grow older—in reality become more diverse. It is appropriate to examine issues related to aging and work, given the multiplicity and diversity of concerns with an aging society, the visible increase in the numbers of older persons, their diversity as a group, and society's changing economic and productive needs. Through such a research focus, policy-makers, researchers and practitioners can devise appropriate strategies for making long-term decisions. The design for such an approach, however, has not been forthcoming.

Implementation of recent guidelines such as the Age Discrimination in Employment Act, prohibiting employers from discriminating against persons between the ages of forty and seventy, has apparently clouded the issue of who is or is not considered aged or old. In the business community this particular piece of legislation has created a degree of consternation concerning retention, promotion and retirement policies. The popular American definitions of aging people as a homogeneous group has resulted generally in the following:

1. a tendency to mask political, social and economic issues associated with aging
2. a lack of cost efficiency in programs designed for the aged
3. lack of a coherent and coordinated Federal policy on aging stemming from a short-sighted Congressional approach to the problem.
4. widespread uncritical acceptance of the notion that individuals who reach a certain chronological age are to be set aside from the mainstream of society ostensibly to make room for others, e.g., Toffler's "throwaway society"
5. the belief that government should assume the major responsibility for the care and maintenance of older people, similar to stockpiling or putting into mothballs outdated and obsolete military equipment

These last two points are a somewhat jaundiced and

inhumane view of persons who contributed their work, energy and money to the development and expansion of today's society which has allowed Americans to enjoy a living standard unequaled in history.

Paralleling the increased numbers of older Americans and the prospect of living longer is a pervasive belief that persons who reach a certain "magic age" can no longer be productive and contributing members of society, especially on the job. Older Americans are caught in the time trap of "obsolescence," which W. Wirtz, author of *The Boundless Resource*, referred to as ". . . a human convention that became a reality because it first became custom." J. O'Toole, author of *Work in America*, identified this "time trap" as "Retirement, the activity of the aged. . . ," and went on to assert that this activity ". . . occurs increasingly in 'leisure communities' cut off from the rest of the world, both spiritually and physically." Both these views assume that the "linear life plan," referred to by Stern and Best in the book, *Relating Work and Education*, is a functional way for society to behave, and that all persons go through life in a similar linear fashion—education for youth, work for adults, retirement for the aged. More importantly, the linear assumption leads to a "reactive" style of problem-solving—dealing with problems as they arise—rather than a "proactive" style which anticipates problems in terms of developing programs and activities based on available knowledge, such as population statistics.

AGING AS A PROCESS _____

All persons experience the aging process, beginning at birth and terminating with death. Thus, a paradox is introduced as part of aging, which is important for some on theoretical grounds, but not always so important for practical purposes. Some aspects of aging do begin at birth and are simultaneous with the individual's development, especially if one examines the process from a purely physiological perspective. But it is more logical to think of aging as a process that begins soon after the initiation of growth and more convenient to think of aging as a process which becomes of concern when one has become an adult. Regardless of when one perceives aging to have begun, *it is a process which is a common denominator for all people and an experience with which both individuals and groups can identify, regardless of age, sex, ethnic persuasion, or point of onset.*

The rapidity and degree to which the onset of aging is manifested and realized varies from person to person and is influenced by unique genetic characteristics, lifestyle, health, environmental press, and often uncontrolled chance factors having an impact on society, such as economic recession, war and epidemics. Because aging is common to all persons—as well as being uniquely individual—and because the number of those who are simultaneously experiencing this process will continue to increase for at least the next twenty-five to fifty years, society—as well as the individual—is facing crucial issues. These will affect the welfare and future of society. They will influence changes in social as well as individual values, especially as these changes affect our perceptions of older people. They will certainly, through development of social institutions, influence society's manner in dealing with an increasingly large dependent sub-group of the population.

The physiological, social and emotional changes one experiences during the aging process are, for the most part, gradual and often not realized until some outward manifestation is evident, such as the first gray hair, first facial wrinkle, physical slowdown in bodily reaction time, reaching age forty, fifty or sixty, death of a parent, family member or close friend, retirement of close associates at work. When these as well as other manifestations of aging are realized as occurring to self, they are usually unique to the individual, influencing self-perception in relation to society and the lifestyle with which the individual identifies.

Scholars, researchers and theorists from a wide variety of disciplines have attempted to describe, research and state postulates concerning the aging process. These activities are necessary to clarify which decisions need be made concerning the older person's rights and place in society, as well as to recommend programs implementing these rights for the affected persons. Developmental psychologists such as Erikson and Havighurst describe human development and life changes as growth stages. Others have attempted to account for and explain special change components affecting the person's progression through life, e.g., career decision-making, intelligence, physical development and socialization.

These theorists—and others with similar interests—originally formulated their constructs to apply to understanding the development of children, adolescents and young adults. At the time their postulates were formulated, older people were acknowledged but accorded little attention. Since World War II other theorists have recognized that there is more to living than education, work, retirement, death. They are beginning to question the rigidity of the linearity of life notion and the "one-life, one-career" imperative. They are recognizing that the range of styles and contexts within which an individual develops can be—and indeed is—variable across individuals and their life spans. The conditions of living are varied and social change is so volatile and rapid that traditional formulas for problem-solving appear to be becoming non-functional and subject to re-examination. This observation is emerging as true, especially in terms of the traditional views expressed about the process of aging, views upon which new social changes and value orientations are intruding.

Traditional opinion as to how society views who is or is not old is also in a process of change, and it is this opinion which determines what rights and entitlements should be established and implemented for the care and maintenance of older citizens. The implication of these traditional perceptions is that older citizens need to be cared for and to have certain activities done for them. Such a view does not seek strategies to work *with* older persons so they can continue to be in control of their lives in their aging process.

Several theorists have attempted to attend to these societal and value changes and their impact on older persons. Since the late 1940s, theories which have enjoyed the most popularity in the aging and adult development field have been called Activity Theory, Disengagement Theory, Adult Socialization Theory and Developmental Field Theory. Researchers have attempted to describe older adult behavior. Their descriptions and research have suggested programs concerning older Americans which in turn have influenced Federal policy concerning old age. Such theorists have helped to focus on a segment of society previously ignored and thought by some to be anonymous. They continue to be helpful in articulating economic, social and personal problems with which an aging society is attempting to cope. Finally, research generated as a result of theorists' postulates has revealed previously little-understood facets of aging—issues and problems never before articulated—and stimulated extensive research and new theorizing, and helped to stimulate the initiation and maintenance of economic, social and psychological assistance programs for older Americans.

Since the early 1950s, there has been a rising interest in and concern with studying the later stages of life. Accordingly, more researchers have investigated these theories and, in turn, refuted some postulates while supporting others. Through this scientific process, researchers have provided decision-makers with guidelines to enhance the legitimacy of aid programs for older Americans. In addition, this proliferation of research and the knowledge which results will encourage new theories and sub-theories which can only enhance our understanding of this aging process and the relationship of older persons to society.

Theories are heuristic devices, of course, used by researchers attempting to understand and explain the phenomena they are studying. As such, their findings are reported for others to read and use. Value judgments and inferences which result from theorizing are frequently influenced by the researchers' own beliefs and particular views about life, and the time in history that the theory was conceptualized and postulated. Theories on human development and subsequent research arising from them, however, are subject to a high degree of unaccounted variance which is not always clearly identified. Therefore, predictions about human development and behavior do not achieve the degree of precision one would hope, and are not carved in stone. What is of concern is that on the basis of researchers' results—which in turn influence changing attitudes—decision-makers suggest laws and programs which affect people in ways not always anticipated. This is especially true for older people who are dependent upon such decisions and laws for the quality of their existence. In turn, lawmakers are dependent upon those theorists and researchers who are perceived to have credibility.

While this may be interpreted as a simplistic view of how theory interacts with actions and assumes an over-inflated importance for theories and their attendant research, that is not the intent. What is intended is to raise a note of caution about research findings concerning human beings, since most actions that decision-makers have initiated and implemented concerning older people are designed to do something *to* or *for* older people, as long as they meet certain conditions. The result is that we are developing an increased dependence on our legislated social institutions to make the critical life decisions when someone reaches an arbitrarily-defined age, rather than assisting individuals to independently pursue their constitutional freedoms. In the past, programs and activities designed to assist older people to function in society frequently have been imposed on them without their having been consulted. Recent activities of groups such as the "Gray Panthers" and the National Association of Retired Persons are demanding some voice in whatever society is doing *to* or *for* older citizens. They want to be part of the "action" concerning themselves. In essence they are beginning to demand that they not be denied their inalienable rights to live their lives as they see fit. The key elements in maintaining individual autonomy regardless of age, however, are economic independence—which continued participation in the labor force makes possible—and the maintenance of good physical health.

SOME CAVEATS

It is appropriate and logical here to cite some caveats underlying this book's rationale, and to provide a base for understanding its plan. These caveats are:

1. Man in a democratic society is a free individual and as

such is able to make appropriate life-governing decisions. These are made in such a way as not to infringe on the rights of others. In freely making these decisions, man is willing and eager to assume the responsibilities and the rewards which are associated with this freedom.

2. Social, political and economic forces in an increasingly complex society are intruding on and pre-empting man's individuality and freedom to act independently.

3. Man both acts on and is acted on by his environment.

4. Man is denied a significant portion of his identity when he is forced to withdraw from his work for whatever reason, and when society pre-empts the decisions as to when and how he chooses to work. Without some form of work, man is unable to establish or re-establish his identity and place in society, a condition which results in social, psychological and eventual physical termination of life.

5. So long as man is physically, psychologically, and emotionally able to function in his society, then he is able to continue to learn and master those tasks he chooses and to employ those learnings in productive activities of his own choosing.

6. Mastery of tasks within developmental life stages is dependent upon one's perception of self to be able to master those tasks, the power and control one perceives he is able to exert in his environment, and the functional ability to perform both physically and psychologically in relation to developmental expectations as society allows these expectations to become manifest.

7. Human beings develop and age differently throughout the life span; thus, the older they are chronologically, the greater are the individual differences both within and between groups.

These caveats are the assumptions and tenets upon

which this book is based. The chapters which follow are intended to present justification for these assumptions and for ensuing recommendations.

Note: The term "man" is used throughout this book in a global sense and is not intended to discriminate between the sexes. The sex-identifying pronouns, e.g., he, she, him, her, will be used where appropriate.

2

WORK, THE CORE OF HUMAN EXISTENCE

Historically, the activity of work has been a focus in human beings' lives. Work has influenced a person's development both as an individual and as part of a social system. It has been the means by which individuals have striven to achieve higher-level needs for self-expression. As such, work as a traditional and ancient life activity has involved the expenditure of physical or mental energy in order to produce those goods and services which allow one to live, survive and express himself in his environment.

For most forms of work today, use of human physical energy has been reduced or replaced by machines, with the major output of energy for production of goods and services being mental. How and when an individual is to begin and terminate producing goods and services have been questions of only recent concern, and arose essentially as a result of the interdependence of individuals as a result of the division of labor, the development of industrialization, and attendant technological advancement. Today—and more importantly, in the future—these questions will become of increasing concern both to the individual and to society.

The onset of a person's work-life, while generally proscribed by age, physical development, education and training, and social mandate, is filled with anticipation, is socially approved, is encouraged and is monetarily and emotionally rewarded. Constructive participation as a productive worker at whatever age is perceived as a social "good." The key to such positive attitudes is the perceived social as well as self-approval of one's productive contribution to self and society. It is in this way that an individual develops an identity, senses his worth.

At the latter end of the spectrum, essentially in industrial and technologically advanced societies, the individual generally has been terminated as a contributor at some arbitrarily-defined chronological age. Ostensibly, an industrial society determines when an individual is "too old" to continue to contribute to the social "good." In a sense, this form of termination is society's statement of when the individual is no longer worthwhile: when he is to give up his identity, when he can no longer contribute to the welfare of self and others, and when he ceases to be able to make decisions surrounding his working life.

THE WORK CONCEPT — HISTORICAL EVOLUTION

All human activity continues to occur during the aging process. However, concern with aging has become more vocalized as the population increases, as this burgeoning segment of the population strains existing natural resources, as it becomes more visibly pronounced, and as it affects individuals personally, economically, socially and politically. Nowhere is the aging process more evident, more misunderstood and more discriminated against than in the employment sector which occupies a major portion of a person's life.

Although work has had meaning, value and status since the beginning of civilization, there was a time when it was recognized as important to individual as well as collective survival, so everyone—including old and young—was expected to work. The social value of work as a distinctive sphere of activity did not emerge until specialized work activities or, as some would express it, "division of labor," became important for the social group (e.g., some persons were more adept at making tools for community use whereas others were recognized as being more adept at hunting). As the techniques of herding and agriculture began to be developed to the point where production surpluses over immediate needs were common, there systematically emerged different kinds of specialized work as well as distinctions between workers (those who toiled) and non-workers (those who were chiefs). As these distinctions between workers and non-workers became more pronounced, the value component of differential work activities began to emerge. (These distinctions arose only when, due to ample and stable food supplies for some individuals, freedom from full-time work became possible). The code of Hammurabi and the Judaic code are early examples of values attached to work and of regulations set down to govern working behavior.

The concept of work being considered as toil, and thus to be avoided, evolved from the formation of ancient societies which began to develop class structures. In ancient Greece, and later in Rome, work was perceived as toil and not an activity engaged in by the ruling class. In both Greece and Rome, slaves were used to do the heavy labor and relieve the citizen from the "curse of work." Both Greek and Roman societies believed that citizens should own businesses and supervise agricultural efforts, thus work, but never labor as did the slaves. Handicrafts and the work of artisans were held in low regard and were to be avoided. Free men were to engage in more lofty activities, such as thinking of the great truths or practicing virtue.

The early Hebrews believed work was a painful drudgery but was necessary as a consequence of Adam and Eve's transgressions. Thus, as H. Borow said, "labor was a divinely imposed sentence" to expiate spiritual wrongdoing. Since early

Christians were Hebrews, Christianity followed the Judaic tradition in believing that work was a punishment imposed by God to atone for the "original sin." There was a positive note injected in this concept in that work was a means to accumulate wealth in order to share with others who were less fortunate. Sharing the fruits of one's labor was considered a way to enter into God's grace.

There were challenges to the early, more debasing views of work. Prior to the Christian era, Hesiod wrote, "Work is no disgrace," while Ovid, Christ's contemporary, is cited as saying, "When I die, may I be taken in the midst of work." The negative views of work as debasing did not change abruptly from generation to generation or from one era to another. Earlier value systems gradually were absorbed, adapted and extended from society to society and as social need dictated. After the demise of the Roman Empire, the decline of cities gave rise to two contrasting views concerning work. The landholding aristocracy of the Middle Ages believed that any form of work was ignoble, whereas the Benedictine Order felt that both manual and intellectual labor were religious duties.

As society developed through the Middle Ages, skilled artisans and craftsmen sold their services to the highest bidder, enabling them to experience a degree of freedom and autonomy. The concept that work was ennobling began to shift from the monasteries to the artisans, craftsmen and merchants as these groups emerged and were more in demand during the latter part of the Middle Ages. The path to wealth and power for these groups in the rising society was through work. What is important to remember about feudal society is that the only basis of human dignity for the "common man" was work. The nobility had the land; the common man had the brawn. Thus, if one produced, he had dignity, regardless of personal cost or degradation.

Religion was certainly a contributor to the evolving concept of personal dignity through work. It was the development of guilds, influenced by St. Thomas Aquinas, which demonstrated the value of work to the well-being of society. Under this system, profit was permitted, but only barely so. However, the ultimate goal under Aquinas's system was the hereafter. As the feudal system began to slowly disintegrate, there emerged a class society: the nobility and wealthy, the upper class; the artisans, craftsmen and merchants, the middle class; and the lower class, composed primarily of serfs, menial workers and servants.

The Protestant Reformation under the leadership of Martin Luther was a powerful force in spreading the concept that work was the universal foundation of society and formed the basis for social classes. Work, under Luther's interpretation, became the universal reason for living and to achieve the highest level of perfection in one's work was the ultimate service to God.

John Calvin also espoused hard work as the route to religious piety. Calvinism, however, added the dimensions of free choice of an occupation and the belief that it was morally acceptable to become wealthy through work. C. G. Wrenn, author of *Human Values and Work in American Life,* pointed out that a new dimension was added to the Christian work ethic as a result of Calvinism, the dimension of profit. The morality which emerged concerning work was that one could "pile up credits with the Lord" through hard labor and doing "good works," while still making a profit.

Puritanism, evolving from Calvinistic doctrine, expanded the work concept to include one's obligation to work. Puritans preached that it was one's moral duty to extract the greatest possible gains from work. It was considered a disservice to God in a most sacrilegious sense to wish to be poor. To prove that one lived within "God's grace," one worked hard, succeeded in his trade or profession, and demonstrably showed a profit. This brand of Protestantism considered that one had a "holy duty" to aspire to occupations and class status above that to which one was born.

The basis for modern industrialism and modern capitalism emerged from the value attached to hard work, the need to work, and the justification of profit. The original purpose for the more positive change in the value of work—from the pre-Christian concept of work as toil to work as an intrinsic good—was lost during the post-Reformation period. Work as a "good" became an activity to enhance and advance the self in society as opposed to work as a means to enhance and advance the self in "God's grace." This transition which took several centuries paralleled the transitions from a two-class to a three-class society. It occurred also as industrialization and advancing technology occupied society's concern for profit. As a result, fewer people were needed to produce the basic foods for sustaining life.

As society began believing in work as a "good" and as it moved from an agrarian to a manufacturing base, it began to invent subtle meanings for work and to specify divisions of labor. There began to appear degrees of "goodness." Work hierarchies began to form and to reflect one's status in society. The outcomes of these shifts resulted in the social values assigned to work on the basis of the kind of work performed rather than on working in and of itself. The social value attached to work provides an individual with an important social identity.

THE WORK CONCEPT —
19th AND 20th CENTURY
IN THE UNITED STATES _____

The value of work as a virtue was inherited from Europe and transplanted to the New England colonies by Puritans seeking religious and commercial freedom. The concept that one must work to survive resulted from the rigors of early pioneer conditions experienced by settlers in the New World. Those individuals who were non-productive or non-socially responsible were considered to be liabilities in their communities, to be shunned and ostracized. Not only was it necessary to work for self-survival, but also for the survival of others. The early settlers were mutually dependent in terms of sharing their knowledge, skills and physical abilities to work in order to establish themselves in a sometimes harsh and unyielding environment. The land was bountiful only in response to increasing toil. Thus, regardless of age, all persons as members of a family and of larger social units were considered to have worth and importance so long as they were able to productively contribute to self and society's welfare.

The concern for education and training of youth began intruding on an evolving work ethic as the expansion of the New World colonies progressed, as the colonies prospered, and as they recognized the opportunities that unlimited land and natural resources provided so long as they were willing to work hard and learn. No longer were those individual and social benefits which arose from the concept of "work as toil" so much a condition for survival. The emergence of class distinctions began to be evident as colonists perceived a lowered need to "brave the hardships inherent in colonizing the New World," and as the basic needs for survival (food, shelter, clothing) were reasonably abundant and surpluses could be exported.

With the institution of education in its many forms and at many levels, both in the home and established institutions, there began a shift in the work concept. Hard work combined with education and skill-training was the route to a successful life; hard work alone, while necessary, was no longer seen as sufficient. The traditional European forms of work role and social position were drastically altered in the New World colonies. The belief in hard work combined with the availability of seemingly unlimited arable land and natural resources—as well as the availability and desire for education—were principal factors in removing constraints toward upward mobility, status, wealth and prestige. These beliefs began to be more ingrained after the Revolutionary War. The establishment of the American Constitution set forth the four basic freedoms. These were interpreted literally throughout the loosely-woven Confederation of States. The westward expansion in the early nineteenth century reinforced and speeded up the belief that with hard work one could be and could achieve anything he chose, with education facilitating the process. However, throughout all the changes taking place, *all persons*, regardless of age, were still expected to contribute to the welfare of self and society. Only the young people began to experience a lessening of demand for their labors as formal education began to be available and consumed some of their time. Older people worked until they died, much the same as some older people today who still live on their own farms or are self-employed. Regardless of the changes occurring, the fundamental belief that work—especially hard work which resulted in externally observed products—was seen as something morally good in itself. This belief continues to be persistently glorified. Current writers are challenging this view as being relevant for the 1980s and 1990s.

That success and security came through hard work and that the concept of work as an intrinsic "good" persisted in the settlement of North America are obvious for several reasons. The fundamental belief in the Protestant Ethic was a basic value for the early colonists and continued to be the dominant ethic throughout the early development of this new nation. With the exception of black slavery in the South, the European concept of agrarian feudalism had little chance for success due to physical conditions encountered by the colonists and the nature and background of the colonists themselves. The non-technical development of the North American Indians restricted them to the hunting and gathering stage, making them susceptible to relatively easy domination. The concept of indentured labor— while introduced to early colonial society—did not succeed very effectively due to the extreme scarcity of labor, the abundance of open land, anti-aristocratic opinions, and the rise of manufacturing and trade. The rough frontier life of early colonial days and the rigors of the westward movement re-warded the combination of both physical and mental work. This combination led to such inventions as the steam engine, revolutionizing transportation and reducing the value of human muscle power for work; and the cotton gin, which led to a reduction in the need for large numbers of field workers and increased the production of cotton for export. This was quite different from European traditions where manual workers were not expected to think and thinkers were not expected to do manual work. Underlying these changes in work concepts was a continued pervasive religious connotation that the activity of work was sufficient in itself to provide meaning and fulfillment in life.

The rise of industrialism in America engendered further developments in attitudes toward work. The status and worth of individuals became not only a question of work but of the kind of work. Brain or mental labor took on a new value and status, displacing the importance of human muscle power. This shift set in motion the establishment and importance of work hierarchies which undoubtedly were established as a result of mental activity taking a preeminent position and machines preempting human muscle power, paralleled the movement from a pioneer agrarian society to an industrial society. These changes toward industrialization, originating in the fourteenth and fifteenth centuries, accentuated the division of labor, prompted harnessing steam and water power for mass production of goods, and led to the increase of commerce and trade between states as well as with other countries. However, the factor which perhaps affected individual workers most during this movement was the intensification of the division of labor. The implication was that the increased fragmentation of the work process, while increasing productivity, removed the worker from participating in forming the final product and firmly established the interdependence of workers and various forms of work as a condition for individual's as well as society's survival.

The shift from an agricultural to an industrial society and from the holistic work concept to the fragmentation of work into specialized components (which led to the concept of mass production) was gradual. The War Between the States brought greater focus on the need to develop technology (work of the mind) to increase mass-produced goods in orderly and systematic ways, and to accommodate a national social need. It logically can be concluded that for the first time the individual worker was subordinate to the welfare of the system in an industrially-oriented society. The very survival of the United States as a political entity envisioned by the founding fathers necessitated this form of individual subordination in order to resolve civil strife. It was during the next half century that the major changes in society and the American work ethic took place. Many historians perceived this time period as a most critical era, since major political, social and industrial reform movements began to take hold.

It was during this era that the concept of work was replaced by *occupation* as a means of determining the individual's status. It was at this point also that the *kind* of work one did—and not merely the fact of one's working—was the route by which individual success and status were evaluated. The more one used his brain to reduce or avoid physical work, the more one was esteemed and the more value attached to mental rather than physical activity.

The alteration of the work concept paralleled the social alterations which were occurring. The movement by workers toward industrial centers led to the demise of autonomous, self-sustaining small communities. The migration of people from rural environments can be attributed to two factors. Mental work resulted in a developing technology which allowed for fewer persons to produce more food for an increasing population and also created food surpluses for export to other countries. But in order to produce those industrial goods necessary for increased food production, there was a need for workers to congregate in central locations, thus forming urban nuclei. The need for more workers to produce an ever-expanding manufacture of a wide variety of goods at the expense of individuality began to erode the traditional work ethic and individual autonomy. Another factor affecting this erosion was the increase in immigrants who were willing to work at lower pay in the anticipation of advancing in a new society. In a sense this behavior was not too dissimilar to that of the indentured servant of early colonial days. As did the indentured servants, these new immigrants moved out of their bondage as quickly as possible to establish themselves as active participants in society.

It is logical to assume that with the rapid occurrence of social change combined with changes in the nature of work itself, the work ethic in America was also undergoing modification. Work was no longer a private affair in which the worker got satisfaction in seeing the finished product of his labor. Instead, workers were now in a "glass house" under the watchful eye of a supervisor who, if dissatisfied with efforts of the workers, would replace them. They were also under the impersonal surveillance of others who evaluated their worth by their performance.

These changes—which began during the latter half of the nineteenth century—gained momentum at the turn of the century, and came into full flower during the first half of the twentieth century. The more rapidly innovations such as automation became employed in the mass production process, the greater the profits to the manufacturer. At the same time that technological advances were being introduced in the industrial/manufacturing sectors of society, workers were experiencing greater fragmentation and specialization of their efforts with a corresponding decrease in the need for manual labor, reduction in hours worked, increases in leisure time, and an increase in workers' wages.

The freedom from "work as toil," experienced by most workers in the form of a reduction in hours worked, had led to an increase in free time. However, freeing workers from "toil" through industrialization also deprived them of ". . . involvement in the total production process as well as the possibility of self-realization," as cited by H. C. Kazanas, co-author of *The Meaning and Value of Work*. This has created problems far beyond any perceived by those who felt they were freeing man from back-breaking toil, problems with which we are still attempting to cope. It was believed that the modern age of machines would be a humanization of work, the humanization that today's "New Breed" of workers is demanding as their right.

Two world wars have led to increased job fragmentation and an accentuation of the individual subordinating self in the work setting for the good of the larger society. In order to produce the goods needed for war, increased mass production was mandatory. In order to bring both wars to successful conclusions, therefore, it was both patriotic and desirable for workers to suppress dissatisfaction with job fragmentation, since they perceived their efforts as contributing to an outcome with which they could identify. Another factor contributing to job fragmentation was due to the large influx of workers attracted by high wages into urban manufacturing centers. This was especially true during World War I, and seemed to reach a peak during World War II. This migration of workers from the farms to the cities was similar, in many respects, to that of the immigrants who flocked to developing industrial centers forty years earlier. These immigrants had to contend with poor working conditions, long hours, and substandard housing. (Project housing was built to try to relieve housing shortages during World War II, but in turn created social problems and instant slums with which cities were poorly equipped to deal.) The major differences experienced by the World War II immigrants from those of an earlier era was rate of pay. Pay for factory work during World War II was the highest in the country's history, providing an unparalleled affluence for the average worker.

The traditional work ethic was further eroded by these conditions, but this was not at issue during the war. Once the patriotic connection was removed, however, these same jobs became the breeding ground for job dissatisfaction. The mass production techniques developed for war production and then extended to peacetime production were to become the source of irritation for workers whose only means of retaliation was elevated absentee rates. Such attitudes were further exacerbated by the introduction of automated production techniques and, more recently, by the cybernetic revolution and advancements in high-speed computer technology. Traditional workers were becoming less and less in demand, which resulted in increased non-product-oriented service workers and reductions in hours. As the worker became less and less involved in the production of a product and as he perceived a lessening of importance of his role in the production process, there was seen a corresponding reduction in his personal involvement and commitment to work. Work began to take on the characteristic of a necessary activity to finance leisure time activities, rather than an activity which had intrinsic worth and dignity.

The American worker appears to have rejected that aspect of the traditional work ethic that work in itself has intrinsic worth. There have emerged two contrasting concepts as the work week has been reduced and wages have increased: hedonistic reactions and anti-materialistic reactions. The several forces of a modern society combined with automation and the elimination of traditional jobs have encouraged early retirement and other forms of either temporary or permanent withdrawal (increased use of drugs and alcohol) from active partcipation in the labor force. The changing work ethic, or at least its weakening, has led to workers experiencing identity confusion and a need for role clarification.

IDENTITY AND WORK _____

S. B. Sarason, author of *Work, Aging, and Social Change,* has stated that, "Work is one of the two major ways (our sex is the other) in which we define our personal identity and on the basis of which others presume to know what we are . . . Indeed our society encourages postponing the choice of a 'work' identity for sixteen or more years. . . ," thus delaying how the individual is defined by self and others, at least in the context of work. These two conditions—identity and delaying one's work identity—to which Sarason refers, are unique to modern society. It is questionable whether, prior to establishing work hierarchies, man was overly-concerned with his work identity. He was perceived to be either a worker or non-worker. As work hierarchies became established and later refined, however, one's position in the hierarchy became all-important in terms of social status and upward mobility.

The concept of job hierarchies established new criteria of "good" in terms of social value and esteem. A person's identity and worth were defined by his aspiration to a given level on a hierarchy of jobs within a given job cluster. The higher the job on the hierarchy, the more education was required, and the more intellectual activity was economically and socially rewarded. Thus, the traditional work values set forth through the Protestant Ethic of amassing wealth, influence and prestige were continually reinforced. Since industrialization, manual work has emerged to be a social negative, while intellectual work emerges as a worthy aspiration (shades of the ancient Greek and Roman civilizations). The moral virtues associated with working which identified earlier societies seem to have given way to more modern socially-assigned levels of prestige. There has been a vocabulary developed to distinguish between work which is valued, has status and prestige, and work supposedly lacking in such qualities. *Job* and *work* have become associated with some form of manual effort which holds a low level of prestige, whereas *career* connotes some higher level of effort which involves extensive training of the mind and is, therefore, worthy of aspiration and associated with a socially-sanctioned "good."

Sarason has presented a detailed description of how the above concept has been instrumental in instilling in children upwardly mobile aspirations and concepts of prestige toward work. Parents have never had difficulty in describing what they do not want their children to be. Their description is usually based upon their own backgrounds and experiences—positive or negative. Even today's parents who espouse the notion of non-interference in their child's ultimate career decision have some fantasized ideal of what is or is not acceptable. Parents are never neutral in this decision-making since almost universally they project early on at least two aspirations for their children: that they will receive as much formal education as possible, and that one day in the ambiguous future they will "be something" in some career. The imposition of these views by adults usually takes the form of a question posed to a young child: "What do you want to be when you grow up?" as if children have already formed detailed fantasies of how they view themselves as adults. This form of question stems from the "one-life, one-career imperative" view of Sarason, which assumes that once one makes a career choice, this is what he will be doing throughout his working life. Thus, the work identity one develops is assumed to be unchanging, and it influences the individual's relative social position and how he is perceived by self and society both now and in the future.

Daniel Yankelovich in his chapter, *The Meaning of Work*, presented four themes around which workers are identified within the context of the work ethic rooted in the Protestant tradition: good provider, independence, success and self-respect. The degree to which one has achieved to an acceptable level the standards related to those themes is quite readily determined by the work one does and the social group with which one identifies. Most people who work within a given career cluster and at some point in the work hierarchy of the cluster have some knowledge—to a greater or lesser degree—concerning the nature of the work performed. They are aware also of the economic rewards associated with that work effort. Thus, when strangers meet at a social function, they usually ask each other what they do for a living. On the basis of the response, they classify each other in terms of the nature and hierarchical level of the work as well as evaluating individual worth according to Yankelovich's four themes. While this may be a simplistic approach in the identification process, its effect on the socialization process is important. Decisions are made such as duration of the contact and how much and to what extent one chooses to make a future personal investment in the other. These decisions are especially important for those groups who are aspiring to high levels, both in their work and in society. Perhaps the group least affected by this form of identification are older adults who are more concerned with the quality of an individual's character than the work he does.

There is some evidence that the way individuals are identified within the context of work is changing. Younger adults seem to have a lowered preoccupation with the tangible assets resulting from one's work. The more important factor to identify others is the degree to which they are living self-fulfilled lives. Personal satisfaction has become the important criterion. It is evaluated in terms of personally fulfilling and meaningful work. This in no way is a rejection of the traditional work ethic of making money and achieving occupational status. It does diminish the traditional importance of material goods as the accouterments of success. Whereas in past years the size and cost of one's car, as well as the number of cars, and the size and cost of one's home were the material means to identify one as a success, today one is valued more highly if he owns an energy-efficient car (usually small) and smaller energy-efficient homes. The "New Breed" which Yankelovich describes is currently redefining how a person identifies self and how he is identified by society in relation to work. These changes affect how an aging America and the older person's perception to his relationship to the world of work are perceived and understood.

AGING AND WORK DEFINED _____

Both terms—age and aging—have about as many shades of meanings as there are definers. Both evoke different feelings and connote different concepts, depending upon one's experiences with life events associated with the terms, as well as an unquestioned acceptance of what is considered to be society's final authority: the dictionary. These definitions are helpful in that they provide a shorthand for communication in an agreed-upon way. As such, their definitions are the "rules of the game" in the meaning and use of language. However, language and its use, as well as the definitions of language, reflect the culture as the dictionary compiler and various authorities perceive that culture to be. Generally, the publication of agreed-upon definitions suffer the shortcoming of a time-lag relative to new usages, meanings and interpretations. These, I suspect, will become more pronounced as communication technology speeds up the usage of words, and as social change speeds up the different meanings associated with word usage. This is most relevant regarding the usage of "work," "aging," and their various synonyms, since their usage will undergo even more radical changes during the 1980s, and probably will in the 1990s.

Such highly-regarded authorities as the *Oxford English Dictionary*, and compilers of *Webster's Third New International Dictionary of the English Language, Unabridged*, have presented numerous definitions for work and for aging which can be presumed to reflect the commonly-accepted usages prevalent from the mid-1950s to the mid- or late-1960s. In essence, these authorities define work as an activity in which something is done or accomplished over a given period of time as a result of an expenditure of energy either physical, mental or both.

Aging implies change over time accompanied by a loss in essential qualities or forces which limit the degree of an object or organism's functioning. At this point, it is enough to state that aging is perceived to be a process which all humans experience.

The process is not uniformly experienced by all, however, which creates a problem in specifying who is or is not old. For our purposes, aging is not exclusively related to chronology, though that aspect is certainly an important component. Therefore, it would be erroneous to specify that when one reaches a certain specified number of years in age he is old. Rather, it is appropriate to specify for now that aging is a process which all persons experience differentially, and the process is related to their chronological, physical, psychological, social and emotional development.

Work, on the other hand, needs more elaboration. It has been said that the concept of work has been evolving slowly since man has attached value to it. The moral imperatives associated with work sustained man throughout the centuries. The moral imperative of work as a "good," signifying man's worth and dignity to self and society, sustained our colonial forebears in the building of this nation. As with most concepts, however, changes occur in their moral precepts, and with these changes come changes in definition; so it is with a definition of work.

As one examines the literature on work, regardless of theoretical orientation or academic discipline, one is struck by the almost uniform relationship of work as an activity in which people engage to produce a product or render a service for which they are remunerated either in money or personal gratification. Various scientists, sociologists, psychologists and economists, among others, generally define work as having these dimensions, although each discipline elects to emphasize different facets. Thus, the physical scientist sees work as a transfer of energy, physiologists focus on the amount and type of muscular energy expended by the organism, sociologists will refer to the energy expended by the person as he engages in the production of a product or delivers a service, and the economist sees work in terms of its effect on the economy, especially its production of goods and services. The psychological perspective of work emphasizes its continuous nature, whereas A. Tilgher, author of *HomoFaber: Work Through the Ages,* continues to impart the more religious connotation that man's natural predestination is to work. O'Toole denies the ennobling aspect of work as it is engaged in today, but rather sees work for most people as drudgery to be avoided whenever possible and engaged in in order to purchase those goods and services needed to sustain life and to enhance leisure activities.

Kazanas, *et al* conducted an extensive analysis concerning the meaning of work in American society. They concluded that a definition of work includes seven recognized and accepted factors. They are:

1. Work is continuous and leads to additional activity.

2. Work results in a production of goods and/or services and in some instances carries the connotation of the "efficient" production of goods or services.

3. Work is performed for a personal purpose, but these purposes may be:
   a. *intrinsic:* performed for self-satisfaction,
   b. *extrinsic:* performed for pay or to secure other forms remuneration.

4. Work requires physical and/or mental exertion.

5. Work is performed on a regular or on a scheduled basis.

6. Work has socio-psychological aspects in which certain relations must exist. Among those are:
   a. The macro-sociological aspect which deals with the relations of the worker to the society as a whole; and
   b. The micro-sociological aspects which relates to the worker's relationships within his immediate society of fellow workers.

7. Work involves a degree of constraint which is either externally or internally applied.

When these factors are examined closely, it is clear that a definition of work is not a simple matter. Therefore, the meaning and definition of work one uses must recognize the purposes for which the term is being used.

Our concern with work and its meaning is with regard to the aging process. Since aging is a life process and work is continuous in its nature, encompassing both internal and external human and societal factors, it is this theme we will follow as we examine the relationship of aging and work.

3

AGING AND WORK IN AN EVOLVING SOCIETY

The process of change, especially when it is abrupt, can be traumatic, full of risks, and sudden. Just as often, social change can be slow and peaceful, allowing society a period of time in which to adjust to new values, attitudes, beliefs and living styles. One such evolutionary change currently being experienced is the transition from a youth-oriented society to one that is more mature and adult-focused.

This transition may or may not be traumatic. Since demographers have been predicting it for some time, it certainly is not unanticipated. Yet, all social change is full of risks for those experiencing it. New values, new ways of viewing people, new lifestyles and new social institutions can be expected to result. Many difficulties will emerge as a result of change, due to the social meaning attributed to that change.

Work is still a major preoccupation in modern adult life, since its rewards provide the wherewithal to live and survive.

As such, work becomes a very personal and individual experience due to the decisions which are associated with it—what to work at, where to work, when to work, for how long. The process of aging is also a very personal experience which, when interacting with work, has a profound effect upon an individual's life course. Both these experiences occur within a social context.

The activity of work and the aging process can be conceptualized as occurring within two social contexts: internal and external. The internal social context is defined as having two components: 1) that aspect of the individual which is perceived of as the self and generally unique to the individual, and 2) that aspect which includes interactions with family, family units, friends and the immediate significant work and social settings with which one personally identifies. The external social context includes the larger and more ambiguous society to which the individual belongs, either through birth or self-selection, a society including his community, geographical region, state and nation. Thus, a person works at a job in a given work setting and the resulting material and non-material rewards of this effort have immediate impact on those with whom he is associated, and on the significant personal and social interactions which he experiences. Simultaneously, the energy expended in work affects the community, state, region and nation with which the individual identifies. The further removed one's work and personal life are perceived to be from the external social context, the more indirect are their perceived effects. In modern industrial societies the effect of collective action in the external society has a greater direct impact on the individual in his immediate context. This external social influence becomes more predominant as the social milieu becomes more complex and as governmental initiative supercedes individual initiative. Legislation, therefore, will have different effects on an individual (internal social context), although this legislation is intended to respond to individual needs and be uniformly implemented across the board to all individuals. The further removed one is from exerting influence on the external social context, the less potency he has on actions affecting daily living. It is this perceived social impotence and being acted upon as a uniform group that increasing numbers of older Americans are beginning to articulate and resist.

The Social Security Law with its various amendments and the Age Discrimination in Employment Laws are examples of society's impact on the individual. The larger society has legislatively determined—in an undifferentiated manner—at what point in time the individual can no longer be a productive worker and contribute to the economy, as well as how much economic support the individual can receive as a result in lieu of continued work. In some situations, especially when physical and psychological conditions would permit continued participation, social pressure influences individuals to retire from active labor force participation. As the external society's actions and social attitudes are formulated and institutionalized over time, individual autonomy and decision-making in controlling one's life directions are more and more eroded, resulting in a miniscule social impact by the individual. The proliferation of Federal legislation, especially during the last decade, affecting older people, is evidence of the larger society usurping the individual's autonomy under the assumption that older people are unable to engage in the decision-making process. This is especially true with regard to their continued participation in the labor force.

In any examination of the internal and external social context in which the individual works and ages, it is important to remember that society is not static nor stationary. It is in a continual state of evolution which is fast or slow depending upon the exigencies of different generations. These changes are experienced differently across generations and, similarly, within generations. They are similar in that social change is caused by and experienced by all in a given generational group. Changes are experienced differentially in that each individual and generational group experiences and affects social change from its own internal frame of reference and particular time in history. Consequently, different aged generations experience discontinuities with each other and with the external society as to values, lifestyles, individual worth and place in the social order. Uniform application of the larger society's rules and mandates rarely accounts for individual differences both within and between generational groups, and time in history tends to exacerbate differences and create generational discontinuities.

IMPORTANCE OF
SOCIAL CHANGE

Social scientists long have accepted the importance of reciprocal interaction between the individual and his environment, however, its effect is not equal. It appears to be tilting away from individual needs and concerns and toward those of the larger society as it becomes more and more complex and as government intervention, technology and industrial conglomerates exert more and more influence over society and its institutions. This is especially evident in times of national emergencies such as war and economic recession, which have intruded upon people's autonomy and development.

Erosion of individual autonomy has been aggravated in recent history as a result of industrialization, modernization, urbanization, the accelerated rate of new product development, and increasing Federal involvement, all of which influence daily life. Society has no precedent to suggest how both the individual and society can function and cope with changing social problems and the human needs which emerge as a result of modernization. Such problems as rapidly-changing employment, rising welfare costs, high inflation rates, increasing numbers of older citizens and changing values and lifestyles are examples of constantly changing social concerns and their attending problems. The speed with which society's changes are emerging outstrips and lags behind its ability to deal with and find solutions for the changing human condition. This, of course, assumes that society is responsible for dealing with or taking care of the individual who effects and is affected by these changes. Yankelovich perceives these changes as resulting in an emerging psychology of entitlement, ". . . the psychological process whereby a person's wants or desires become converted into a set of presumed rights" which "assume a growing belief that because the individual is born into the larger social environment, then that environment is obligated to fulfill those rights collectively."

Changes are accepted by society because of the meaning attached. Full acceptance of the resulting changes do not occur until long after they are part of the social system. What is more difficult for society to understand, deal with, and accept are the consequences of these changes and resulting changes in life-style, such as: drastic alterations in work, the increase in popu-lation—more especially an older population—reduced possi-bility of long-term job stability due to job obsolescence result-ing from technological innovation, and increase in leisure time.

Within the context of social change and changes in the nature of the work force, the work environment, and the nature of work itself, is the new phenomenon of old age. L. W. Sim-mons, author of the *Handbook of Social Gerontology*, reminds us that in pre-industrial societies old age was rare. Old people rarely comprised more than 1 or 2 percent of the population when age sixty-five is used as the delimiter. In 1948, India's older population was only 2.2 percent of the total. In the United States old people comprised only 4.1 percent of the population at the turn of this century. While social definitions of age vary from society to society, the phenomenon of aging is new as a social issue in modern industrial societies.

Social rites and roles in primitive societies were dictated by the degrees of contribution a tribal member continued to make to the total group's well-being. When the individual became a liability, his relationship to the group was terminated. While physical death is not the direct outcome in modern societies, a ritual of termination is often practiced through company retirement dinners which commemorate long and productive service. This form of ritual is modern society's method of ousting the assumed non-productive member from the social group with which the person has identified and to which he has contributed for a major portion of his adult work-ing life.

In more settled agrarian societies, the social rights and roles of the aged are more developed and articulated. This is due to their having stable food supplies, stable family structures, an organized community life, and generally agreed-upon lifestyles. All labor which is perceived as contributing to the maintenance of self as well as of society is perceived as valuable.

The nature of the work activity for the aged in such societies would be comprehended as a demotion by modern standards and thus the maintenance of self-esteem and status might be in question. However, if the work performed by the elderly in those societies is seen by others to have merit and worth, contributing to the family or the "social good," then work status might change without a reduction in self-esteem.

It may be that where physical work activity was valued at one life stage, the knowledge accrued over time or the ability to direct others becomes more valued with age. Of course, age alone does not qualify one for a responsible social position. Demonstrated past ability is an important attribute for an older person to gain high status in a social group. In most stable pastoral societies, the older group members are expected to perform those tasks which the social group identifies as necessary and contributory to the social and individual good. These older societies defined—through work performed—the role of older group members.

R. A. Ward, author of *The Aging Experience*, has concluded that "Older persons are better off in societies which allow for the acquisition and exercise of property rights and in which property is institutionalized and guaranteed by law." Acquisition of property is based upon rights rather than upon strength or abilities which can decline with age. In this way, ownership of property helps the aged exert power over younger members of the social group. This allows the older person the right to expect or demand deference. Youth are dependent upon the aged for the transmission of wealth and resources. This form of dependence is not as evident in hunting and nomadic societies where accumulation and retention of wealth and property is dependent upon physical prowess. The more prestigious position of the aged depends upon a stable society where changes involve normal and gradual transitions from generation to generation. Any social upheaval, such as revolution, epidemic, severe and prolonged economic recession, can upset this balance.

The respect an extended family accords older people contributes to their status, authority and respect received. The respect and position of older people in China and Japan, as a result of Confucianism and of ancestor worship, which antedates Confucius, is well-documented. The concept of "filial piety" was the cornerstone of the primarily agrarian Oriental societies. Since the family unit was believed to represent the larger society in microcosm, any negative act against the elders in the family was, in a sense, an act against the leaders of the society, thus to be avoided.

I. Rosow, who wrote *Socialization to Old Age*, suggests that a system of mutual dependence is one reason for the importance of the concept of the extended family in American society. The concept may involve repayment for services which older family members rendered earlier in life or may provide for continued opportunities to give and receive mutual support, whether the support be economic, social or psychological. In stable agrarian societies family size dictated whether this mutual support was located primarily with the nuclear family or in the extended family. The larger the nuclear and extended families were in pre-industrial societies, the greater the degree of security, status and respect the aged experienced. Apparently with the changing society, the aged have lost the security, status and respect previous generations assumed were their rights.

In *Aging and Human Development*, I. Press and M. McKool, Jr. condensed the bases of an older person's position in society into four prestige-generating components. They are:

1. *Advisor component:* older people have generated expertise which is useful to others.

2. *Contributory component:* valued contributions can be made to cultural, familial, or economic activities by older people.

3. *Control component:* Older people exercise a mono-

poly over necessary objects, property, ritual process, or knowledge which can have direct control over the behavior or welfare of others.

4. *Residual component:* older people retain prestige associated with previous statuses from which they retire.

In earlier society, age alone—while a necessary condition—apparently was not in itself sufficient for older people to receive respect, status and authority.

Since World War II, a small proportion of older people (5 percent to 10 percent) have been relegated to institutionalized ghettos called retirement or nursing homes. Once these people reach a given age range, they are arbitrarily placed into some labeled category, such as young old, or old old. The only apparent alternative the person has is to move from one restricted category to a more restrictive category, all the while being sentenced to the "slag heap of life." D. O. Cowgill's model of "Aging and Modernization," suggests that four major societal trends are the underlying causes for the negative effect upon older persons. They are:

1. the rapid developments in health technology,

2. the expansion of scientific technology, which has affected the nature of work, the work environment, and the work ethic,

3. rapid urbanization, and

4. education.

Cowgill believes that an obvious by-product from modernized societies to contemporary developing societies is its modern health technology. This process has been most evident since World War II, with the introduction of modern forms of sanitation and control of communicable diseases. Such developments have drastically reduced infant mortality and have prolonged life at all stages. One consequence of improved health technology is that rapid openings in the labor force are no longer created by death, a fact which has increased competitive generational pressures in the labor force. The social substitute for death has been the practice of retirement and, more specifically, pressure for early retirement. Since a strong work ethic characterizes the work role as an individual's major life role, and since both material and non-material rewards are allocated accordingly, retirement from the status-giving activity of work is accompanied by a reduction in rewards, including monetary income, psychologically-satisfying status and respect.

Cowgill points out also that modern economic technology creates many new occupations which are filled by young workers. They are rewarded both economically and psychologically for filling these highly-valued positions. Older workers remain in the more traditional work roles with accompanying loss in status, obsolescences, and less pay. Both youthful competition and job obsolescence combine to create pressure for older workers to retire from the labor force and to accept the inevitable loss of income and status. "Thus, health technology and economic technology separately and in interaction conduce to the restriction of the roles of the aged in society and towards their relative financial and psychological deprivation."

The third element of Cowgill's "Aging and Modernization" model is the impact of urbanization on the aged. The young—who are highly mobile—flock to urban centers to take the new jobs created by economic development. This migration, which produces physical separation from family, contributes to "... breaking down the extended family in favor of the nuclear conjugal unit. Neolocal marriage becomes the norm in a modernizing society. Residential separation fosters social and intellectual separation of the generations." The occupations generated by new technology result in social mobility for youth from which the old are omitted; this in turn exacerbates the social distance between generations. The residential segregation resulting from youth's mobility and the social distance which job status differences create combine to promote social segregation between generations and foster a "cult of youth." Demographic changes, modifying social attitudes toward the aged, and economic and political pressures seem to be working together to partially neutralize the reverence toward youth, especially in the United States.

Education is the fourth component in Cowgill's model.

Modernizing societies strive to promote literacy. As it is introduced, there follows a desire by the society to provide for progressively higher levels of education, as well as for advanced levels of technical education, in order that youth may move into the new occupations created by the developing technology.

Since the target for all such education efforts is the young, youth become more educated than their elders, a development which constitutes an inversion of status. The consequences of this inversion are most pronounced during the early stages of a society's modernization, during which time children are literate and parents are illiterate. This form of youth-elevated literacy contributes to an intellectual and moral segregation of the generations. As youth become more literate, adults tend to lose most of their power and influence within the family unit. Cowgill has concluded that education ". . . contributes to the down-grading of the elderly in modern societies." There does seem to be some evidence that this element in Cowgill's model may not continue to be a major factor. The elderly of the future may be expected to be educated at about the same level as their youth, at least with regard to the number of years of education. What will be at issue is the time in history when the education was acquired and its relevance to the current and future needs of an aging society.

CHANGES IN THE UNITED STATES

The aging/working relationship in the United States is complex. In many respects the evolution to an industrial society is quite different from similar transitions other societies have and currently are experiencing. Reasons for such differences in the United States are: 1) historical longevity, 2) geographical space, 3) political structure, and 4) diversity of ethnic and racial sub-groups.

When compared to other industrial nations, the United States is relatively young in terms of political identity. Its history and traditions as an independent political unit are over two hundred years old, although colonization of its eastern boundaries occurred over three-hundred-fifty years ago. This relative newness has freed the United States from certain rigid adherence to national dogmas, values and lifestyles, which are part of the more traditional, longer-existing industrial societies. It was pointed out earlier that in Europe, position in life was determined by whether one used brains or brawn in terms of his work. In the United States, individual and social survival depended upon all persons using both brain and brawn, regardless of their age or station in life. It was not until some were able to amass wealth and invest it in a growing technology that differential work activities based upon status and ability were to emerge. The amassing and investing of wealth led to the formalization of work hierarchies and to increased leisure time for workers. The formalization of work tended to glorify youth.

Social changes were not uniform across the young nation and were not to solidify until the westward expansion became commonplace during the late nineteenth and early twentieth centuries. Those seeking manifest destiny, those venturing farther westward, were the youth of America, mainly because of the rigors of travel and the attending deprivations during that era. Youth were concerned with their own social positions and status in the growing nation and were, therefore, willing to put up with the stresses of moving and the changes affecting their lives.

Older persons in the more settled regions of the new country had control over the wealth and property, which rarely got transferred to youth until the older persons died or reached a stage of life where they were either physically or psychologically unable to exercise control. Youth's only alternative in a conservative agriculturally-oriented society was to either inherit an older person's property or move to unsettled areas and develop their resources.

A third factor in the relationship of aging and work concerns the political structure of the United States, which emphasizes the quality of the individual as a basic article of faith in the Constitution. It is this fundamental belief, along with a strong belief in the Protestant Work Ethic, which was conducive to autonomy in one's personal life. The result was an emerging social behavior pattern, different from the more traditional European societies, which allowed the individual to work in whatever capacity, create whatever could be created by one's own labor, and develop a hierarchical society within which the individual was valued by what he did and not by the station in life to which he was born.

In this sense, those who were physically able to survive the rigors of independent living, contribute to the welfare of self and society, and reach an old age were accorded a degree of filial piety. Others were either ignored or ostracized from society, in hopes they would die, a custom similar to that of the tribal societies of an earlier era.

The emergence of ethnic and racial sub-cultures also contributed to a different social evolution in the relationship of aging and work. The migrations of people during the 1800s and 1900s from other countries to the United States further contributed to the changing character of society. Most immigrants were young, poor and willing to fill those positions in the work force which were relegated to the lower levels in the hierarchy, but of a higher order than that which they left behind. They also brought with them their cultural heritages which influenced change regarding the relative position of the aged within their sub-groups. The degree of influence on the total society with regard to the aging experience varies from one sub-culture to another, and one generation to another. The contribution to a changing attitude toward work and aging by ethnic and sub-cultural minorities is not well understood although some have begun to explore the question.

Some of the aged in colonial society who were in elite positions—such as church elders—were venerated, whereas those who were destitute and without families were often mistreated, ignored and scorned. Due to lack of medical knowledge, old age was often a time of extreme physical suffering. So long as the aged (and we must remember that they were few in number at that time) were physically healthy, active and able to continue working in some capacity, they were accorded great respect and authority. Those who were not, endured great suffering.

Colonial Puritans made age a cult that had religious overtones. The Elders ran the church and were accorded preferential seating in the meeting houses. The literature and sermons of the day preached veneration toward the aged. In the more respected occupations of religion and education people tended to die in office since there was no generalized concept of retirement at that time. Positions of community leadership were usually occupied by older citizens who also made the ultimate decisions in times of crises.

Several social forces combined in colonial American society to bring about changes in the veneration of the aged. As colonists became established in their new environment, as the rigors of living and making a living began abating, as individuals began amassing wealth and property, and as man began to perceive that his basic needs were being met, there emerged time for individuals to contemplate the future course of their lives.

D. H. Fischer's *Growing Old in America* points out that several trends emerged near the turn of the century which eroded the veneration of the old and enhanced the status of youth. Wealth, rather than age, began to be the criterion for preferential treatment in the meeting houses. Terms of respect (gaffer) for the elderly gave way to terms of derision (codger) and people began to dress to enhance youth rather than emphasize age. Political, ethical, economic and demographic changes resulting from the American Revolution combined to create fundamental social changes. The stability of a society which placed the aged in a pre-eminent position gave way to an emerging equality of youth, followed by a dominance of youth.

Roles both within and among generational groups began to differ as society began to industrialize and modernize. One's sex and position in a work hierarchy began to preempt the more traditional notions regarding role. As these differences began to emerge, the relative position of age groups also began to differ.

Cowgill and Holmes pointed out that as society modernized, changes emerged in roles and status that were detrimental to older people. They concluded that modernization was associated with 1) later onset of old age, 2) chronological age being the criterion to define old, 3) increased longevity, 4) the emergence of an aging population, 5) higher proportions of females, widows, and grandparents in the population, 6) lowered status of the aged, and 7) an increase in the extent of disengagement of older people from community life. All these changes contribute to a lowered status of the aged in modern society.

Sarason theorized that much of this status decline that began during the post World War II era, was dominated by four developments:

1. a population explosion which set in motion an economic expansion with which society was not equipped to deal,

2. the rise of poverty, civil rights, racial and women's movements,

3. the World War II G.I. Bill which provided for new and expanded educational opportunities for millions of veterans, and

4. an explosion of scientific and technological innovations which rendered obsolete traditional ways of dealing with human, economic, and health problems.

These trends emphasized a youth cult and denigrated the aged. The impact of a youth-oriented society was so strong, old people began to deny their age; such denial served to mitigate against effective socialization to old age. Activity Theory arose as a theoretical attempt to explain the phenomena of aging. Disengagement Theory was conceptualized for the same purpose. There were few compelling reasons for Americans to accept an aged role in society. "Younger people perceive the aging as old; the elderly readily agree to the classification of *other* aged, but reject such a definition for themselves personally." The answer to a query to a ninety-year-old man by this author, as to when he first perceived that he was old exemplifies how some older people perceive their age. He responded:

I'll never forget the day. It was my eighty-third birthday and I was getting out of bed when I realized that I just was not moving as fast as I used to and my bones ached and I really was in no hurry to do anything. I seemed to have lost my pep, my desire to want to face another day being quite as active as I had been once. I thought this must be what it's like to be old. I didn't like the thought then, but now I accept the fact that I am old.

In his perceptual view, this man was not old until long after the time when younger people perceived him as old, and long after our social systems defined him as old. His role perception, until he believed himself to be old, was that of an active and involved human being who essentially was living the way he thought he should, contributing to society and the maintenance of self. He had no role models to emulate. He was himself a role model for others.

Rosow has categorized ten dimensions of the socialization process in modern society, none of which is appropriate for old age. These categories are summarized below.

- *New Role Sets:* Concerns status succession from one role set to another. As the person ages and the number of possible new role sets shrink, the tendency is to remove old people from the socialization process. As people age and become old, ". . . there are few pressures on them to observe many norms, for few people have any stake in their conformity—beyond their incipient dependency and these by the maintenance of their self-sufficiency and health."

- *Rites of Passage:* Involves explicit status change, marked in time and observed by ceremony. Aging is a gradual process with few dramatic changes to mark transitions from youth to middle age to old age.

- *Isolation from Former Groups:* Socialization is the process of losing contact with one age group when identifying with another age group. Aging involves a gradual loss of group membership and a gradual erosion of the supports associated with that membership.

- *Ignoring Other Status Differences:* Concerns ignoring past differences when moving from one age group to another. It assumes that all individuals entering a given generational group age homogeneously. Older people, in an effort to counteract forced homogeneity, try to emphasize and value their past achievements and status, thus delaying or denying movement to an impending old age.

- *New Conformity Criteria:* Involves a basic principle of socialization which concerns that taking on new roles and meeting new norms as one gets older are rewarded. This is generally true throughout middle age. When one reaches his fifties the rewards begin to diminish, e.g., salary growth rates slow down to a sustained level throughout the sixth decade. The older one gets the more he is judged by his age rather than by his performance. There is little incentive for older people to conform to new criteria since there are few rewards available to them and the criteria for the few rewards available are ambiguous.

- *Role Clarity:* The more clearly new roles are defined and described, the easier it is to move from one generational group to another. The culture provides clearly-defined roles when one moves from a teenager-student status to young adult-worker status to middle adult-work-parent status. However, old people have no such clearly-defined role definitions; hence, they must create their own private role definitions which may not be in harmony with what the culture loosely believes the role to be.

- *Role Rehearsal:* Involves practice of socializing into a role either through direct experiences or through facsimile representations. Supervised clinical training is an example of socializing to a given professional work role. Old people have no patterned experiences for which to rehearse, not only because the role is devalued to such an extent that there is no incentive to practice, but also because the role is so indefinite and diffused.

- *Committing Activity:* Concerns commitment and involvement in a new role as well as changing one's self-image to conform to the new role. Since there are no special skills necessary to be old, there is no incentive for ego involvement into that life stage.

- *Other Committing Forces:* Includes such dimensions as positive aspiration to role, voluntary participation, anticipatory socialization, fixed or finite training period, and the like. Since the aging person does not usually desire to be old, preparation for old age does not stimulate one to actively mobilize and engage in these activities.

- *Successful Performance:* Successful experiences in role rehearsal and performance facilitates socialization to new life roles. In old age there is little basis for successful performance except in non-age related terms.

For adults, socialization to new life roles generally revolves around their work. Therefore, when older individuals are denied involvement in the work arena, the socialization process as well as their perceived self-worth is diminished. Our ninety-year-old man who first perceived himself as old at eighty-three (he had a full work career as a plant maintenance manager), also terminated his part-time business at about the same age he began believing he was old. He had already outlived most of his social group with whom he primarily identified. For him, there were no more possible roles to emulate or aspire to except his inevitable death.

4

WORK AND HUMAN IDENTITY

In general, idealized old people are portrayed as "beloved and tranquil grandparents, wise elders, white-haired patriarchs and matriarchs." The opposite image perceives aging as "decay, decrepitude, a disgusting and undignified dependency." Social policy and programs designed to assist older citizens mirror these conflicting views. Yet, the life force in old age—no less than in youth—needs to be continually reaffirmed as something positive and socially contributory. We find popular encouragement of this need for youthful reaffirmation through the many television commercials and magazine and newspaper advertisements which focus on covering up or delaying the aging process. Examples are creams to cover skin pigmentation changes commonly called "age spots," soap commercials glorifying its use for maintenance of youthful skin, dyes to cover graying hair, and foundation garments for men and women to help maintain the illusion of a youthful figure. Emerging from this commercialization is an implicit goal to define the aging process in terms and behaviors as benignly as possible. The personal identity to be associated with the aging process—which commercial advertising projects—is that of a youthful, active, productive person who is valued by society regardless of age, not an image of either beloved tranquility or undignified dependence. In a sense, Americans—regardless of age—are encouraged to project a false identity of youthfulness and to deny the aging process for as long as possible.

The dimensions of self which a person actually projects are those perceived as the most positive, those which collectively form one's identity. Usually the most desired personal characteristics a person possesses are those which are displayed to others and upon which value judgments regarding personal worth and social contribution are made by self and others. Throughout the ages people have worked to sustain themselves and the society or group with whom they identify. It has been through work in which the individual most often is engaged that his identity is defined, molded and maintained and through which most social rewards are forthcoming. Regardless of the cosmetic effects portrayed by commercial advertisements, it is the work that an individual performs, work which is value by self and others, which determines the social status and degree of respect accorded to the person. Wealth amassed as a result of work can be influential in determining one's identity. It is, however, the perceived value accorded the work activity and the visible result of that work effort—rather than the wealth itself—which act in combination to determine one's perception of his own worth as well as society's perception of that worth. If the individual is perceived to be productive and self-sufficient, then he is accorded society's respect. If he is perceived to be dependent upon society's largess, then he is at best tolerated.

J. O'Toole, citing Albert Camus, describes the importance of work in an individual's life: "Without work all life is rotten. But when work is soulless, life stifles and dies." O'Toole goes on to point out that ". . . to be denied work is to be denied far more than the things that paid work buys; it is to be denied the ability to define and respect one's self." Rosow has also addressed this issue. He states, "Work is at the core of life. Consider the deeper meanings of work to the individual and to life values: work means being a good provider, it means autonomy, it pays off in success, and it establishes self-respect or self-worth."

It is assumed that for most people the economic rewards of work will also provide for leisure activities as well. Less obvious are the psychological purposes or functions of work, those which contribute to an individual's self-worth and identity. O'Toole has summarized them:

1. Work contributes to self-esteem; through mastering a task, one builds a sense of pride in one's self.
2. Work is also the most significant source of personal identity; we identify who we are through our jobs.
3. Work is a prime way for individuals to impose order, control, or structure on their world.

Work, then, is important in how man is defined by himself as well as by his society. Without this activity, man lives in a state of ambiguity, is directionless with regard to his future, roleless in his society, and loses the feeling of mastery over himself and the environment. When older people are denied access to the work activity, whether this denial of access is through mandatory retirement, overt discrimination, or benign concern for the well-being of the older person, they then become individuals without purpose, roleless in their society, and dependent upon the largess that society chooses to offer.

IDENTITY AND IDENTITY CRISIS

The singular and invariant attribute through which one's identity is maintained and influenced throughout life is his or her sexual gender. It is a biological given and the one attribute of a person's identity which is stable across the life span. Socially-sanctioned norms determine how one displays his sexual identity during various life stages; he does so by dress, hair style, and cosmetic use, regardless of recent trends labeled as the "unisex" movement. Physiological characteristics project positive sexual identity.

Other attributes of human identity are not as stable. Physical characteristics, as well as age, allow one to be identified as a child, adolescent or adult. The distinguishing differences between young adults and older adults are usually physiological: thinning or graying hair, wrinkles and sagging muscles. These characteristics are not uniform by age and sex, however, and are often cosmetically modified to maintain an illusion of youthfulness. An individual is most apt to be identified in the context of such roles as husband, wife, parent, grandparent, friend, student, scholar or worker. Within these multiple contexts, the individual holds a view of self which he projects to others, as well as a view which others hold of him in a particular context. These views are constantly changing, depending upon life circumstances.

Other than sexual gender, the work which people perform is the second most consistent and clearly-defined aspect of their identity. It is through an identifying work title that we define ourselves in social situations, and by which others classify us according to the values associated with such labels. One's work, its value and the social position and human interactions one enjoys as a result of it comprise the identity subscribed to by self and through which it is projected to others. Thus, the higher one's work is on a job or career hierarchy, the more positive is the self-image and the more esteem the individual is accorded by others.

The formulation of a person's identity—other than by sex—is never established as a static or unchangeable attribute. Identity formulation is a process which is always changing and developing and can be described in psychological terms as follows: ". . . identity formulation employs a process of simultaneous reflection and observation, a process taking place on all levels of mental functioning, by which the individual judges himself in the light of what he perceives to be the way in which others judge him in comparison to themselves and a typology significant to them; while he judges their way of judging him in the light of how he perceives himself in comparison to them and the types that have become relevant to him."

Since one's identity is linked to individual as well as social values, work and the work setting comprise an important dimension of how one perceives his identity. After all, work consumes a significant portion of one's adult life. To be denied access to it whether by means of forced retirement, poor health or whatever other means, is to be denied access to developing or maintaining one's identity and place in society. Our older citizens are being denied such an environment under the aegis of benign benevolence, the denial of which intrudes upon continuation of their identity development and associated values and rewards.

When older people are denied access to those activities and environments in which they previously have experienced the rewards and acceptances of their worth, they may experience an identity crisis. Depending upon how an individual copes, it can be temporary or permanent. It may be conceptualized as a kind of "psychosocial relativity." Whenever an individual experiences an intrusion in his psychological world or social environment, a discontinuity, he can be said to be experiencing an identity crisis. For most people, intrusions in their normal life pattern are temporary and—for the most part—non-debilitating. For older people, however, who experience retirement, death of a spouse or significant friend, or any event which carries with it a sense of permanent change in their life pattern and their perceived status, a disequilibrium is experienced for which they have little or no preparation or previous experiences to help them cope.

INTRUSIONS ON
IDENTITY DEVELOPMENT _____

In modern society it is apparent that children and youth are the only social group for whom non-traditional work is an accepted way of life. Education and training is assumed to be their expected work role, a role which is non-productive in terms of goods or services and which is costly to society. The economic drain on society in support of children and youth is accepted in the anticipation that it will yield a future return in terms of socially- and economically-productive adults. All other dependent people—such as unemployed workers, aged retirees, and the disabled—are perceived to be less than accept-able, people whose value to society and to self is suspect and tolerated as a necessary evil.

Continuity in one's life as well as the continuity of a society is dependent upon work and the stability work offers. When uncontrolled life events intrude on an individual's and/or society's stability, then discontinuities are experienced which disrupt the normal process for identity development. During the past half century, three major time periods included uncon-trolled events which have intruded on the development of a traditional and stable life pattern and have created situations in which both individuals and their society experienced discon-tinuities. These were the Depression years of the 1930s, World War II and its aftermath during the 1940s and 1950s, and succes-sive wars and recessions during the 1950s, 1960s and 1970s.

These events or intrusions on both the individual's and society's normal developmental processes have created a life situation in which traditional values are under re-examination, question and change. New ways of establishing human identity are being experimented with, and certain generational groups, such as retirees and the elderly are struggling to identify and establish their place in the social order. (See *Toward a National Policy on Aging*, Vol. I & II, 1971; Harris, 1975, for detailed account of this struggle.) More personal intrusions in one's life—such as death, divorce, retirement or critical illness—usually demand that individuals experiencing these crises realign themselves in new relationships with their family, society and self in order to create a new or modified identity. Whether intrusions are cataclysmic to the society or individual, the common denominator for establishing or re-establishing a person's identity is the stability of the work one performs which is perceived to be contributing to the maintenance of self and society.

Those who are retired and whom society defines as old, enjoy no such work setting in which to maintain or re-establish their worth. Current labor force practices deny them access to the work place where their identity was formed, developed and maintained in the past. Retirement is not seen as a viable alter-native for maintaining one's importance in either one's internal self perception or external social world. Without work which is perceived to have value to self and society, older people no longer have a forum within which to justify their continued existence or be accepted as valued and contributing members of American society.

Most employed persons work in a system where some form of retirement is mandatory. While it is acknowledged that there possibly may be good business reasons for a worker retirement policy, such may not always be good for the person. This may be especially true for those who have a need to maintain their position because of the social or personal role definition, or because of economic reasons. For others, the shock of being forced to move from a well-defined and stable role category (work) to a more ambiguous role (retirement) is more than they can tolerate. The sudden confrontation with excessive leisure time results in personal discontinuities for which there generally has been little preparation or training.

Some people welcome retirement. It provides an opportunity for involvement in a variety of time-consuming activities previously held in abeyance. For others, retirement may be viewed as one of the losses which accompany the aging process. This latter group may be experiencing some loss of competency or body image, as well as a loss of self identity. Their status as a worker did, after all, afford social contacts or a group identity associated with productive activity. The concomitant economic loss of income or a drastically reduced income resulting from retirement may limit mobility, lead to living in less physical comfort, or in a strange environment.

Many researchers have indicated that in more traditional societies several social and institutional forces interplay to provide a sense of stability as well as a sense of future which affirms an older person's identity and social position. These forces are property ownership, strategic knowledge, productivity, mutual dependence, tradition and religion, kinship and family, and community life. It is when these institutional forces are reasonably stable that older people's identity in their social systems are assured. This stability has been shaken, however, creating an unstable environment in which the older citizen's worth is yet to be defined.

CONSEQUENCES OF AGING _____

The aged are less and less valued as society becomes more and more modernized. Younger people seem to develop negative attitudes, relative indifference, or outright rejection of older persons. This is more apt to occur as younger persons, in order to accommodate the changing nature of jobs and new work environments created by advancing technology, move into those work arenas for which they have been educated or trained. It is also apt to occur in those traditional work environments where a changing technology has made the older worker obsolete. Younger people have difficulty in understanding that it was the creative work efforts of their older counterparts which created the situation wherein a newer and more modern technology was developed so that new and more interesting careers, jobs and work settings could flourish. This devaluation of the older person, then, may be attributed to 1) ignorance on the part of youth with regard to the previous contributions of their elders, 2) fragmentation of work so that the results of older workers' contributions are not visible, and 3) youth's impatience with the "system," coupled with their desire for quick entry into society's mainstream. The devaluation process, be it overt or covert, is a way to move older workers out of the labor force.

The stereotyping of older people is a form of "agism." The problem with it is that individuals are seen more in terms of a representative of an age group rather than in terms of their uniqueness. Consequently, when a member of a given age group behaves in atypical ways, there emerge discontinuities both between and within age groups in terms of actual vs. expected behaviors. Social conditioning has done an efficient job of convincing members of a given age group, especially the older groups, that only certain ways of behaving are appropriate, and members of that group have come to believe that they are incapable of behaving differently. If an older person elects to break out of the socially-imposed stereotype (not retiring at the expected age, etc.) he risks the censure of both his own age group as well as that of younger age groups. As a result, expected behavior, regardless of how ambiguously it may be defined, tends to be rewarded via group or family acceptance; whereas non-conforming or non-accepted behavior is accompanied by social sanctions. In this way, stereotypical conceptions of age-related behaviors are reinforced and any desires for change by older people are disparaged.

Another consequence of aging results in older people being excluded in many of life's rewarding activities, especially those associated with work. It is here older people are excluded from a source of social contact and the attending social rewards and status which contribute to maintaining an accepted identity in society. Income loss resulting from retirement reduces the potential for participating in social engagements previously enjoyed, thereby excluding retirees from sustaining the level of socialization necessary to maintaining their identity with members of their "social class, ethnic or racial group." Participation in family activities, especially with children and grandchildren, may occur with less frequency as one gets older. Older people, especially the retired who are on fixed incomes, may find they are unable to afford—either for financial or health reasons—the associated travel costs necessary to maintain close family ties with younger people who have relocated. As older retired persons age, their economic base erodes as a result of normal inflation, their physical mobility starts to become limited, and their social interactions are reduced, resulting in their being systematically excluded from the social participation and stimulation enjoyed by younger people. This situation further erodes their already precarious role identity and importance.

Role loss can occur as a result of such events as poor health, widowhood or retirement from one's work. As a result of lowered income after retirement, lifestyles are altered. As a result of general decline in health, independence may be impaired. Most role losses experienced by older people are unwelcomed and involuntary. In the final analysis, role loss affects an older person's previous group membership, lowers his prestige, and reduces the number of options for group membership in which his status is identified and maintained.

As family and work responsibilities are lessened and as physical functioning becomes limited due to growing older, role ambiguity and confusion results. In earlier societies, older citizens experienced no such ambiguity in their lives. Even in tribal societies, the aged knew what functions they were expected to perform and the associated rewards. Rosow has described role loss in old age:

> It may be defined with a maximum of personal preference and individual choice. This seeming boon, however, calls heavily on people's initiative and inner resources in the absence of definite role expectations by others. Such negative demands are not always easily met and may generate as much strain as do conflicting role pressures. Indeed, role loss and ambiguity are generally quite demoralizing; they deprive people of their social identity and frequently affect their psychological stability. The apparent freedom is often a burden because earlier in life, roles typically structured expectations, requirements, and activities for them. Most workaday routines do not result from intention, but merely from occupying a particular social position and from several decisions at crucial points in the life cycle. The unstructured situations of later life are inherently depressing and anxiety-generating. Older people must fill the vacuum of social expectations with personal definitions, and they must develop private standards in the absence of established norms for them. Many of the elderly respond to their devaluation and ambiguous role by clinging to youthful norms as a means of dealing with the new uncertainties.

Throughout recent years the literature on aging has been replete with references to the aged retaining youthful self-images long after society has defined them as old. This perception of age by older people has been one of the more consistent findings reported. Perhaps what older people are saying when they cling to youthful self-images is that being old is a "state of mind" and is not based upon the number of years lived, regardless of what institutional forces—like Social Security Laws and the Age Discrimination in Employment Act—might dictate. B. L. Neugarten in an article on aging recognized this when she classified older people as being "young old" and "old old." This suggests that the "young old" can still be active and fully participate in society. E. H. Erickson, in describing life's developmental stages, elected not to specify stage as being linearly related to age. Rather, he described or proscribed the life events needing to be mastered in any given life stage as part of an individual's normal developmental pattern. L. Harris, in a report to the National Council on Aging, reported surveys indicating retired people prefer to be referred to as senior citizens as opposed to terms suggesting "old," "aged," or "elderly." Apparently older citizens, especially those who cling to behaviors which reflect youthful self-images, are unwilling to accept society's standards of who is or is not old. It is anticipated that as the number of persons over sixty-five increases during the next few decades, and as this group becomes more vocal with regard to its concerns, resistance to socially-imposed aged definitions will become greater.

THE HUMAN IDENTITY DOMAIN

A set of conditions which can be used to define the domain within which human identity is formed, developed and maintained may be broadly identified as social, physical and psychological. Collectively they form the domain through which human identity is expressed. Older citizens experience significant intrusions in these conditions; these intrusions, in turn, create situations disruptive to maintaining their identity and place in modern society. The conditions of this identity domain are conceived to be theoretically mutually exclusive, even with the realization that operationally they are interactive.

Physical Condition

An important characteristic of one's identity domain is

one's physical condition. Cellular theory advocates have argued that during the life span of a species there are a finite number of cell doublings, after which the organism deteriorates until morbidity and death occur. Practically speaking, cellular deterioration does not generally impede human functioning in most life situations until the latter half of life, and then only gradually. J. F. Fries, as cited in the *New England Journal of Medicine*, has demonstrated that during this century the average life span for human beings has risen from forty-seven to seventy-three years. He concluded that this increase is due to control of infectious disease and, more particularly, to the significant reduction in neonatal mortality during the same period. With further advances in controlling chronic illness on the immediate horizon, Fries has calculated that by the year 2045, people will die naturally and that life longevity can be expected to average eighty-five years, at which time the organism will simply wear out and die.

There are significant advances being made in improved community health, physical conditioning and diet, along with reductions in critical physical debilitation and mortality previously brought on by chronic disease. These medical advances have contributed to improvements in the physical vitality and stamina of older people as well as to an increasing longevity. This fact suggests that survival throughout the aging process has been extended to such an extent that traditional perceptions of who is or is not physically old must be modified. Modern society's ability either to postpone or drastically reduce chronic illness creates a situation in which deteriorating physical health has been reduced to a point where personal autonomy and physical vitality can be maintained until very near death for larger numbers of people. It seems reasonable to assume that those who retire from the work force (either voluntarily or involuntarily) can look forward to good physical health and vigorous, active minds and bodies; but they have few outlets through which to expend their energy in what they may deem as productive and fulfilling, unless some of our social and institutional systems are modified or changed. Given the changing nature of older people's improved health status, recent Federal legislation raising to age seventy the point at which people can be forcibly removed from the labor force is a move in the right direction. Using Fries' figure of physical vitality to age eighty-five suggests that people who retire at age sixty-five or seventy have, on the average, fifteen to twenty additional years of non-productivity to look forward to with no previous preparation on how to be inactive. Assuming that social and institutional systems designed to assist older people in later life are not modified or changed, any increase in life longevity places an economic burden on American society which goes far beyond the intent of the framers of old-age assistance programs. For many older people, some form of productive work may be an appropriate outlet both to satisfy their identity needs and to relieve their economic burden. To deny that older people are physically healthy and able to continue to function in socially-approved and productive work activities is to deny them both continued access to an arena of their identity and to full partnership in their society.

Social Condition

A second condition for maintaining a person's identity has to do with the social conditions under which he lives and the role and functions performed in his society. Rosow outlined the necessary conditions for maintenance of those social roles to which older citizens are currently denied entry when they leave the heterogeneous work environment for the more homogeneous environment of older Americans.

Retirement is often accompanied by certain losses with which our social and institutional systems seem unable to deal. Some of these may be associated with the stability of routine associated with most traditional work activities and environments. While the routine of work may appear boring to some people, there is a certain stability associated with the semblance of order, security, and life planning that such routine brings to one's life. It has been this writer's observation that in most academic settings where, except for meeting classes, an orderly time sequence for conditions of work are not necessarily mandated, productive individuals still have a tendency to plan their schedules in an orderly way in order to establish a routine. Even professors *emeriti* will frequently continue lifelong routines of work, providing order, stability and a sense of security in their lives, as well as maintaining their scholarly (work) identities in an academic environment. Personal discussions with older retired people reveal that they generally continue to arise at the same time each day, go through their usual morning ablutions, and plan their daily activities in time sequences similar to those they had when they were working. A retired self-employed shoemaker reported at age ninety-seven that he still read his morning newspaper from 8:00 to 9:00 a.m. daily. He experienced a day of unrest and a sense of incompleteness and loss when if, for any reason, this routine was disrupted.

The work setting is an important environment in which socializing activities occur, activities which are often extended to include leisure time. The quality and importance attached to this form of socialization contributes to a sense of self, a perceived self-worth, and a sense of belonging. Older persons who are removed from a work environment and have reduced opportunities to engage in socializing activities suffer from a loss of place in the social milieu. Accompanying this is the loss of continuous associations with others who comprised the older person's supportive social network in the past. Socializing activities and the maintenance of supportive social networks to identity development has emerged as important in recent years.

Psychological Condition

A third condition in which one's identity is formed, developed and maintained involves the psychological perceptions one has of self. As the individual ages, his personality changes. One can assume that as this occurs, a person's identity also changes. The age/change view is that human growth is a process of adaptation to various life stages and that personality development suggests that as a person ages, he will choose a lifestyle that offers the greatest degree of ego involvement and life satisfaction. This, of course, assumes a reasonably supportive social environment. These age-related personality changes reflect the changes in one's identity. Life span developmental psychologists have wrestled with these notions and have postulated stages of development and psychological tasks which influence how individuals perceive themselves and, in turn, are perceived by others. They focus attention on psychological development in the second half of life and, for discussion purposes, divide the second half of life into "Middle Age" and "Old Age." They postulate four aspects for normal development in "Middle Age": valuing wisdom and physical powers, socializing, emotional flexibility, and mental flexibility. For "Old age," three aspects: ego differentiation vs. work-role preoccupation, concern with one's physical health, and dealing with one's imminent death. Apparently the key elements for successful aging include acceptance of self as a changing being, flexibility in dealing with the exigencies in one's life, and seeking new ways to maintain one's identity. Life span developmental psychologists assume that at some specified age (currently, socially determined as age sixty-five) individuals will withdraw from active participation in the labor force and assume a new status in their internal as well as external world. What this new status is or will be is clouded. The ambiguity has led older citizens to raise their voices concerning their role and to demand recognition as to their past contributions to society and to their current worth and dignity. One can conclude that not only are older citizens voicing their views in local, state and national forums, but they are attempting to express a new self by coping on a day-by-day basis. Some forms of their coping result in their contributing, in disproportionate numbers, to society's mental health statistics.

Enforced withdrawal from the labor force—especially during economic recessionary periods—can contribute to an older person's sense of identity confusion. Manifestation of this is seen in increased alcoholism, suicide, depression, psychosomatic illnesses, and other negatively-defined behaviors not previously evidenced in older people. Frequently, through lack of understanding, medical personnel treat these behaviors as signs of old age and further exacerbate the problem through prescribing inappropriate drug treatment programs which then lead to excessive drug dependency and little understood iatrogenic side effects. In one sense, an enforced labor force withdrawal experienced by older persons who are ill-prepared for the changed status they will be experiencing can be likened to Kubler-Ross' five stages of grief: denial, anger, bargaining, depression, acceptance. Denial and anger may be associated with guilt in that the independent and previously self-sufficient worker who is thrust into a non-worker status is dependent upon others as well as upon social and institutional systems for his daily sustenance. The bargaining and depression states may be forms of denial of the fact that one has been socially defined as old when in reality he continues to think of himself as young. Finally, the acceptance stage may become resignation that one must be old, therefore he is. It is at this stage that we can speculate that an older person may choose suicide or some other form of non-functional withdrawal as an alternative to living.

The importance of the psychological domain in the maintenance of human identity as related to work cannot be minimized. When one is perceived and defined as old by his society, and he is forced to accept this definition, especially in terms of work and productive usefulness, he experiences a sense of worthlessness, thus, loss of identity. To be both physically and psychologically denied access to the work environment after some forty years of inclusion is to be denied access to an environment in which one's identity is known by self and others.

5

OLDER PEOPLE AS UNTAPPED RESOURCES

Progressive automation and a society which minimizes the physical drudgery of work have given rise to a throw-away society in the United States. In the past, the availability of inexpensive and an apparently inexhaustible supply of fossil-based energy and a belief in the availability of unlimited natural physical resources have combined to create an era of unprecedented economic influence. For quite some time a rising birth rate combining with significant reductions in infant mortality, an increasing life expectancy, and a past history of high immigration rates (especially between 1880 and 1920) have influenced and fostered the view of an apparently inexhaustible supply of human resources. But more human resources still are needed to perform work and produce the goods and services demanded by a growing and changing society, regardless of the strides made by industry to reduce the physical drudgery of work. Current world-wide energy problems, a growing realization that physical natural resources are exhaustible, a rising inflation rate, and apparent lowered worker productivity, suggest a need for conservation strategies to be implemented vigorously on all of society's resources if the quality of life is to remain high.

RESOURCES

J. O'Toole, author of *Work, Learning and the American Future*, has proposed three categories of resources. They are 1) land, including energy and all other natural resources, 2) capital, including machines and all other man-made sources of wealth, and 3) labor, which includes all aspects of human skills, intelligence, ingenuity and other abilities. O'Toole speculated that the first two of these resources—both factors of production—may be approaching a point of maximum exploitation. He suggests that we must make better use of our human resources. He believes that: "... it is the intellectual powers of the race that constitute an immense reservoir of productivity and advancement."

It would seem that the problem with which we are confronted today is that of identifying, defining and exploring those strategies which maximize the potential of our natural, capital and human resources if the quality of life is not to stagnate and then diminish. The ultimate goal, at least in the United States, is to continue to advance the quality of life for everyone. After all, this continues to be "The American Dream." Conversely, when we cast aside older people through retirement or social welfare programs, we deny them work and assume that at some arbitrary point in time they have little left to contribute; then we are being discriminatory and we are casting aside a valuable human resource.

Natural Resources

While we are depleting mature human resources,

engineers, chemists, product development specialists and others are actively engaged in identifying strategies whereby stockpiling and recycling natural resources are feasible as well as cost-effective. Some are also searching for additional natural resources, as yet undiscovered. And still others are uncovering and defining the potential of newly-identified natural resources and redefining ways to use currently under-utilized resources. Some examples include: 1) identifying and developing non-fossil-based energy sources such as nuclear, thermal, solar, wave action, water, wind and others for economical mass consumption, 2) developing an underwater technology for food production and extraction of usable natural resources, and 3) exploring outer space for its long-term potential for improving the quality of life on earth. Billions of dollars of public and private funds are being invested in these activities.

Capital Resources

Individual financial institutions, multi-national corporations, and governments throughout the world are endeavoring to find new and creative ways to generate the capital necessary for 1) product development which utilizes natural resources, 2) job creation, and 3) increasing the level of productivity. In the United States, investments for the generation of capital resources—both public and private—range in the billions of dollars in the anticipation of an increased financial return and the desire to assist industry to be competitive in the world marketplace. It is assumed that such investments and the development of creative ways to generate capital will contribute to job creation and the raising of living standards, thus improving the quality of life for all. But if, as O'Toole has suggested, we may be reaching the maximum potential of capital resources, does this suggest anticipating a future decline in the quality of human life similar to what some fiction writers have envisioned? It has been suggested that the solution to this issue is of world-wide concern and involves decisions as to whether capital investments will follow the labor-intensive format of emerging nations or the energy-intensive formats of Western industrialized nations.

Human Resources

The investment in identifying and developing our human resource potential pales in comparison to that for natural and capital resources. It is only a recent—and still little-understood—realization that human beings are a natural resource whose full potential has yet to be explored. Essentially, we have not wisely utilized or developed human beings to the extent that we have our other resources. Apparently, a major belief in and commitment toward developing the human resources across the life span has not reached a level of importance in modern society as has the commitment toward developing the natural and capital resources. This is perhaps due to the seemingly unlimited availability of inexpensive energy, which in the past has negated the need to be concerned about broadening and nurturing the use of human resources to offset rising energy costs. Concerning investment in the human resource potential, there has been one notable exception since World War II: the G.I. Bill. Financial aid for the education and training of World War II veterans was of such a magnitude that it made a significant difference in the quality of life in America, contributed to an unprecedented era of economic affluence for individual citizens, and contributed to the generation of capital to be used for the development and use of natural resources. As a partial result of this investment, the United States experienced a fifteen-year period of unique economic prosperity and job expansion as well as a more highly-educated and affluent society. The residual benefits to other nations are incalculable.

Human Resources Defined

Perhaps we should examine the term "human resources." H. S. Parnes has indicated that resources are defined as ". . . the collective wealth of a nation or its means of producing wealth." This, of course, is a more general definition than the one proposed by O'Toole. Parnes goes on to state that "it follows that when one talks about *human* resources, one is talking about human beings in their productive roles—in their wealth-creating roles." Defining human resources in this sense does not assume that the productive role of people is in any way more important than other life roles, e.g., spouse, parent, citizen. Defining human resources in this way does assume that a person's productive role in society is interrelated with all other roles because ". . . it yields income which conditions the performance of other roles . . ." and this productive role ". . . serves as a means of self-expression and self-fulfillment."

We have now introduced a paradox into this thesis. If human resources assume that man functions in a productive role which creates wealth, then he, in order to continue to be needed to produce wealth, must also be a consumer of that same wealth. As a consumer of the goods and services produced, man's objective is to acquire the best quality goods and services as well as the largest quantity at the lowest price. Man as a producer has a goal to earn the greatest amount of money possible for his efforts, while at the same time making the productive activity (work) a pleasant experience without excessive expenditure of physical energy. Parnes stated that a human resource policy will need to deal with this paradox.

OLDER PEOPLE AS HUMAN RESOURCES _____

In the United States, nurturing human resource potential has centered around the education and training of youth and, more recently, young adults. This is understandable in a youth-oriented industrial society. However, this rationale has led to an assumption that educational investments should be focused only on youth, who are not only perceived to be able to learn the new technology more easily than older adults, but are expected to work and be productive longer than older adults: thus, turning back to society a greater return on its investment. The tenability of such an assumption has never truly been demonstrated. On the contrary, such an assumption has emerged historically as an article of faith in society's move toward industrialization, rather than on the basis of any hard evidence. An argument can be made that education for adults at all ages and in a variety of fields can lead to greater economic returns to the society, as well as personal satisfaction and feelings of well-being for the workers. Evidence of this is the success of older individuals who returned to school—especially graduate school—to be competitive for higher paying, more professional-level jobs. Some have even changed their occupational fields to meet and be prepared for a changing vocational structure.

But, there is a generalized belief that society should invest its financial resources in developing the human resource potential of youth. Parents have come to believe that it is important for their children to receive as much assistance as possible, especially through education, on the assumption that the more education they pursue, the better their chances of living productive and rewarding lives. In order to assist their children to achieve their potential, parents often will sacrifice material goods or the development of what is accepted as the "good life." What is important is that this form of parental behavior attests to the belief that the future will be better than the past for today's youth who, in turn, are expected to behave similarly toward future generations. (A detailed examination of this value concept suggests that ethical and moral beliefs of earlier generations still actively dominate society but are being manifest in different forms. So long as this and other traditional ethical and moral beliefs persist in a society, then one will have difficulty supporting the notion that social ethics and morals are degenerating and/or disintegrating. They are not. They are assuming new forms to accommodate a changing society.) Because of this confidence in the long-term potential of youth, adult society has been willing to sustain and tolerate the burden of an increasingly longer youth dependency which some would call a capital investment in human resources. It eventually will yield an increased productive potential of workers. It is believed, too, that this lengthy dependency will result in higher economic returns to society and expand on the continuing development of an improving quality of life.

Belief in the investment in youth as a human resource potential is such an article of faith in American society that youth dependency ratio figures—which are used to estimate the costs of maintaining the aged in society—are rarely discussed by economists, actuaries and the like as a factor about which we need be overly concerned.

The underlying belief in youth's human resource potential leads to an implicit assumption that aging adults eventually will reap economic rewards in the form of increased retirement entitlements. Another assumption is that there will be continued improvement in the quality of life as one grows older. It is taken for granted that in this way society not only recognizes but also rewards older people for their past productive efforts upon which modern society is built. When proportionally fewer individuals were surviving to older age groups, society was willing and apparently economically able to support an age-dependency population regardless of individual need. Apparently this tenet as applied to today's older adults is being challenged, e.g., challenges to rising Social Security costs, modifications in mandatory retirement, enactment of age discrimination in employment legislation in order to keep older people working, and a beginning attitudinal and political shift away from the early retirement practices prevalent during the 1950s and 1960s.

During the last half century, society's solution to an existing older worker population has been to deny people at a given age the right to continue in economically-productive roles. For many years, writers and researchers from a variety of disciplines have questioned how much longer American society can or will continue to afford to scrap older workers through mandatory retirement, social sanction or benign neglect.

The general view projected by some researchers is that older people should be retained in the labor force as long as they are able and willing. They do not deny the concept of retirement from the labor force at some point, but neither do they suggest that all people are unable to continue to function in productive ways or should be forced to retire at some arbitrarily-fixed time. Collectively, they seem to suggest that such a decision is uniquely individual and that a forced withdrawal from the labor force is a waste of human resources which society can ill afford, as well as being a denial of an individual's rights. Further, it is discriminatory behavior toward a specific segment of the population.

Prior to modern technology, withdrawal from productive activity was a voluntary decision by individuals, often in consultation with their families or clan. During the last sixty years, legislative fiat has usurped this voluntary decision-making through such actions as the Civil Service Retirement Act of 1920 and amended in 1929, the Railroad Retirement Act of 1934, and the Social Security Act of 1935.

More recently, such legislative action as the Comprehensive Older Americans Act Amendments of 1978 and the Age Discrimination in Employment Act Amendments of 1978 suggest that Congress is beginning to recognize the heterogeneity of older workers and the need for more flexibility in determining the age at which one ceases to be economically productive. Congress seems to be acknowledging that older adults' human resource potential must be utilized more efficiently and effectively if society's economic problems are to be resolved, and if existing capital and natural resources are to be maximized.

Perhaps we need to re-examine our earlier definition of human resources as related to our other resources. Such an examination would shed some light on the assumption that at some arbitrary point society can assume an individual's potential is no longer valuable and that society then must support a rapidly-growing dependent older population. The human resource potential appears to be cyclical in terms of its relationship to natural and capital resources. This cyclical relationship is depicted in Figure 1.

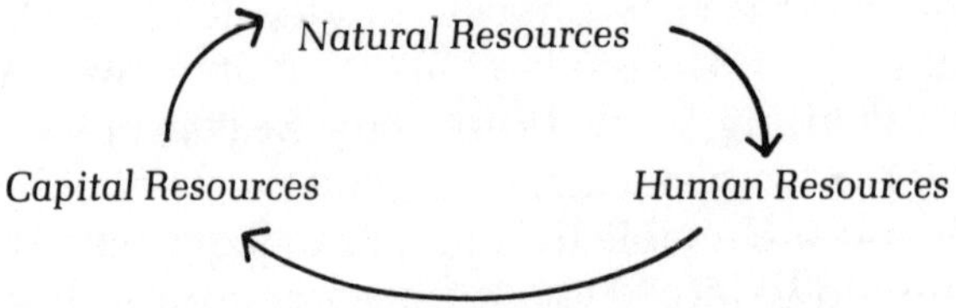

Figure 1. Cycle of Resource Interaction

The three factors are perceived to be mutually related in that any imbalance in one will create discontinuities in the other two. Recent energy problems, especially shortages during the 1970s, created severe discontinuities in employment. Unemployment problems caused a reduction in the purchase of manufactured goods as well as in purchase of services, which in turn reduced the amount of capital available for investment in the development of natural resources. This concept is often popularly referred to as a "ripple effect," which permeates the entire society and results in economic slowdown. The same phenomenon is observed throughout history when one of the three factors of resources is out of balance with the others. The phenomenon most often referred to is the Great Depression of the 1930s, which resulted from a temporary collapse of capital resources.

The cyclical concept is also applicable to human resources who—in our definitional sense—may be perceived as both producers and consumers. A worker who produces generates wealth which, in turn, generates the wherewithal to purchase goods and services produced by others and which also creates jobs for new workers as well as capital resources. When, for any reason, this cycle is interrupted, either temporarily or permanently, and when a significant segment of the population is so affected—such as the marginal worker, poor, handicapped, and aged—then an economic breakdown occurs and everyone is adversely affected. In our case, older workers are perceived to be the most adversely affected since they find great difficulty in being employed or being re-employed after a period of high unemployment.

This concern with unemployed older workers was clearly delineated by Frances Perkins, Secretary of Labor during the first Roosevelt Administration, when she unsuccessfully argued before the Congress that the forty- to sixty-four-year-old group should be considered in the Social Security legislation then under debate. Parenthetically, it can be concluded that the earlier retirement concept so popular during the late 1950s and 1960s finds its early roots in this apparent legislative disregard for the mid-adult group who were too young to retire and receive economic assistance and too old to be eligible for entry-level jobs usually reserved for youth. Obviously, non-workers are non-producers who also—at least theoretically—become non-consumers unless they are subsidized for their non-productive behavior. P. A. Haber, author of *Our Future Selves: A Research Plan Toward Understanding Aging,* points out that the marketplace has not yet discovered older people as major consumers.

The post-sixty-five age group who, as a result of formal retirement policies, are removed from the labor force as producers and perceived to be able to consume without working, given the economic support assumed under Social Security, private pension plans for some, and personal savings. It is questionable whether the quality of life under such a retirement policy is sufficiently high to be other than marginal for most of the oldest age group, thus reducing the impact of their being consumers of goods and services. If such be the case, and the numbers of older retired people are increasing, we may be heading for a rather severe disjunction in the production-consumption cycle. This, of course, assumes that modifications in our current system of economic support and under-utilization of human resources continue.

The Myth

In twentieth-century America, many myths remain surrounding the productive potential of older workers. The myths have had a negative impact on understanding and accepting the human resource potential of older workers. These myths began to be accepted as fact during the 1930s when severe economic depression created an unprecedented unemployment problem in the United States. One solution which gained favor prior to and during the 1930s, was to remove potential workers from the labor force through the introduction of mandatory retirement policies similar to those existing in European industrialized societies. Such policies effectively removed some individuals in the upper age groups from unemployment roles. Also, such a policy formally defined who was or was not old. At the other end of the age spectrum, youth were effecitvely eliminated as unemployed workers. This was accomplished by raising the age at which employers could employ them, especially in non-agricultural work. Until they reached age sixteen, youth were denied entry to many jobs under the aegis of reducing youth exploitation by unscrupulous employers or under the claim that the work was too difficult or dangerous. It was simultaneously assumed that youth would need more education over a longer time period to be employable in a developing and expanding technological environment. The social institution of public education was firmly established throughout America at the time, a fact which made it relatively simple for society to impose employment sanctions on youth. There was, after all, a proscribed activity in which they could be occupied, and who could argue against more education for youth? Legislative action effectively reduced some of the pressure associated with the unemployment problem during the 1930s without creating new jobs or getting more people to perform productive activities. Through legislation it was also effectively defined exactly who was young and who was old.

R. B. Calhoun, in his book *In Search of the New Old,* suggests that the influence generated by late nineteenth-century romantic writers gave an inaccurate picture òf elderly people. Not only were writers guilty of misrepresentation, but medical research taking place at that time—research in cellular aging—as well as medical practices and health treatment also had an unintended effect. Older people were described as worn out, crotchety, unable to work as effectively as younger adults, or sickly. Thus, under the economic stresses of the 1930s, society willingly accepted the myth of the tired, worn-out worker who deserved to be retired from the labor force after many years of hard work. (At this point in history, work as toil was still a prevalent concept.) This action created a growing dependency population who, through subsidized retirement, ostensibly was being rewarded for years of productive activity. Many contemporary writers—most notably Butler—have strongly and persuasively argued against this view, suggesting that what truly resulted was a benign neglect of older Americans who were asked to be the focus for resolution of society's economic problems. (It is interesting to note that a paradox emerges when society perceives it has need to rapidly expand the labor force to meet a national emergency, such as was experienced during World War II. Social and legal sanctions against employment of under and/ or overaged persons are significantly ignored, reduced, or set aside, only to be reinstituted after the emergency no longer exists.)

Since 1950, research from such varied disciplines as economics, history, medicine, psychology and sociology, among others, implies that the myths surrounding the non-productive potential of older workers has little basis in fact, and we can expect that these myths will become less relevant for the vast majority of older people. Business and industry more and more appear to be reassessing their past policies regarding placement, retention and termination of older workers, stimulated in part by Federal legislation concerning job/age discrimination. We seem to be moving into a transition period which is calling for a re-examination of the human resource potential of older workers and a re-evaluation of the truth of previously-accepted myths. F. R. Eisele, writing in *The Annals of the American Academy of Political and Social Science*, alluded to this transition as the "iceberg tip in the history of social policy." The tip has been known for several decades, but only now are we beginning to recognize the depth of the iceberg.

There are many myths and stereotypes surrounding older people which have influenced social attitudes and social policy:

1. physically slow in movement and thinking.

2. not creative

3. rigid and inflexible

4. unable to learn new concepts and ways of behaving or, at best, they learn them slowly

5. distrustful of change

6. traditional and conservative

7. prone to live in the past

8. egocentric and demanding

9. irritable and cantankerous

10. given to reminiscing and being garrulous

11. failing, both mentally and physically

12. often ill and unable to work

13. feeble, uninteresting and awaiting death

14. a burden to society, to family and to self

The entire spectrum of such views which, when considered collectively, form a negative perception of older people, especially as related to their human resource potential. Many writers and researchers have addressed the various elements surrounding the potential functioning of older people.

Within the context of human resources potential, it is helpful to cluster the many myths into three categories: individual differences (including intelligence and cognitive performance), physical health and mental health. While this scheme does not exhaust all possible ways to categorize the myths, it is helpful in terms of understanding where we are regarding beliefs about older people. It is essentially within these three categories that the detrimental myths are based. It is to the minimization of these myths that the White House Conference on Aging (Toward a National Policy on Aging, Vol. I & II, 1971) addressed itself and later the call for major research commitments was made in the monograph, *Our Future Selves*.

Individual Differences.   Differential psychology has contributed much to a basic understanding of how individuals function—both intellectually and cognitively—within and between groups. In a comprehensive literature review, A. Anastasi reported on the nature and extent of our knowledge as related to the psychology of aging. She set forth three major conclusions concerning intelligence which are important for our discussion. These are:

1. Individual differences within any one age level are much greater than average differences between age levels.

2. When considering the performance of older and younger persons, it is important to differentiate between age differences and age changes. Age differences may reflect educational or other cultural differences between generations rather than the physiological or psychological effects of aging.

3. The activities in which one has engaged over time

have influence on whether abilities increase, decrease or remain stable. Educational and vocational activities are two examples she cites which influence the selective improvement of some abilities and the decline of others. What emerges as important is what one has been doing during his life span, not how long he has lived.

What is significant for an understanding of the human resource potential of older workers is that their intellectual abilities are on about the same level as those of other groups. Since intellectual ability appears not to be negatively correlated with age, we can assume it has minimal influence on an older person's job performance or work productivity.

Cognitive Performance   Cognitive performance generally includes problem-solving tasks, learning performance or thought processes which translate into some activity. These dimensions previously have been thought to be significantly slowed in older adults to a point where their productive work capacities are judged to be below some performance criteria set by employers. While it is conceded that *at some age* and for *some older persons* cognitive performance is below an expected standard, the accumulated evidence since World War II strongly supports the view that this is not true for all older people. Research on cognitive performance categories indicates older people perform at about the same level as younger people, in some cases better. Only in response performance are older people slower, though long-term physical exercise as well as past experience may moderate the effect of age on reaction time. Such a slowing, which is not excessive, does not seem to adversely affect an older person's rate of productivity.

From the mass of available evidence reported concerning older people's cognitive performance, one can conclude that denying them continued participation in the labor force beyond an arbitrarily-defined age is discriminatory and represents a loss of a valuable source of experienced workers. This practice was instituted by society through its elected officials and sanctioned by the electorate to regulate the size of the labor force, rather than allowing the marketplace to dictate worth and continued participation. The enactment of the 1978 amendments to the Age Discrimination in Employment Act has only recently begun to acknowledge the fact that older people are able to participate productively in the labor force long beyond the time previously felt to be socially convenient for their withdrawal. The effect of this legislation has yet to be evaluated with regard to its full impact on society in general and on older people specifically. Preliminary statements as reported in the popular press, however, indicate that some older people are taking advantage of continued work beyond age sixty-five, but their work is beginning to take on new forms and new configurations.

Physical Health.   Perhaps the most negative attitudes emerging in industrial society and used as justified sanctions against older people's continuation in work are related to their physical well-being. As stated earlier, non-industrial societies recognized declining physical ability of aging people and accommodated those changes through reassignment of work tasks within the individual's capabilities without an accompanying loss of esteem. With industrialization came impersonalization of work assignments, job fragmentation and formation of work hierarchies which have left little room to allow for physiological changes.

Modern society's solution, retirement at some specified age, demeans the older worker through loss of pay, hours worked or of an esteemed position in the work environment.

Attitudes associated with the physically debilitating characteristics of work have evolved in part from two sources: 1) belief in the concept of work as toil, and 2) the physically debilitating nature of work and extremely poor work environments. A. Anderson, author of *Old Is Not a Four-Letter Word*, reports that a recent U.S. Department of Labor study indicates that only 14 percent of industry's jobs require much physical strength. This leaves 86 percent of industry's jobs requiring a low degree of physical strength and assumes the probability for the need to develop higher intellectual and cognitive processing levels. We found from Anastasi's review that older groups function at about the same level both intellectually and cognitively as do younger age groups. Combining this with the knowledge that the service sector and government agencies are employing more persons than the so-called strenuous goods-producing jobs, we are left with the notion that the majority of productive activity requires only a minimum of physical strength and stamina. If this concept is accepted, as it should be, then the traditional myths surrounding physical decline in relation to work and age have no real substance and are invalid.

The real meaning of physiological decline which accompanies the aging process for all people—particularly as it relates to older people—can now assume a new and far less pejorative meaning. (This new perspective intends that study of bodily function and physiological decline leads to better health practices throughout the life span, which in turn leads to healthy functioning adults.) There are many physiologically-based theories which have been formulated to explain the aging process. Wantz and Gay, authors of *The Aging Process: A Health Perspective*, have summarized the most prevalent ones as "Autoimmune Theory, Nutrition Theory, Wear and Tear Theory, Waste Product Theory, Radiation Theory, Cybernetic Theory, Virus Theory, Stress Theory and Evolution Theory." Each of these has merit and each explains some aspect of the physiological dimensions of the aging process.

The physiological theory which seems most relevant for our purposes is the "Wear and Tear Theory." The others have contributed their share to the negative physical view of aging, though this was not their intent. "Autoimmune Theory," for example, is derived from cellular mutation theories and suggests that cellular deterioration and disease are related to the aging process and reduce the potential productivity of the older worker.

The "Wear and Tear Theory" basically assumes that at some point in time the human organism simply wears out and dies, similar to any machine. If the organism is properly maintained throughout the life span, we can expect it to function effectively until all the parts wear out simultaneously. As with any machine, however, peak efficiency of the human organism cannot be maintained throughout its life with the same degree of consistency as when it was new. Many factors contribute to a functional decline over time of humans as well as machines, among them over-use, improper maintenance and poor construction, for which suitable compensations are made. The point at which the human organism can profitably maintain its efficiency varies from individual to individual for many reasons, such as genetic makeup, life situations at birth, accidents and uncontrolled environmental forces. It is this variability which has given rise to the numerous physiological theories of aging. It is enough to recognize that the "Wear and Tear Theory" of aging has led to the assumption that we can legislatively predetermine when the human organism needs to be retired. This is the same philosophy employed by business and industry to estimate the longevity of machines they are using in order to make decisions as to the most profitable time to replace them. New models (young workers) take over productive functions unless an emergency necessitates reactivation of the older retired machine (older worker).

It is recognized that this analogy is not the most pleasant way to view human beings in their productive roles. Nevertheless, it is a reasonably accurate view, given the way older people have been treated during the last fifty or more years and have been "mustered out" of the goods-and-services-producing activities of our society. As R. N. Butler, author of *Why Survive? Being Old in America*, and others have pointed out, however, what is not understood when employing a decision-making philosophy as described above is that older people become more heterogeneous as they age. This heterogeneity is not only physiologically, but also economically and psychologically, a characteristic of human beings. It is the very nature of this heterogeneity that precludes continued acceptance of the belief that we can, with any real degree of accuracy, predict when at some arbitrary point in time the individual will physiologically wear out and be unable to continue to function as an important human resource.

Mental Health. A third category of myth concerning the functioning of older people relates to a mental health perspective. As with the other categories, there has emerged over time a popular belief that as one ages, his mental functions become impaired, making it risky to maintain him in productive activities. Often, visible manifestations of forgetfulness, reminiscing, becoming more assertive (some would call this being cantankerous), being repetitious in describing events, desiring to be quiet at times and over-active at other times, being overly talkative and the like are signs to which others point to justify identifying an older person as being in a state of mental decline. Apparently, any behavior which younger age groups (in some cases the same age group) identify in older age groups as not conforming to some preconceived perception of behavior is a sign of mental deterioration and disorientation.

Often these behavioral indices are pointed to as the onset of "senility." Yet, as stated earlier, there are few if any socially-agreed-upon roles for older people in modern society. Then it is not unusual to see older people exhibit behavior which in the past has been rewarding for them and which assisted them in coping with life's discontinuities, even though some ambiguous external criteria suggest otherwise. The irony is that this same behavior—which is perceived as socially unacceptable in older age groups—is perfectly normal and acceptable in younger age groups. Clinical and social gerontologists are actively engaged in research of these dimensions and in developing intervention programs in an effort to ameliorate the mental health aspects of the aging process. The gerontological literature is a testimony to the active interest and concern in this area.

The most difficult mental health problems encountered by older adults and their families are depression and dementia, more commonly recognized as senility. High suicide rates among older adults are seen as symptomatic of excessively depressed states, especially among white males. One can also conclude that higher-than-normal rates of alcoholism and drug abuse among older adults are also symptoms of depressed states. The popular media—especially television—have often portrayed older people in these conditions, contributing to the popularization of the mental health decline myth as being applicable to all older persons.

In reality, feelings of depression among older people may be expressions of or reactions to personal losses such as job and career, loved ones, home; the loss of any one of these could trigger such behavior. Such losses are not uncommon across the life span and similar feelings exhibited by younger age groups (the young express this as "feeling down") are not viewed negatively and are tolerated. Such toleration is not accorded to older people who experience similar feelings and perhaps do not perceive any alternatives in their future. B. J. Gurland was referring to this when he reported that older age groups (sixty-five and older) manifested higher rates of *depressed symptoms*, whereas younger age groups (twenty-five to sixty-four years of age) exhibited higher rates of *depressive disorders* as diagnosed by psychiatrists. In a work setting, the possibility of alienation from other workers can have a negative impact on job performance and co-worker cooperation. Such behavior, when exhibited by older people over a protracted time period, could be claimed as evidence justifying termination or forced retirement from work rather than evidence which indicates the need for a program of counseling and therapy to help overcome depressive feelings and to bring about the readjustment of one's life to accommodate losses.

"Senility" has become a popular catch-all phrase to categorize dependent or deviant behavior exhibited by confused older adults. Once such a label is placed on an older person he is often powerless to challenge it. Such labels have been used to remove the "troublesome" older person from his environment, especially his job. In the book *Aging in the 1980's*, author M. Gatz concluded that "neither the mental health system nor the aging network has developed adequate programs to identify and serve older adults with organic brain syndrome."

Several factors exacerbate the ambiguity surrounding misconceptions associated with this "senility" label: 1) lack of research on the etiology and treatment of organic brain syndrome, 2) lack of coordination in psychological, social and physical treatments, 3) legal issues regarding competency, 4) assumptions of responsibility regarding persons so diagnosed, and 5) poor representation in the "interest group" political process. Such ambiguity associated with popularized attitudes about "mental problems" suggests that extreme caution must be exercised in labeling older people as senile or as manifesting the early stages of senility, especially as related to their productive potential.

There are far too many exceptions to this attitude reported throughout the literature on aging and generally observed throughout society to warrant assumptions of older people's inability to functionally perform based upon mythical misconceptions of declining mental health.

Misdiagnosis of either depression or organic brain syndrome can and often does lead to treatment error, especially from a medical-pharmacological perspective. This can lead to iaotrogenic complications which aggravate, rather than alleviate, possible mental health problems and which can interfere with the continued productive activity of older adults. In the human resources context, our argument is that misconceptions, errors in judgment and voids in knowledge concerning the etiology of mental health issues among the aged do exist. Due to these errors, we risk omitting from productive self-sustaining activity many persons who otherwise could and perhaps would like to continue making positive, productive contributions both to themselves and to their society.

Policy Issues. The longer they are in place, the more often most myths associated with the human condition are accepted as fact. They are unquestioned assumptions offered to explain the unknown, to resolve a perceived problem at some point in time, or to satisfy a vested interest for some reason. Myths about aging, which have been developed and nurtured over time, have intruded on the formation of public policy designed to assist older people in the transition to and in living later life stages. Public policy based upon mythical assumptions presumes that decision-making concerning the individual's productive efficiency and worthwhileness rests with society; it is not negotiated by the individual with his employer. Such a policy is punitive rather than rewarding for most of the people who have spent a lifetime in productive self-sustaining efforts. The many myths about the productive functional ability of older people are invalid as criteria to be indiscriminately applied to all people at a specified age.

As we try to live through the economic stresses and strains during the 1980s, situations which we inherited from the 1970s, and as the full impact of declining birth rates of the 1960s and 1970s begins to result in a declining labor force during the 1980s and 1990s, we will—in all likelihood—turn to our older age groups to assist in resolving social and economic problems which may result. Certainly we have done so in the past when we experienced other national crises. Older people will be positively looked upon as human resources whose time has come.

There are five interrelated policy domains which merit consideration and also relate to the importance of the older adult's human resource potential. The first policy issue concerns the fullest development of the productive capacities of human beings. This includes not only development of technical skills necessary for job performance, but also what H. S. Parnes refers to as "labor market skills," which include such areas as "a basic understanding of the dimensions of the work world; the occupational alternatives open to individuals and the education and training these occupations require; how one goes about looking for work; how one presents one's self to an employer." Included here is also the development of a set of attitudes, habits and behaviors consistent with employment in an industrialized society.

In the past, society has assumed these skills, attitudes, habits and behaviors as the learning province of youth. There is such a deep and pervasive belief in the importance of "labor market skills" that a new emphasis in Career Education was introduced as part of public school education in an effort to sensitize youth to these skills.

It appears to be an assumption that when one reaches adulthood—especially older adulthood—and has been in the labor force for a period of time, he has mastered these labor market skills and has no further need for keeping up with changes. This assumption may have been valid in the past when several job changes over a lifetime were exceptional, but with the changing nature of work and with the expectation for several job changes being the current and future norm, it may no longer be valid. Deficits in the knowledge within an adult population do not manifest themselves until they are forced to stop work for any reason, e.g., a lay-off due to economic slowdown, the company's going out of business, or forced early retirement.

Under these circumstances, some older people are faced with a job search after working in one setting for several years. Many adults of all ages find re-entry into the labor force a trying and traumatic experience for many reasons; there may be family responsibility, difficulty in uprooting to move to a new community, or loss of income. The older the adult is, the more likely he will be to take early retirement. This brings with it all the attending financial losses and social and psychological stresses, but these may be preferable to the struggle to find new employment which, if found, often results in considerable reduction in income and loss of status.

A second category for a human resource policy has to do with allocation of resources. This policy area is concerned with assuring that individuals who have mastered both vocational skills and labor market skills are allocated among those occupations, industries, firms and localities in which their contributions will be maximized. This means that work incentives are consistent with the economy's needs and that workers have adequate as well as accurate job information. This will necessitate the development of appropriate institutional arrangements, which promote functional occupational and geographic mobility. The implication here is that there will need to be closer cooperation between business, industry, educational institutions, public and private placement agencies, and all other institutionalized groups who have concern about people and work.

It is essential that more and expanded job training be developed and also retraining programs for older workers, programs which build upon previously-mastered vocational and labor market skills for all workers. Future workers will need to think in terms of multiple careers during their work lives rather than the one career which has been the norm. Life-long training and retraining will become a necessity rather than an exception if workers are to keep pace with rapidly-changing job demands. If we accept the concept that we are moving toward a stationary population, then proper allocation of older workers as a resource assumes a high level of importance in order for us to meet future labor market demands, a level only recently being recognized.

Human resource utilization is a third category for a human resource policy. Proper use of human resources is designed to eliminate waste by the employer. The most significant waste concerns discrimination—overt or covert—based upon age, sex or race. Discrimination is bad policy not only because it is immoral, but because it is wasteful of vital resources and has no justifiable basis.

The fact that myths about aging workers in the labor force are without any real foundation suggests that older people are singled out for massive discrimination. Similar arguments can be made to support the elimination of discrimination based upon race and sex. This policy area does imply that a form of discrimination is proper, that of productive capacity. The difficulty here is that employers are assumed to be able to clearly define acceptable limits of productive capacity as related to different jobs, as well as having the ability to correlate these limits with age.

Because previous wasteful practices concerning the use of human resources assumed an unlimited supply of workers, employers have not needed to attend carefully to issues associated with productive capacity, age and time utilization of workers. A human resource utilization policy involving older workers will have to consider the need for defining what the limits are of productive capacity of all workers relative to job performance needs. In addition, more effective personnel and industrial relations policies designed to minimize waste—such as absenteeism—will need to be developed. Recalling Yankelovich's theory, it may be that future generations of older workers who subscribe to a modified work ethic different from their predecessors' will be motivated to be more deeply involved in this issue.

Human resources maintenance or conservation is a fourth policy consideration. This relates to maintaining and conserving the health and vigor of people. It would include such issues as adequate nutritional programs, preventive health care, and industrial safety and hygiene, as well as income maintenance schemes such as unemployment compensation, workmen's compensation and disability compensation. In a paper written for the Center for Vocational Education in Columbus, Ohio, H. S. Parnes stated that these areas are important "not only because of their humanitarian implications, but also because they protect valuable investments in the productive capacities of human beings during periods in which they are not working."

In a sense, this was Frances Perkins' objective during the 1930s, as it was an earlier concern of settlement house workers. At issue is the maintenance aspect as it is currently being practiced. Past and current policy conceptualizes maintenance in terms of government action to provide the basic care for individuals experiencing temporary dysfunctions, but such policies do not take into consideration how this "down time" is to be used. For older workers, these maintenance programs often turn out to be the prelude to early retirement. J. M. Kreps, *et al*, suggest in a paper put out by the U. S. Government Printing Office than when (and if?) we experience a stationary population, there will be little need for concern with early retirement.

A stationary population, however, is not anticipated until the middle of the next century. In the meantime, two to three generations of older citizens will have experienced the latter life stage with all the attendant stresses which such an increasingly large group can be expected to experience if there is no change in current aid programs for older adults.

When considering unemployment problems which result from economic slowdown, business failure or any discontinuity in the normal resource cycle, perhaps we might conceptualize this as "down time." Such time can be used for job retraining programs, upgrading job and labor market skills, and in similar activities in which both the public and private sectors work cooperatively. This concept is not dissimilar to what is currently the practice in business and industry when there is any temporary interruption in the productive flow. When such an event occurs, workers are temporarily re-assigned to other work activities until these situations are rectified.

A final policy area which needs careful attention involves maintaining a high level of demand for employment. This is, of course, a matter of general economic policy of concern to all facets of society and of serious concern to the nurturance of a human resource potential. So long as there continues to be a high demand for employment, we can assume that the production-consumption cycle will not be interrupted. If there is not maintenance of high employment levels which stimulate the production-consumption cycle, then concerns with maximizing a human resource potential become irrelevant and the traditional approach of restricting who will or will not be able to be employed will continue.

This means later entry of youth into the labor market (already occurring through longer educational experiences) and earlier exit of adults through such mechanisms as early retirement. Continuation of the latter policy can be a danger to society because problems arise concerning time utilization and attending economic costs. In the rise of youth crime, increased antisocial behavior, experimentation with alternate lifestyles at younger and younger ages, we can see that excess leisure time may be counterproductive for youth as well as for society. Can we expect similar societal problems with older adults if the system forces excess time onto them without some alternative ways to use that time? It is essential that they perceive their activities to be valuable and that these activities be rewarded.

6

RETIREMENT:
AN ARTIFACT OF
INDUSTRIALIZATION

Thoughts of retirement from formal work are as old as man's living in stable, organized societies. Historically, retirement from paid work was not entertained as a possibility for most people until the modernization of society. An ancient exception was Homer's reference to Laertes—father of Odysseus—as being retired from heading his estates in order to perform more simple agricultural activities when he became old. Other exceptions have been noted throughout literature and history.

The actual removal of oneself from formalized work for which there was financial remuneration was rare for most people. If the event ever did occur, it was limited essentially to the affluent or infirmed. There were at least three reasons for this: few people lived long enough to consider an adult life without some type of formal work, few people could afford to maintain themselves for lengthy periods without working, and since the Reformation most people accepted the sanctification of work as the way to enter God's grace. *Not working* was a contradiction of this ideology.

In early agrarian societies, the reality of retirement from formal work was reserved primarily for those who had accumulated sufficient wealth and property to allow them leisure. Those who were able to "retire" altered their work roles rather than give them up. The majority—regardless of age—continued to engage in some form of labor until death or physical infirmity.

As civilization matured, work for those who had "passed their prime" was modified to some extent, but rarely was terminated. For most individuals, the notion of retirement was an idealized dream, to become a reality only with society's industrialization. Modernization reduced the amount of work one had to perform to sustain himself. It also resulted in the desanctification of work as a moral good, an idea from the time when society had more human resources than it knew how to or was willing to accommodate.

With the use of machines to perform worker functions, people began to enjoy more leisure, earn higher incomes, amass estates, and experience better health. These factors have led to realizing the retirement concept to the extent that today, most people believe that retirement from work is their right—a right to be experienced with comfort and dignity. Whether this expectation has yet been achieved by most people who have or will be retiring has been the subject of much speculation and debate.

The concept of a modern-day "superanuated man" who is ostensibly to receive a few years leisure in later life as a reward for many years of employment is widespread. However, with the inception of more formalized systems to remove workers from the marketplace there have emerged social and economic problems for which there has been little preparation for long-term care of non-productive workers.

Displacement of older workers from the labor force to solve social and economic problems is not a new idea. Many procedures have emerged, been tried, and discarded over time. Early retirement systems were predicated on a concept of employee reward for long and faithful service and as a way to make room for younger workers. These arrangements were generally individually devised between employer and employee and were quite satisfactory for some workers. They emerged at a time when employee-employer ratios were small, when small business was primary, when life in general was quite simple, when few people survived to an older age, when labor-intensive work was the norm, when daily work demanded physical rather than mental stamina, and when capital resources were at a minimum but human resources were increasing in number. With the advent of mass production concepts and an increasing youth population, employee-employer ratios grew quite large. They now have become so large that the personalized retirement plans of the past are no longer efficient or effective. More impersonal retirement arrangements have been introduced to accommodate the change.

However, being retired or non-employed for pay is essentially a new phenomenon and has become a new phase in the human life cycle for the average worker. Retirement from work is a direct result of moving from a human labor-intensive work force to a more efficient machine labor-intensive work force. But as more people are retiring at earlier ages, there arises a large dependency population living longer, one that is expected to be consumers (assuming economic wherewithal) rather than producer-consumers. Others who are younger are expected to produce enough to sustain non-producers in their consuming roles. Should all the countries of the world convert to technology to produce their goods and services then all people would become consumers who would need to expend very little energy in productive work as we conceive it to be. Then perhaps we would not need to concern ourselves with retirement issues. All people would live in a semi-retired state throughout their life span. As it stands, however, reality and past history suggest that such a Utopian state is very unlikely to emerge during the foreseeable future.

Issues surrounding any form of retirement surface periodically, since the possibility that attaining such a stage is within reach of most in industrialized society. How to live in such a stage of life in a manner agreeable to all persons has never been resolved satisfactorily. Perhaps one reason is that we are badly in need of theoretical models which can systematically study the complex interaction of work, retirement and aging. These complexities entail life satisfaction, roles, self-images, status, economics, family and marriage dimensions, as well as political and health realities. As society evolves, questions associated with the systematic removal of an experienced segment of the labor force at a given chronological age continue to be a topic of concern. Certainly, the lack of resolution of these issues is related to the issue of chronological age versus functional age as the determinant of who should be retired, and at what age. What is really needed is an unambiguous definition as to what is meant by "aging," "aged," and "old age" so we can be more precise in resolving the ever-spreading conflicts and divergent (sometimes counter-productive) views and actions concerning the life stage called retirement.

RETIREMENT: WHAT IS IT?

Retirement means many things to many people and its definition depends upon the definer—the individual or society. It is a term used to denote a concept or an attitude which—in the United States—seems to be universally accepted and agreed upon as a life stage all persons are entitled to experience, at least superficially. Even if a person reaches the turning point in life called retirement, what is it?

Writers from many disciplines have traced the evolution of a retirement concept but they avoid offering clear definitions. One explanation which seems to arise uniformly is that when an individual is not working for pay and is the recipient of a pension or Social Security benefits, he is retired from active participation in the labor force. In their book *Aging in Mass Society*, however, Hendricks and Hendricks pose several unsettling questions:

> How do we classify a person if he or she returns to work next week? Does it make a difference if the work is only

part-time as opposed to full-time? Is a person retired if he
or she has not worked for a full year prior to the time of an
interview? What if one is unemployed but cannot now
claim retirement benefits? Should an individual who
was forced out of a lifelong job at age sixty-five (we can
also include ages sixty-two, sixty, fifty-five and for some
military personnel forty or forty-five as points for early
retirement, enforced or otherwise), was unwilling to
leave and is currently seeking full-time employment be
classified as retired?

We can ask similar questions related to part-time workers, part-year workers, and the like. Should they too be considered as retired? In an article in *Social Forces*, E. Palmore
suggested that as an alternative, retirement could be calculated
on the number of weeks worked during the previous year. This
would allow retirement to be a matter of degree rather than the
dichotomy which most writers seem to consider it. This adds
another dilemma, however; how many weeks worked or not
worked would constitute being in a stage of retirement? Who
would make such a decision? In what jeopardy are financial
entitlements when one does elect to be a paid worker in a partial
stage of retirement?

As stated earlier, the possibility of universal retirement
is a recent phenomenon resulting from the modernization and
industrialization of society. This has resulted in older people
experiencing a non-role in their retirement for which history
provides no precedent and which, until lately, has been
ignored. It has been only in recent years—as society has begun
to perceive the increasing numbers of older people who suddenly have become visible—that attention is being devoted to
the life stage called retirement. This new awareness of older
people has contributed to the ambiguity surrounding retirement's meaning. C. E. Bennett, in his *History of Manual and
Industrial Education*, attempted to define retirement as a:

> life stage, an event, and a process of adjustment. As a life
> stage, it is a period of economic activity socially pre-

scribed for workers in later life. As an event, it is characterized by the separation from paid employment which has the character of an occupation or a career over a period of time. Finally, as a process of adjustment it begins when retirement is first considered by the individual and abates when the individual has achieved a new distribution of his energies and new modes of behavior in the absence of his work role. Thus, retirement can be viewed as both an institutional arrangement in society and as an experience of the individual.

With this view in mind, we can define retirement *as a permanent nonworking-for-pay life stage which most people can expect to experience at some chronological point in time.* In this sense, retirement is a distinct life event and represents a stage of the life cycle. Because of inherent ambiguities, it is a stage which may be traumatic for some and looked forward to by others, and it may occur early or late in one's life. Retirement as a termination from paid employment is, in reality, a convention bred of necessity. It is a concept and activity designed to accommodate or resolve social, political and economic problems which have resulted from the centralization of work environments, the fragmentation of the work activity, a rapidly rising youth population, and an erosion or the work ethic.

THE EVOLUTION OF A CONCEPT _____

The concept of retirement from paid employment as it has spread in the United States essentially was a program that was implemented to move large numbers of people out of the labor force, to ease economic stress, and to make room for growing numbers of more youthful workers. As such, retirement was incidental to a person's age. It is only a recent phenomenon that age has become synonymous with retirement.

After the Civil War, according to W. A. Achenbaum in *Old Age in a New Land: The American Experience Since 1970,* only state judges in some states were forced to retire because of advancing age. Other individuals who survived to older ages were valued for their insights, their knowledge of farming, and their moral guidance for youth. Rigid retirement concepts did not exist since older adults were perceived—at least superficially—to be functional and able to be just as productive as the young. On the other hand, Achenbaum raised questions about this view when he pointed out that old people seem to have been valued for little more than their knowledge, advice and guidance. In this sense they may not have been perceived as functionally equal to the young, but neither were they forced to withdraw from their work environment, since being old carried with it no social stigmas.

With the rapid depersonalization of the work environment came changes in the work structure itself, changes in economic organizations for the production of goods and services, and the institution of corporations which bureaucratized modernization. R. H. Wiebe, author of *The Search for Order: 1877-1920*, pointed out that these rapid alterations in industrial systems brought with them the formalization of governmental —as well as industrial—bureaucracies which in turn, served to bring into sharp relief the plight of workers and their families who were crowded into metropolitan districts. The adverse living conditions served to justify the initiation of social reform movements; formal retirement structures became an outgrowth of these movements. Prior to the formalization and institutionalization of social reform movements, older workers tenaciously retained their positions in the labor force during the early phases of the industrial movement. They generally had little savings and were without community ties. The more anxious they became about getting old, the more they clung to their positions. Without formal retirement systems, corporate and government bureaucracies became holding institutions and informal retirement mechanisms for thousands of older workers. In general, the new industrial worker had no family farm to retire to. Retirement from formal working arrangements meant a marginal existence in a crowded tenement district of an urban community.

W. Graebner, in *A History of Retirement*, pointed out that by 1900, the United States entered an era of state capitalism ". . . in which the power of government was brought to bear on problems too intractable for the cooperative solutions of private enterprise." The regulatory agencies of an expanding government bureaucracy were instructed to devise systems to solve the problems of retirement. Such legislation as the Civil Service Retirement Act, the Railroad Retirement Act, and the Social Security Act were the result. This series of legislation was basically designed to solve unemployment problems in particular work sectors, as well as to solve—for corporate and government bureaucracies—the issue of employment settings acting as holding institutions for the elderly worker. Simultaneously, stigmas were attached to being old, such as staying in a job too long is to be looked down upon and perceived as depriving employment for a younger person. This attitude was further exacerbated by the romantic writers of the previous generation who glamorized old people as sweet, white-haired, loving, grandparental, rocking-chair types, as well as by the medical researchers who were only recently beginning to make inroads concerning knowledge regarding public health, cellular deterioration and the like as they related to longevity.

Graebner posits three changes experienced by capitalism which had impacts upon retirement. "First, consumption replaced production as the most important solution to the nation's economic problems." As a result of this idea's introduction between 1890 and 1930, older people were expected to retire from work (cease being productive) and spend newly-acquired financial benefits (e.g., savings, pensions, Social Security). In this way they would become consumers, stimulate the economy via consumption, and make room in the labor force for the young. Retirement itself had become a commodity to be sold. This is, of course, antithetical to the human resources model.

His second point concerns the belief that unemployment problems were somehow different from those of poverty, and that unemployment was a problem for which the state had some responsibility. Fears associated with unemployment problems in a free market system served to justify age discrimination rather than to develop strategies which utilized the resource potential of all workers in a tight labor market situation. The retirement theory—which reduced worklife—became a national policy by which to reduce unemployment problems and relieve government and industry from functioning as detaining institutions for older workers who did not have the resources to retire.

Formal retirement programs were introduced originally to solve unemployment problems within specific labor groups as technology reduced the need for human workers more rapidly than did their dying off (e.g., railroad workers, civil service workers, teachers). This type of national policy was so enthusiastically endorsed that retirement legislation today affects nearly all occupational groups in American society.

Finally, the third major change felt by capitalism which has had an effect on retirement policies and practices relates to the post-World War II decline in America's international competitive position. To deal with competitive losses stemming from post-war recovery programs among Western technological nations—and to take advantage of cheaper labor—American manufacturers began producing in other countries. It was believed that this action would help make the American economy more efficient. It was to compensate for reduced labor demands from the American labor force that early retirement concepts were introduced and hawked via "Madison Avenue" advertising. People were being wooed, cajoled, induced or pushed to remove themselves from the active employment scene, ostensibly to indulge themselves in leisure life activities to which they were entitled. The "retirement dream" was promoted and belief in its possibility for all Americans became a reality. This, of course, was another manifestation of a national policy designed to solve either real or imagined unemployment problems. Older people—not necessarily *old* people—were once again being called upon to solve a social, political, and economic problem: remove self from the situation and the problem is resolved. It was almost as if it were un-American to wish to continue employment when one reached the "magical age."

Universal retirement has emerged as a social convention established in order to solve economic problems in rapidly-changing technological societies. Bismarck, the first chancellor of the German Empire, was well aware of this when he introduced the concept in the German social democratic states, as did the Danes, who were the forerunners of the universal retirement concept. The United States only half-heartedly accepted the idea until the "Depression" years, at which time retirement was perceived as a way to reduce the effect of the unemployment crisis.

With the liberalizing of the mandatory retirement age (Public Law 95-256, 1978), the relationship between retirement and productive efficiency was reversed. Employers—both public and private—were now forced to make employability decisions on the basis of merit, not age. Such a change in national policy assumes increased productivity, while at the same time relieving financial burdens for public and private pension systems. Apparently, this is to be a more humane way to deal with a rapidly rising older population while still accounting for the uniqueness of the individual. At this writing, it is too soon to estimate the affect of this national policy upon the older American population.

However, what is beginning to evolve as a result of a changing national retirement policy is perhaps a higher order concept which truly recognizes the worth of individual workers and their contribution in a continually-emerging society. Retirement, as originally conceived and designed to eliminate or reduce the size of the labor force, has been punitive toward and non-discriminating of an individual's past and potential productivity. Perhaps now that we are beginning to realize that we are entering a post-industrial phase of American society's development we are also recognizing that retirement—as a national policy designed to solve society's social and economic problems—is no longer relevant.

As a society, we seem ready to see the more coercive forms of retirement disappear. As a national policy designed to solve economic problems associated with increasing life longevity, retirement has become a welfare system of grand proportions, having the effect of warehousing a large cadre of human resources, people we have not been willing to understand nor continue to include as part of the "American Experiment." As a political issue, the "Graying of America" seems to be having the effect of influencing politicians to address those issues concerning this population segment, thus altering—or at least influencing—social policy legislation.

What seems to be needed is a re-evaluation of the retirement concept which accounts for individual differences to which we will need to adjust, rather than continuing to expect a predetermined segment of the population to adjust. This, of course, calls for new ways to interpret retirement—what is it, at what point in the life cycle should it be introduced, should it be introduced at all, who is affected and under what conditions? These are knotty issues which will take time and debate to resolve and will call for major shifts in thinking as well as longitudinal research if this transitional life stage is to be understood.

GROWTH OF THE
RETIREMENT MYTH _____

As more and more people began to realize benefits from the Social Security system to which they had contributed since its inception, the belief in retirement from paid work and the expected economic support systems became a reality. For the first time, a non-working-for-pay lifestyle for most older citizens was beginning to be looked upon favorably. In post-World War II America, people came to believe with an almost patriotic zeal that when they reached the "magic age" it was time to relinquish their place in the work force to the rapidly-increasing population of youth. Not to want to retire at the "magical age" was almost un-American. Society's acceptance and economic support of a non-productive-for-pay lifestyle was a complete reversal of traditional views and values of older people's place in the productive activities of society. It paralleled changing work ethics and the growing acceptance of views associated with Yankelovich's analysis of the "Psychology of Entitlement." It was during this same period that social-psychological theories of aging were being developed, which tended to add credence to retirement being a normal life stage in human development.

With all the changes transpiring since World War II, regardless of the lip service given to the acceptance of that life stage called retirement as a right, R. A. Kalish in *The Later Years: Social Applications of Gerontology*, reminds us it was today's ". . . Mr. Citizen, Sr., who emphasized the importance of . . . avoiding dependency, of being productive, . . . of being meaningful to others and avoiding self-centered actions, of being future-directed and avoiding past-directedness." We see here a built-in contradiction and conflict which society has not truly confronted until recently, when the enactment of the 1978 amendments to the Age Discrimination in Employment Act took place. Hard work associated as part of the Protestant Work Ethic helped society realize the retirement experience as fact and also glamorized certain behavioral attributes of older people. This same adherence assumes that once that life stage is reached, one will continue to abide by that ethic even though life roles identified through its application are ambiguous and the available environments in which such an ethic can be practiced are limited. *When one is old and retired from work and the work environment, it is difficult to maintain independence with reduced incomes, continue to be productive in the sense that energy expended is revered by self or others, and continue to be meaningful to others, since one's value in the eyes of others has been diminished.* These are the problems of role identity Rosow was discussing and to which we referred earlier. To be retired from one's productive role in society is to become a member of an ambiguous and heterogeneous social group which has few identity points other than chronological age, little shape or form which is valued by the larger society, and a relatively minor place in the social structure. The loss of one's work or productive role in society which accompanies retirement suggests the need for role realignment when one reaches this later life stage.

In *The Later Years: Social Applications to Gerontology,* G. F. Streib has identified four factors which need to be considered for role realignment when one retires: a) new life roles need to be formed since loss of work, which may have been the individual's major focus of attention throughout life, is a reality which accompanies retirement, b) loss of income or, at best, a severely reduced income, which limits the individual's ability to maintain the living standard to which he had become accustomed, c) some older individuals either had health problems which influenced the retirement decision or they suddenly experienced declining health which is a new problem (any significant decline in physical condition suggests the need to drop certain roles and assume others which are less familiar), and d) changes in the family structure due to children having left home, the death of a spouse, parents being dependent upon aid from children rather than the reverse, which in earlier years had been the norm.

We have alluded to the notion that certain institutional arrangements in society—along with an adherence to a strong work ethic—have given rise to the reality of retirement as a way of life. Retirement as an experience which can be expected has brought with it a new leisure life role. Acceptance of leisure as a way of life and as different from the high activity levels demanded in the workplace helped to redefine both old age and retirement as a form of disengagement. Disengagement Theory served to perpetuate the retirement myth and was used to justify the withdrawal of workers from the labor force, as well as to introduce and justify early retirement practices which emerged during the 1950s and extended into the 1960s and 1970s. On the other hand, Activity Theory posited that complete disengagement was socially and individually destructive. While one may retire from the formal work environment, one needs to stay active and involved in life. Developmental Theory assumed that retirement was a normal progression of the life cycle and attempted to describe human behavior which represented that life stage. These and other social-psychological theories did much to reenforce and solidify the institutional arrangements which led to retirement from work being assumed to be a normal part of life. They all implicitly agree that role changes and realignment are normal progressions confronting individuals who chronologically reach the retirement stage of life. These theories also seem to accept the idea that *all* individuals can and should expect to behave in an identified pattern. However, these theories seem to ignore or not address the issue of socially-accepted environments in which new and socially-revered roles can emerge, develop and achieve a significant place in the social milieu. Retirement communities, nursing homes, etc., seem to be emerging as warehousing institutions similar in some respects to the work setting prior to formalized retirement programs.

Most people want to remain in the work environment since this is where their identity continues to be defined. Therefore, most retirement is involuntary and, we can add, serves to perpetuate and satisfy institutional (public and private) needs. Further, since a person's identity is sustained by several life roles, the work role being one among many and no longer the preeminent one which it once was, adjustment to retirement will pose few problems. Retirement today is in marked contrast to an earlier time when at the least later life brought with it the roles of family sage, historian, and guardian of the family wealth as well as a degree of filial piety.

In all likelihood, full- or part-time retirement from non-paying work activities is desirable for some and not for others. There is no one ideal life role for all older people; there are many. The problem is to define these roles so they are perceived by both self and others to be emulated by younger age groups. True retirement advocates argue that retirement is the period of life in which "one can take it easy" and enjoy the leisure to which one is entitled. Leisure advocates neglect to explain, however, how the majority of retirees—after having lived a life of self-dependence—will be able economically to afford this state of living without being a burden to society. The other position is that one should work as long as he or she can and, if retired by one employer, seek other full-time work, since the most important life role one enacts is in the work environment. This position assumes that older persons can find other work to perform, whereas the evidence overwhelmingly points to the opposite direction.

The activist movements of such groups as the Gray Panthers and the Association of Retired Teachers are asserting that the individual has a right to some say in the decision making regarding when and under what conditions he is to retire. The underlying theme of the various White House Conferences on Aging has reflected the view that the traditional myths about aging are no longer relevant. Society will need to accommodate the view that older Americans are not worn out, used up and unable to continue active participation in productive endeavors at some arbitrarily-defined point in time. The traditional institutional arrangements for retirement from work—which have also formally defined who is or is not old—are no longer appropriate and are a liability to society.

ECONOMIC SUPPORT

Uppermost in the minds of most older people trying to preserve their autonomy and maintain their independence during their retirement years is maintaining good health and economic well-being. Medical research has made a significant impact on eliminating or reducing the effects of numerous fatal illnesses, and has had the effect of extending the life span. The formerly terminal diseases have been reduced to such an extent that most people in modern societies live without fear of premature death due to bacteria. During the past few decades, significant reductions in death by cardiovascular dysfunctions and cancer have been made. The medical advances have been so spectacular in some cases that most people live without fear of dying prematurely. This realization is unique in the history of man and has resulted in longer-lived, healthier and more active older adults.

Physically, older people are not "used up" after four decades of work as were their predecessors; they can and often do maintain activity levels that are far more strenuous than the demands made on them during their working-for-pay years. For many, an involved and active lifestyle has had the effect of extending their longevity beyond the years suggested by estimates published in actuarial tables. Using Fries' estimates, it is not unreasonable to assume that by the year 2040, older people can expect to live active, healthy and productive lives until they are eighty-five. Given our current institutionalized retirement patterns, this means twenty to twenty-five years of not-for-pay activity during one's adult life stage. Combining these estimates with the not-for-pay activity years for youth, we are left with living an estimated forty to fifty years in non-working-for-pay lifestyles. This is potentially one-half the expected life span. The real question now is whether the individual or society can economically sustain this form of non-productive lifestyle. Is society willing to sustain this form of lifestyle? This is an issue society has not confronted yet. Whether a long-term dependency population is affordable is an economic question. The two questions are not mutually exclusive. Yankelovich's thesis suggests that the maturing World War II babies are questioning whether they can or are economically willing to sustain such a long-term dependency population.

J. J. Spengler, in a government paper, has estimated that by 2030, the population growth in the United States will have stabilized, assuming no immigration and assuming that fertility rates will stabilize at the replacement level. When and if this occurs, we can expect an increasing proportion of older members in the society. As has been cited, we are already experiencing a visible increase in the numbers of older citizens. These increases are straining the social systems which were designed to reduce the trauma of aging in an industrial society. If Spengler's estimates are correct, the economic stress and strain American society is experiencing—given no drastic modifications to existing economic support systems—will far exceed the estimated budgetary outlays that will be needed by the turn of the century to support a continuing rapidly-rising older dependency population. If this is so, according to R. L. Clark, by 2050, the tax rate required to maintain the present economic standard for people under Social Security will need to be 17.55 percent. This estimate assumes the retirement age stays constant at age sixty-five. Clark also reports that his figures are compatible with the Social Security Administration's long-range estimates of 17-18 percent tax after the year 2025. He further asserts that in order to raise the present Social Security level from a replacement of 40 percent to 60 percent, it would be necessary to raise taxes by 50 percent. Regardless of which direction public policy elects to follow, the economic cost to society in maintaining a large and growing older population will be exceedingly high. At the same time there will be no corresponding increase in purchasing power or improved living conditions. This will have the effect of further eroding the nation's resources, which can have a devastating effect on the total society and which is of major concern to the aged. At a time when resource conservation and recycling are in the forefront of a nation's conscience, it seems appropriate to re-examine the continuation of an economic support system which was introduced originally to solve a labor crisis.

SUPPORT SYSTEMS _____

Retirement and attendant financial entitlements have become an accepted way of later adult life. It is a system which, until recently, society has believed it economically could and was willing to sustain. Current economic support systems (public and private) which are contractual arrangements between the worker and society and the worker and employer have evolved concurrently with the acceptance of a retirement way of life and their adequacy is beginning to be questioned. The amount of retirement income derived from these sources is dependent upon the dollar amount contributed by the worker and/or employer, as well as by the number of years worked and the age at which retirement is initiated. In addition, it is tacitly assumed that upon retirement the individual will have some savings to augment his income from retirement arrangements. In theory, this combination of financial arrangements is thought to be sufficient for older people to provide for themselves financially at some reasonably comfortable level. This pluralistic theory seems to be an article of faith that when one reaches his or her retirement years, that person will live a life of reasonable comfort with a reasonably adequate income. This, of course, is an idealized dream and the view pitched by Madison Avenue advertisers when, in reality, quite the opposite seems to be true for many. The number of older people living in poverty has been estimated at from 4 percent to 21.6 percent, and apparently there is no clear estimate of the number living at the near-poverty level. In their book, *Aging, Agism and Society*, G. M. Barrow and P. A. Smith report that in 1975, over one-fourth of the elderly were categorized as "near poor." Depending upon whose estimates one elects to accept, we can conclude that 29-40 percent of the elderly in the United States live at an income level below what many might consider reasonable if they are to experience a comfortable retirement in our current society. This does not seem congruent with the retirement policy perceived by many in our country to be desirable, believed by most older adults as their right, or consistent in a society that has been estimated to be the most affluent in the history of man. Nor is such a condition a true reward for those adults who have worked hard to help develop and contribute to this nation's growth.

It is assumed that for most Americans who reach retirement age, their income support system is a combination of their contributions to the Social Security System, participation in a pension plan (public or private), and personal savings. Theoretically, the distribution of the tripartite economic support system would appear as depicted in Figure 6-1a, which suggests an equal balance of income support.

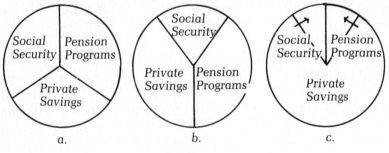

Figure 6-1

Since Social Security is conceived as being only a small aspect of financial support, however, the bulk of retirement income is expected to be derived from pensions and savings, as seen in Figure 6-1b. If neither Social Security nor pension programs—especially private pension programs—can meet financial needs in retirement (this does seem to be the case today for many retired elderly), then the bulk of financial support will fall to the individual, as seen in Figure 6-1c. This latter view seems to be looming more and more as a reality unless both the public and private sectors are willing to expend larger amounts of capital to support a growing dependency population which is expected to reach a peak between the years 2010-2030.

Social Security

The Social Security System has been examined in great detail by numerous writers and researchers and has been the subject of numerous debates. Basically, the system is comprised of four parts: 1) basic benefits [OASI], 2) Disability Insurance [DI], 3) Hospital Insurance [HI], and 4) Supplementary Medical Insurance [SMI]. In addition, there is available Supplemental Security Insurance [SSI], paid from general revenues and used to assist retirees whose basic income falls below the poverty line set by the Federal government. The framers of the Social Security System conceived it as a way to insure that older workers who retire would have assurance of a small income to be supplemented from other sources, especially personal savings and family. Social Security was never intended to satisfy all the economic needs of retirees but was designed to help achieve individual equity and social adequacy for older people. With the many amendments and "add-ons" over the years, however, the Social Security System has become a welfare program of grand proportions, and through lack of understanding or misinformation people have come to rely more and more on their anticipated OASI benefits as the major income source during retirement. For many reasons the welfare notion associated with Social Security seems antithetical in American society; 1) affluent individuals who least need the income derive the largest dollar amount since they generally contribute the most, 2) welfare payments to older people are contradictory to the work ethic to which older Americans subscribe and which has been a sustaining moral force in American society, 3) the pyramiding nature of the entire system assumes more workers will enter the labor force and pay into the system than the number receiving benefits. We have ample evidence that "the system" is in difficulty, a) due to more people living longer than when the system was initiated, and thus receiving far more dollar benefits than they contributed, b) due to inflation, which is growing more rapidly than contributions to the system, c) due to declining birth rates which, in effect, place a greater financial burden on fewer people, and d) the "means test" restricts freedom of choice to continuing working for, if retired people do work, they may lose some or all benefits under the system. In effect, to be a recipient of Social Security benefits, one will need to be beholden to the State in order to receive income which he himself contributed and which he has come to believe is his right to receive. There are numerous other issues which are yet to be resolved. Some changes are being considered, though, such as benefits for two-worker couples not sharing equally to their lifetime contributions, and payments to minorities who, on the average, do not live long enough to derive any benefits due to their dying sooner than the majority of the population.

Pension Plans

Private and public pension systems, which have grown rapidly since World War II, comprise the second leg of the tripartite economic support system for older people. These programs have yet to realize their true potential as part of the total income support system for older people. In essence, pension plans are defined as:

> . . . any plan, fund or program established or maintained
> by an employer or by an employee organization, or by
> both, that a) provides retirement income to employees, or

b) results in deferral of income by employees for periods extending to the termination of covered employment or beyond, regardless of the method of calculating the contributions made to the plan, the method of calculating the benefits under the plan or the method of distributing benefits from the plan (ERISA, Sec. 3[2]).

F. P. King, in a report on aging and income, has estimated that about 46 percent of private sector workers and 90 percent of public sector workers are covered by pension plans. Collectively, by 1976, seventy-six million workers were covered by some pension plan. Since many of these plans came into existence only since World War II, however, our experience with regard to income support for the elderly is limited. It has only been since 1974—with the enactment of the Employee Retirement Income Security Act (ERISA)—that retirement plans are insured in a manner similar to the FSLIC or FDIC for savings plans. Prior to that date, pension plans could be dissolved with the demise of a business or industry or through poor management or other catastrophe, with the individual never realizing any benefits after years of contributions.

The rapid growth in private pension plans in the last forty years is encouraging, but for at least two reasons it would be misleading to assume they will meet the financial needs of most retired workers. Not all workers counted as covered will receive pension benefits in old age, due to the fact that a covered worker is not a vested worker. Vesting may be contingent upon long-term uninterrupted employment and does not occur until a worker retires or first uses up his own contributions to the pension program. If a worker terminates employment prior to the vesting date (often between ten and twenty years of continuous employment is required for vesting), future benefits are forfeited since few plans are portable. Earlier, we pointed out that Cowgill suggested that young workers will move to the jobs created by the emerging technology of electronic computerization, thus further jeopardizing the possibility of participating in a long-term pension program until the latter part of their work life. This form of job movement—which is not uncommon in today's work world—reduces the possibility of realizing a substantial retirement benefit being built up over time.

Secondly, the growth rate of coverage under private pension plans has not kept pace with work force expansion. Thus, proportionately fewer workers in the private sector are actually participating in and benefitting from their pension programs than would appear. These problems arise in part because of the lack of pension portability from employer to employer. King has cautioned against over-optimism in believing that private pension plans can provide the much-needed retirement income in most people's retirement years. He is more optimistic with regard to public pension plans fulfilling the elderly's economic needs. Issues of portability, uniform funding requirements, vesting standards, double dipping, and fiduciary responsibility, however, still need to be resolved.

All in all, public and private pension programs are slowly on the upswing. Theoretically, they are beginning to have some positive impact on the economic needs of future elderly, though not necessarily for those retirees who are at the lower end of the socio-economic scale during their working years. P. Drucker, in *Pension Fund Socialism,* has pointed out that pension plans are being relied upon more and more to provide the capital formation for the nation's economy, both in terms of investing pension funds in the economy and as capital expenditures by retirees to pay for their leisure activities. Pension programs' financial resources are certainly one way to generate much-needed capital resources, however, the full impact of pension programs as economic resources for retirees perhaps will not be visible until the turn of the century. Even then they may not be realized unless the problems referred to are resolved.

Personal Savings

The third leg of the tripartite concept of economic support for the elderly is personal savings and family support. Traditionally, thrift has been a highly-revered ethic which has dominated the American culture since this country's inception.

In an earlier chapter, we traced the history of the work ethic and found a close relationship between the profit motive and responsibility for self, as well as responsibility for sharing some profits with those less fortunate. In essence, this aspect of the work ethic is reflected in the individual equity and social adequacy concept of the Social Security System. J. D. Dunn, in *Reappraising Social Security,* has presented a strong argument as to why the Social Security System has failed and will continue to fail to achieve these two contradictory objectives. Both Social Security and pension plans were initiated with the thought that income from them would in a small way supplement individual savings and reduce the financial drain on younger family members supporting their older parents.

Today, such is not the case. Few people save for old age or are able to save to the equivalent degree as in the past. Due to many reasons, since World War II savings in the form of cash or income-producing securities have been eroded for more and more individuals. (Keogh and IRA programs may alter this trend in the future for those persons able to afford participation.) Some of these reasons are:

1. Individual savings for many people have taken the form of home ownership, which is not income-producing in old age. Some retirees who spent a lifetime investing in their homes are finding that rising property taxes and insurance rates are threatening even this source of security, since their basic retirement incomes are not enough to maintain their homes as well as provide for their daily living expense.

2. Shortened work years due to educational requirements during youth and early retirement practices have tended to reduce overall income in relation to rising living costs. This further reduces the opportunity for individuals to save in terms of economic needs in their old age.

3. Rapid inflation during the past decade has eroded the value of fixed savings which may have been initiated during a more stable economic era. Such investments

as fixed-rate insurance annuities do not keep up with rising living costs and drastically reduce one's purchasing power in times of rapid inflation.

4. Various economic recessions have tended to reduce the number of working months per year for the average worker. This reduces the average yearly income, making it difficult to save for the future, and if savings have been amassed, they are used up to meet current expenses.

5. The trend toward smaller and more dispersed family units reduces the number of young to provide supplemental financial support for older family members. Further, it is not uncommon today for childless couples reaching retirement to have no family support, and they must rely on an extended family or a benevolent society for any support.

6. Older adult workers are not as mobile as younger workers and tend to remain fixed geographically. When plant shutdowns and moves force them out of their jobs, they tend to remain geographically stationary and to take lower paying jobs after a period of unemployment, thus reducing their income levels and restricting the possibility of building up personal savings for their future retirement.

7. Two-worker households may modify some of the intrusions in personal savings in the future. Many of the intrusions noted still hold, however, even if only one worker is affected by job layoffs or plant relocations.

Alternatives

Numerous plans have been suggested over the years as alternative income support systems for retired workers. One of the most popular earlier ones was called the Townsend Plan, which advocated a $200 per month across-the-board payment to retired individuals, the restriction being that the amount be spent within a thirty-day period. The premise here was not only that economic support be provided for the elderly, but also that a sagging United States economy would be stimulated through using older people as consumers, hence removing them from their productive work roles. The Townsend Plan attracted many advocates, but we again find in this plan another example of using old people to resolve a labor market problem. Regardless, while the Townsend movement had wide appeal, the Social Security System was well into the planning stage and was enacted into law before the movement gained a firm foothold.

More recently, other plans have been offered as either alternatives to or supplements to the Social Security System as an income support base. Alternative plans have been short-lived, due to the politically negative effect they would have. Two of the more popularized supplemental retirement programs which are gaining some measure of support are the Individual Retirement Accounts (IRA) for individuals and married couples; and Keogh Accounts for self-employed individuals. In a sense, these programs are self-run, self-controlled private pension programs that have an added tax advantage feature which makes them attractive to middle- and high-income workers. Claims of high yield on investments made by individual carriers suggest that these plans can be quite lucrative over the long term, and they are attracting large numbers of the more affluent. With the addition of tax advantages until one reaches age sixty-five, these plans will become even more appealing. One can, of course, raise the question as to why people are participating in these endeavors. Is it to ensure a financially-solvent retirement or to reduce their taxable income during their working years? It is questionable, however, whether the less affluent members of society are equally able to participate in these plans, but they are still viable alternatives for *some* people. With the forced savings concept of Social Security and public and private pension plans making a significant dent in the overall paycheck, one must question how much cash reserve lower income people have left after paying their daily living expenses, money to further invest in these two financially-attractive programs. F. F. Piven and R. A. Cloward, in *Regula-*

ting the Poor: The Function of Public Welfare, offered the thesis that Social Security was not helpful to the poor since the amount deducted from their wages reduced the amount available to pay for the necessities of life. IRA's and Keogh's—as well as other similar plans—do not seem helpful for the poor and near poor. It has been argued that drastic modifications to our existing financial support systems are necessary as part of retirement concepts in order to accommodate a changing time in history, as well as to develop strategies to minister to the needs of the large number of retired elderly living at or near the Federally-mandated poverty line.

The Dunn Proposal

J. D. Dunn has offered a proposal which, by necessity, may gain a measure of support in the near future. He attempts to resolve many of the problems confronting the Social Security System and pension programs. He concludes that ". . . Social Security is rendered increasingly ineffective and inefficient due to changing social, economic and demographic trends that lie largely outside the control of government" and further, ". . . Social Security was designed for an earlier generation with problems quite different from those existing today." His proposal ". . . seeks to transform the existing Social Security System into one that achieves the present system's goals without impeding economic productivity and individual freedom."

Dunn argues that Social Security in its present form cannot achieve the twin goals of individual equity and social adequacy as long as the system is tied to "current-cost financing" in a society experiencing declining fertility. He proposes to permit workers to withdraw from Social Security in return for a compulsory savings requirement in the private sector. General revenues would be used to pay existing benefit obligations to current beneficiaries and for those older workers who desire to remain under the existing system. Dunn's proposal places the burden of economic support during retirement in the free market system, while acknowledging the need for an SSI program (currently in place and paid out of general revenues and not from Social Security) to meet the needs of the poor, disabled and dependent.

The details of Dunn's plan are too extensive to reiterate here. By way of summary, it can be stated that it would be introduced gradually and is estimated to take approximately forty years to be fully implemented. Many key administrative features of Social Security would be retained, but the private sector would compete for the privilege of managing an investor's funds. The issue of the "Means Test" under SSI would be maintained and expanded to alleviate poverty. Income restrictions associated with re-employment after retirement, however, would no longer be in effect for most people. Questions of portability, which currently beleaguer private and some public pension programs, would be resolved, since payments are made to an individual's personal account rather than to a fund account as in current retirement plans. Regardless of the number of job changes one makes during his working years, his account is continually in his name. The amount of retirement income is dependent upon the amount invested and with the current experience of IRA and Keogh, this would suggest that the available amount for the retirement years would be substantial. This program would have the added benefit of making available a significant and stable amount of money for capital formation and investment, a benefit which has been lacking in recent years.

Dunn concludes that the greatest economic risk facing the Social Security System is its large size. "The continued growth of Social Security could itself deter economic productivity because the size of Social Security appears to impact capital formation adversely." If, as O'Toole concluded, we have reached the asymptote of capital formation, then the demise of our economic system as we know it to be today may be near. If Dunn's proposal is seriously considered, then an increase in capital formation can result, with an ensuing need to reevaluate how we use all our human resources.

There are always problems when trying to alter or modify programs or systems which have been in place for long periods of time and which have become a way of life for so many people. This is no less true for the Social Security System, which has withstood many such attempted incursions over the years. However, the Social Security System was conceived and implemented for a generation of people who were experiencing drastic economic deprivation and a society that was attempting to resolve extreme unemployment problems. This is now a different time in history with a different set of problems and needs which also must be confronted. Dunn's proposal attempts to account for time in history as well as the moral obligations which society has made to itself.

Finally, he points out two significant problems which must be faced if modifications to the Social Security System are ever to take place. The first is political. To assure political support of Dunn's proposal, beneficiaries must be assured of uninterrupted benefits. They have come to believe that such benefits are their right, and politicians will need to exhibit considerable fortitude and statesmanship in legislating the suggested changes. Secondly, the problems of misunderstanding how Social Security differs from private savings, how Social Security is dependent upon the political process, and the misrepresentation of Social Security as income security will need to be resolved and communicated both to the public and our policy makers.

A RETIREMENT ATTITUDE

The decision to adopt the age sixty-five as retirement criterion was made at a time when life expectancy was 41.7 years for males, 43.5 for females. If a similar logic were applied today, then retirement from work would not occur below the age of ninety-five to one hundred. We are not suggesting that retirement from work be mandated as age ninety-five to one hundred. What we are suggesting is that our institutionalized concept of retirement and the accompanying implicit assumption of old age is an arbitrary decision not founded in fact, one which contributed to the perpetuation of myths about aging. Since we are in a different era in history and are rapidly approaching the twenty-first century—which futurists suggest will be a century considerably different from anything previously experienced—the concept of retirement from work as a given in one's life needs to be reevaluated.

Traditional retirement and old age concepts are at a crossroads in American society. This situation is due in part to gradual changes toward better health, resulting in longer-lived adults. Another factor is that the foundations for the potential economic security to live one's later life without working for pay are already in place. Also to be considered is the easing of legislative mandates as to when one must retire from work. The implementation of age sixty-five for a retirement concept—designed to make room for younger workers in the labor force—stimulated the initiation of early retirement attitudes during the 1950s and 1960s in the face of a rising youth population. This has since given way to urging later retirement for workers. Later retirement would help to offset rising costs of supporting financial programs designed to fill needs of the aged during retirement years. These needs have multiplied as a result of increasing numbers of older people living longer in retirement.

This beginning move toward later life retirement is stimulating some people to reevaluate when to retire and when to perceive themselves as starting to get old. Certainly for most individuals, age sixty-five is not old today, nor do many feel they can no longer continue to be productive and contributing members of the work force. Apparently, with the easing of mandatory retirement to age seventy, we are again turning to the older segment of the population to resolve economic, social and political problems confronting society. We are again asking older people to readjust their lives to accommodate society's needs, rather than seeking ways to assist older people to exercise greater degrees of freedom in planning their later life stage.

Retirement and the belief that with it starts the onset of old age is a legislated life stage. The concept was set forth as a way to ostensibly reward individuals with a few leisure years after a lifetime of labor. At the time the retirement idea was set forth as universally applicable to all individuals, laboring in the work force was associated with physical drudgery. We saw earlier that the majority of work performed today (86 percent of all jobs) demands very little physical energy, and in the future we can expect even less physical output to perform work. In reality, retirement is an institutionalized arrangement designed to resolve labor market problems. Since retirement from work is legislated, it is not a given life stage, as some social-gerontological theories would have us believe. Legislated retirement—hence, the onset of old age—has restricted the number of social roles available to older people.

Since our work establishes our identity and influences our life roles, denial of access to work and the work environment through legislation restricts the role options in older adulthood and is an intrusion on individual freedom. It is being argued that role ambiguity experienced by many older adults is the result of the legislated mandate to retire from work, a policy which was originally introduced as a way to resolve labor market problems confronting society at a particular time in history. Role ambiguity later in life, as well as the introduction of an old age concept, has little to do with reaching some arbitrarily-defined magical age.

Graebner cautioned against dismantling the retirement system. We are not suggesting such an action. What we are suggesting is discarding the notion that retirement from paid employment is a requirement at any age and that the decision to retire from paid employment belongs to the special province of the individual and not an event justifying legislation. The 1978 amendments to the Age Discrimination in Employment Act was a step in the right direction. However, it still does not eliminate a legislatively-mandated retirement age. To make retirement a truly optional choice as a lifestyle, society will have to change its attitude.

Assuming Spengler's thesis that the population will stabilize around the year 2050 to be true, given no major increases or decreases in birth rates and given stable immigration rates, then the demand for older workers will remain high. When this happens, all forms of forced retirement will be unnecessary for the most part and there will be a normal self-initiated free flow of older workers out of the labor force.

An important barrier toward making retirement an optional choice for people is economic. Americans have come to believe—however erroneously—that Social Security means income security, income sufficient for them to maintain a degree of autonomy during retirement. This was never the intent of Social Security legislation. It is because Social Security payments were economically insufficient to maintain the retiree that political pressure has been exerted in recent years to build an escalation clause into the system, one which will accommodate rising living costs of retirees on fixed incomes. Few retirees have sufficient outside incomes to offset these rising costs and they have expected the Social Security System to supplement this. These additions to Social Security income have resulted in greater dollar returns on one's contributions, with a corresponding increased cost to proportionately fewer workers per retiree than when the system was introduced. Persuasive arguments abound as to why the Social Security System must be modified or changed if it is to be more responsible to social, economic and political conditions of today and—more importantly—the anticipated conditions of tomorrow.

Dunn's proposal offers a reasoned change in order to assure financial security in retirement for all individuals at all economic levels without a corresponding excessive cost to those persons remaining in the labor force. His proposal offers individuals the potential for a greater return on their retirement investment than other existing plans without the need for a continual increase in Social Security taxes which must surely come if no changes are made. A feature of Dunn's proposal upon which he does not elaborate—but which is consistent with the theme of this book—is that a required savings for retirement, housed in the private sector (Social Security and pension plans are forced savings) conceivably would ensure the individual the increased option of retiring when or if he or she wishes. The person must be allowed to do so without social sanctions or economic penalties in the event the individual changes his or her mind at a later date. This option is not currently available without penalty.

A move in the direction for free options to the retirement

decision would help clarify and more clearly specify role options for older people. These will perhaps take on newer configurations than those of an earlier time. What can be expected is that the individual would be in control of those configurations and establish them within a living style of his own choosing, rather than having to adopt a lifestyle imposed upon him via social sanctions or governmental mandate. It is being assumed that as the number of options as to how a person lives his later adult life increases, negative social attitudes toward aging will become neutral and then positive. This concept of change recognizes that as people age they become more heterogeneous. Not all individuals will opt to continue working into their seventies, eighties or nineties. There are, however, those who will. The important factor is that as long as a person has reasonably good health and can function as a worker, the option should exist to continue to work past an arbitrarily-defined age.

Such proposals for economic security as proposed by Dunn, the increasing potential to live in later life as a physically-healthy person, and removal of all social, economic and political restrictions as to when one must retire from work-for-pay makes it much easier for an individual to be responsible for himself. Under these conditions he will also be able to contribute to society. No guilt will be associated with retirement to a life of leisure, the trauma of the retirement from work which some people experience will be eased and the retired person can live the American dream as our founding fathers envisioned.

7

WORK, EDUCATION AND AGING

The "age traps" inherent within the realms of education, work and retirement more and more are coming under question as to their relevance in determining how individuals will progress through the life cycle. Because of the economic, religious, educational and labor hierarchical dimensions by which society is systematized, we have come to believe that there is a correlation between the psychological interpretation of aging and actual chronological age. However, once we unlearn that such a correlation is inevitable, we free ourselves to examine new and more creative uses of time.

Pharmacology, uncovering causes of diseases, as well as other bio-medical advances, and a beginning awareness and understanding of the complex social and psychological dimensions of the human condition are rendering obsolete the traditional concept concerning the life plan with which the time traps of age are associated. The notions of progressing from education to work to retirement, together with the belief in a "one-life, one-career" imperative as a basic framework around which industrial society has organized and influenced the human progression through the life cycle still has utility for social institutional purposes. On the other hand, the belief that this framework is a clearly defined continuum within which age and the psychological sense of aging are parallel for all individuals is being questioned. One area which has been traditionally age-bound and has placed older people into time traps is education with its relationship to work. The assumption that education is the special province of youth and that work is the special province of adults is under critical challenge today.

In recent years, societal change has been accelerating because of the cybernetic revolution. The traditional social arrangements of organized society are being challenged daily and in turn are being reflected in action. For example, women are in the labor force in nearly equal proportions to males, a situation which is altering the traditional male "bread winner" role to that of the more acceptable equal partnerships.

The Graying of America Society has begun to challenge traditional social structures to the degree that the usual ways to delineate older people are beginning to blur. This cohort demands the right of equal participation and recognition in all formal and informal institutional arrangements. One of the more sacrosanct institutions—which in modern technological society has traditionally been reserved as youths' special province—is education.

EDUCATION AND MODERNIZATION

Education in an ever-changing technological society has come to be perceived as the way to enter the work force successfully and demonstrate achievement for progress up the career ladder. The concept of more and more education is deeply embedded in people's minds as a basic tenet of the "onward and upward" progression through life and being able to "live the good life." As education has become more easily available, it has come to be perceived as the "door opener" for those who previously only dreamed of moving up the career ladder. It was during the 1950s and 1960s that people in the United States began to become the most highly-educated people in the world, thus paving the way for upward mobility.

Cowgill felt that massive education of youth lowers the status of society's older members since "adult children are always more educated than their parents." This differential in formal education attainment between children and their parents has led to an inversion of status between generations, as well as the fostering of an intellectual and moral segregation which has given rise to a "cult of youth." When education is primarily targeted toward youth, we foster what has been euphemistically labeled a "generation gap," creating intra-generational conflicts. These become evident in the promoting of young workers over older ones because the younger have more years of education. We saw evidence of this during the late 1960s and into the 1970s through the visible emergence of youth idiom, dress and hair standards, behavior, and experimental living arrangements which confused many adults. It influenced some adults to try to emulate the youth image, and compelled other adults to leave the work force through early retirement. These characteristics are also visible and dynamic conditions of social change and are the cultural characteristics of a youth generation. So, too, at the opposite end of the age spectrum. The cultural characteristics of older people are attributes of that generation. It is difficult and erroneous to describe them as attributes of old age or to demean them as outmoded and relics of a passe generation.

The aspiration of older age groups for new and additional learning experiences are emerging generational attributes that reflect the increased education in their youth. The recent literature on adult participation in educational activities overwhelmingly suggests that the more years of education one acquires in his youth, the more likely he is to want more and continuous education throughout his adult years, well beyond the accepted retirement stage of life. We are beginning to see that educational involvement of adults is a characteristic of a current adult generation and not necessarily of old people in general. In a book released by the National Council on Aging, L. Harris and Associates demonstrated that chronologically-defined older people did not perceive nor classify themselves as old. Generational identity in the past, however, has been at best ambiguous for older adults especially with regard to their role in society. It would appear that with a move toward continued lifelong education, future generations of older adults will begin to identify their own generational characteristics as different from those imposed upon them by the rest of society. Continued education well into later life will also be one attribute which will be visibly demonstrated and help break socially-imposed age ghettoes. Regardless, what seems to be surfacing is that Cowgill's concept of older people becoming diminished as a result of modernization is beginning to be questioned, at least with regard to education.

Cowgill, author of *The Aging of Populations and Societies*, has suggested though, that in the United States the trend toward modernization may have reached its nadir and the trend toward diminishing older people has "bottomed out." We can also add that as the linear life notions are rendered obsolete as a general social characteristic, then older people will less likely be diminished in the eyes of the rest of society. With regard to education, this seems to be an accomplished given due to the increased interest in all forms of adult education. In the near future, older people will be about equal to youth in the number of years of "schooling." This will be due to the mandatory number of years required for youth to remain in school, the increased impetus for extended post-secondary school education becoming the norm, and the large number of middle-aged and older adults who received extended formal educational experiences as a result of the G.I. Bill's influence. Changes such as these, combined with concerns about older people as unused human resources and the obsolescence of formalized work-retirement programs, appear to be early signs that today's neoteric American workplace has reached at least the young adulthood stage of its development and is rapidly moving toward maturity. Some are referring to this shift as a sign of a

post-industrial society. The degree to which all people participate in normal educational and independent learning experiences—as well as the actual types of experiences they are living
daily—seem to be foreshadowing a social change concerning
adult society. This may have significant future impact upon
changing and developing more positive attitudes about old age,
especially as related to the work role.

One-Life, One-Career Imperative

As young and old move toward educational equality in a
more learning-oriented environment, we can assume that new
ways of describing industrial society will come forth. The conventional conception of career, wrote S. Sarasan in *Work, Aging
and Social Change,* has long had a restricted scope: one life, one
career—period. The developmental task of the individual is to
choose from a smorgasbord of possibilities the one vocational
dish he will feed on over the course of his life. This has been
so-accepted a view, reflected in institutional practice and
rhetoric, that from the standpoint of the individual the choice of
a career becomes a self-imposed, necessary and fateful process.
Whatever difficulties this may present, the force of culture
transmitted through parents and schools leaves unquestioned
in the individual's mind the conviction that making a single
choice is a right and proper task, . . . the cultural imperative may
not only be dysfunctional but is increasingly being questioned,
the fact remains that for most people the imperative is ego
syntonic, *i.e.,* it should be obeyed.

"One-life, one-career" is so socially ingrained in our
thought processes that any ideas of "breaking out" can be traumatic, especially among older adults. We can speculate that at
least an aspect of the mid-life crisis, a socially-defined behavioral attribute which has been the focus of so much recent
popular attention, may be associated with this imperative. To
shift careers from the known to the unknown in mid-life when,
developmentally, people in that age range are presumed to be in
the stabilization periods of their careers, can be the cause of
much self-doubt, family upheaval, and the like. Yet, the mid-

life crisis which has spawned much speculation and debate may really be an expression of the desire to break out of the "time traps and age ghettoes" in which social convention has placed us. We discussed earlier that the "New Breed" of American worker described by Yankelovich is challenging traditional life-work imperatives. They are developing their own styles of moving through life. They perceive education as life-long, with the potential to be able to work in several careers.

This "New Breed" of worker who will be tomorrow's elderly are not questioning the need to do something in life, but they are questioning how and when to make the career decision as well as the decision as being irrevocable. These challenges to the social imperatives now in place suggest socially-induced systems like retirement, Social Security, pension plans, and human resource utilization, all of which have impact upon an individual's development and movement through the life cycle and basically assume both the "linear life plan" and a "one-life, one-career" mentality, soon will be more severely disputed.

A Disengagement Theory of aging assumes that life is linear and that at some point in time one will withdraw from the adult working-for-pay life stage and move to a new, less active style of living. Activity Theory essentially reenforces the same life transition belief but suggests continued engagement in activities different from paid work. Other social-psychological theories assume a similar life transition when a person chronologically reaches a later life stage. Each of these theories, in its own way, reenforces the linear life notions and the cultural imperative of "one-life, one-career" as a given. It is being suggested here that these socially-imposed life dicta reenforced by social-psychological aging theories are the result of a social bureaucracy which began to achieve a high degree of refinement at the turn of the century. This bureaucracy spread as a result of rapid modernization and technological advancement in the United States—which sought to omit older people from continuing participation by retiring them from the work force, thus rendering them obsolete. The influences of both increasing bureaucracy and modernization—as well as the surfacing of work imperatives—have influenced social thought and social organizations to such an extent that older people have been expected to go through life in a robot-like fashion, following traditional social conventions, then relinquishing their status to make room for the advancement of youth, who also would presumably follow a similar pattern. This is such an ingrained belief in social thought that programs for older people have been directed almost exclusively toward imposing care and maintenance programs—often designed by younger people— rather than accommodating and assisting older people as they individually go through their life changes. It seems that the sentiment of the individual subordination of self for the good of the society as a whole (identified as having its origins at the time of the Civil War) to solve unemployment problems manifested during economic recessions and depressions has been carried forward and refined to the point where it is the very foundation of social organization today. Our social systems, developed to assist older people, follow a similar philosophical base. Once a person relinquishes one's place in the work environment, he is subject to accommodating himself to the largess of society. It has been only a recent perception that older people are able to participate actively and independently in society's institutions long past an arbitrary age. The post-World War II babies who are the current young adult group—and who will be the elderly group after the year 2010—certainly will have much to say about how society will treat them when they are old, especially if their past and current behavior is representative of their future behavior.

New theories will need to be developed if the aging process in a rapidly-changing social context is to be better understood. We have not yet bowed to rigid theoretical dogmas, so the future regarding theory building looks bright. Development of new theoretical models of aging will need to take into account the realization that human conventions which have become social customs in a modernized technological society do change. Human conventions are not, nor should they be, assumed givens which rarely change. Certainly the massive influx of adults—as well as the increasing numbers of older adults into all facets of formal and informal learning activities—is a visible sign that a traditional social custom—education for youth—is under question. This concept is being tested and is transforming, regardless of the customary ways society's institutions continue to function. Challenges to conventional ways of living were just visibly developing as a result of the world's most affluent society's emergence from World War II and the resulting post-war transitions. This was an early warning to America's public not to get caught in the little boxes of life, which were influenced in part by a sophisticated bureaucracy. Rather, the admonition was to attend to the uniqueness of the individual and recognize the need for multiple lifestyles in order to serve individual need. Instead, we seem to have reenforced the little boxes of time and social systems and placed people, especially older people, into age ghettoes from which there is assumed to be only one exit.

Myths

It is being speculated here that as society began generating the aging myths, it also began accepting them as truths when youth-focused social change became evident. Accepting these myths as truth was convenient in order to explain or justify older persons' behaviors, as well as society's inauguration of maintenance programs designed to care for people in their later years. These myths are now being exposed for their lack of substance and are no longer relevant in evaluating all older people. As myths give way to truth, social dysfunctions between generations have been occurring; new ways of coping, living and socially aligning are surfacing.

The myths related to the education-work concept of age indicate that older people can't learn, can't keep up with changes, learn too slowly, are obsolete and are failing mentally. An aspect of the emergence of these tenacious myths pertaining to work and education is the rising specialization of work, credentialism's growth and refinement, and the persistent belief—regardless of visible changes to the contrary—that older people cannot or will not continue to learn and keep abreast of new knowledge. Nonetheless, this myth is slow to die; both the old and young are reluctant to relinquish it. With the resurging interest in adult education, we may yet see older people once again being respected for their knowledge, insight and intellectual acumen as a result of their demonstrated learning ability.

One of the more salient developments emanating from the technological advancements of American society, and having a direct impact on the aging/education myths, has to do with the rapid spreading of specialized occupations. These are continuing to come forth as an outgrowth of advancing technology and are generally awarded to young workers. These positions may be high risk, assume the need for advanced technical knowledge and often require worker mobility. It is assumed that the young are attracted to the new and will gear up their formal learning to entertain these challenges which will form their career patterns. Status is accorded these moves and youth are in competition for these jobs within their generational group rather than with their elders.

The restructuring and realignment of the work force due to new changes may relieve a potential source of generational friction while at the same time establish a work identity uniquely belonging to youth. This same process, however, may further alienate the younger generation from their elders. How often have parents listened to their children speak in "bits" and "bytes," not realizing that this is computer talk which is related to career-stimulated learning, and not just a new youth idiom? It is to youth that highly-technical job specializations and the required education to perform them are directed. A companion issue is that the specialized jobs and attendant education— which also focus upon the young—issue from knowledge-based industries essentially involved in information processing activities. Adults have grown up preparing for, and are engaged in, occupations which grew from an industrial base and which appear to be becoming less relevant in our advanced electronic-age societies. We are finding that forms of productivity revered in the past appear to be less and less relevant due in part to automation which, in turn, contributes to making older people appear antiquated unless they actively and visibly engage in continuous learning activities associated with the new technological age.

These rapid youth-oriented changes further isolate

adults from those educational experiences which would assist them in moving into fresh careers. The longer the time interval in which adults do not acquire the new knowledge to move into the emerging and changing technological arena, the more likely society in general will accept the myth they *cannot* or *will not* learn. In reality, other factors such as marriage, family responsibilities or home mortgages may be the real mitigating circumstances. These people are placed at a disadvantage with regard to developing the skills and acquiring the knowledge necessary to accommodate these changes—and early retirement is thereby encouraged.

Combined with a rapidly-transforming technology—which is creating new career options with the attendant need for more and extended advanced education—is an advancing wave of credentialism. Regardless of the career to which one aspires, in order to ascend the career hierarchy and, by association, increase one's earning power, one must consider qualifying credentials. O'Toole has suggested that as more and more people are educated the value of education slumps in its prestige and the importance of credentialing soars. He has asserted that "Employers have responded to larger pools of qualified workers by needlessly raising credential requirements for jobs—without upgrading the demands, challenges, or rewards of these jobs."

One result of this is an increasing "Generational Inversion"—". . . the young, though less-experienced, have higher credentials than their elders." Credentialing does assure that an individual has undertaken a proscribed set of learning experiences, but it does not assure competency in job performance. On the other hand, older workers who have been performing the required worker functions successfully and have demonstrated their competency—often without going through a credentialing program—are bypassed for job promotion and pay increases. Thus, a credentialing system based upon education effectively eliminates or discriminates against older people, the less-educated (often minorities), women who have been out of the labor force for a period of time, and other uncredentialed segments of the population.

Credentialing exposes a very real paradox for older workers. There are a number of factors which have combined to contribute to this. It is the older worker who has "toiled" to help develop the technological base which has paved the way for the emergence of a sophisticated electronically-oriented information-based society. And to adequately provide for such industries, in some cases, many companies and corporations have opted to relocate geographically rather than retool or modernize their existing facilities. This has had the effect of abandoning the experienced and more established worker, moving many new career opportunities out of their reach, so to speak. It has also created the need for worker mobility which is more youth-oriented, since the young are not yet locked into the familial and other responsibilities that confront older workers. At the same time, technological innovations—again based upon older workers' past collective efforts—are introduced, procedures with which the young have familiarity due to their up-to-date educational training. Older people who might consider risking a move to new locations find they may no longer qualify for the new jobs unless they are also willing to take time out and return to school to get credentials and, in some cases, renew credentials. As a result, many older workers, rather than giving up their established ways of life, have opted for lesser-paying jobs with lower prestige rather than position themselves where they might fail to meet the new requirements and be forced to re-establish themselves in both their jobs and their social activity.

Under the guise of progress, education—highly revered in modern technological societies—effectively discriminates against older people. When the great majority of the population, both young and old, acquires close to an equal number of years of education, credentialing systems are instituted which are linked to proscribed educational experiences and not necessarily to previous education, job experience and expected job performance. Credentialism effectively discriminates against individuals who do not have the requisite up-to-date educational background. Unfortunately, the Age Discrimination in Employment Act does not address this issue, thus leaving "loopholes" which can be used to discriminate against employing the older worker and perpetuate myths about older persons' inabilities to perform satisfactorily in the innovative workplace of today and tomorrow.

ADULT EDUCATION

The shift since World War II to information-generating and processing work has effectively reduced the human energy drain previously associated with work as "toil." Individual workers have experienced a corresponding rise in available time and energy to engage in more personally-satisfying activities beyond their work environment. The "New Breed" of workers about whom Yankelovich was talking believe that there are other important attributes of living worth pursuing besides work. On the other hand, older workers have been experiencing a rolelessness in the work environment due to these technological shifts, which has resulted in a dramatic rise in early retirement.

One reason for the increasing interest in adult education and a manifest concern with lifelong learning is the increased time available. The newly-found condition is a direct result of machines and electronics performing tasks more efficiently and effectively—tasks which in the past were time-consuming, physically arduous, and contributed to work being perceived as "toil."

As more sophisticated and efficient machinery is developed, there has come a corresponding rise in the demand from business and industry for ever-increasing numbers of skilled and knowledgeable workers to utilize this technology productively and to create new and even more efficient machines to perform future routine work activities. It has been the highly-educated youth to whom business and industry has turned to capitalize on and expand this technology. The decades of the 1960s and 1970s saw the United States exploit the "youth is better" concept to its fullest. We treated our human resources with the "throw away" mentality that cheap energy and belief in unlimited resources fostered. The rapidity of change brought on by the expanding technology in the last three or four decades psychologically outstripped the individual's ability to keep up with the shifts occurring in society and encouraged a sense of psychological aging among the over-forty segment of the population. Perhaps it also furthered the early retirement attitude as a face-saving device for an apparent obsolescence of older workers in the labor force.

After World War II, to be over forty was to be considered as obsolete and to be just tolerated in the labor force. The alternative seemed to be to adopt the accouterment of the youth culture—hair styles, idiom, behavior, dress, slimness through dieting, etc.—in order not to be overlooked for job promotion, salary increases and other benefits. One might also return to school to gain the credentials being granted to the young. Or, of course, one could quietly withdraw through early retirement and conform to a leisure life role, *i.e.*, disengage, an option which was being projected onto the older segment of the work force through massive advertising campaigns. Data from the United States Bureau of the Census on the employment of males age sixty-five and older indicates a 21 percent decline in labor force participation between 1940 and 1980. These statistics suggest that the effort to encourage male withdrawal from the labor force through early retirement practices and a corresponding youth emphasis in hiring practices were effective in eliminating older male workers. Females in the labor market demonstrate a modest gain, 2.6 percent during the same time span, a number which may be an artifact of the recently increased number of female labor force participants. Regardless, male workplace participation after age sixty-five indicates a dramatic decline between 1900 and 1980, 68.1 percent to 21.2 percent, and for females a very modest gain, 8.3 percent to 8.6 percent, percentages which reenforce the assumption that withdrawal from the working environment (essentially through retirement) was socially sanctioned and approved. An alternate assumption can be postulated: with an increased focus on youth and a corresponding emphasis on more and more education and enforcement of credentialism, it was psychologically safer for the older worker to withdraw via retirement than to remain in the labor force and lose in the competition for promotion and advancement.

Society has slowly come to the realization that just because a person withdraws from formal participation in the workplace through retirement, he is not worn out and used up; he need not be cast aside into obsolescence, only to be reactivated during times of extreme national crisis. Adults have long recognized their worth but, as a group, have been reluctant to express this view since it was not popular. They were bombarded with propaganda expressing a prevailing youth-oriented view which in turn shook their resolve in their own belief in self. Those individuals who did venture to voice opposition to the predominant view of older worker obsolescence were accused of being argumentative, garrulous, senile, pejorative—terms used to describe older people. Only recently have such groups as the Gray Panthers and the Association of Retired Persons and such seminars as the various White House Conferences on Aging voiced similar opposition to prevailing views about aging. They have stressed belief in the worth and dignity of older people as contributors in the labor force, a worth and dignity which is only now beginning to be recognized and accepted.

Early retirement and reduced time demands in jobs resulting from technological innovation brought with it an excess of leisure time for older workers, time which travel, gardening and club activities failed to use up and, in many cases, time which was not psychologically nor intellectually satisfying. For the first time, older adults had the leisure and physical and emotional energy to fulfill their dreams, to engage in activities such as acquiring new knowledge which, in the past, may have been denied them due to uncontrollable circumstances. They began to realize that they could continue educational pursuits in both formal and informal learning environments. Older workers were quick to realize the potential for maintaining their place or advancement in their jobs with the use of continued education. From around 1970 on, there began a rise in community college enrollments, learn-at-home programs, correspondence courses, etc., some being job-related and many more for personal development and satisfaction. By far the largest number of participants in adult continuing education programs were in the young adult category.

Older adults—those at or near retirement—appear not to be flocking to learning centers to extend their formal education as are the younger. Perhaps this is due to their unquestioned acceptance of prevailing social standards and customs surrounding retirement behavior and beliefs about old age. Harris and Associates estimated that persons age fifty-five to sixty-four represent 6.3 percent of participants in educational programs and those sixty-five and older only 2.8 percent. They have summarized the reasons for this low level of participation as: the social bias that education is for the young, admission policies in higher education institutions tending to discourage applicants who are over forty, physical limitations, inadequate transportation, lack of money, and inappropriate class scheduling among others. There is also the view that since older persons do not have as much basic education as younger persons, they are unable to compete in the formal learning activity. From reviewing Anastasi's work on individual differences, we found the absurdity of this view. Nevertheless, the current discrepancies in the number of years of schooling between older and younger age groups is very real. This should diminish in importance as our more highly-educated younger population matures.

The recent focus of adult education suggests that older adult participation in all educational forms is slowly increasing. It is still too early to tell whether older adults will be taking advantage of expanding educational opportunities with any significant increase. Higher education institutions, junior and community colleges, as well as other organized learning centers, however, are turning their attention slowly to older learners as a potential student pool, particularly as they experience declining enrollment among the traditional eighteen to twenty-two age group due to the low birth rates of the 1960s and 1970s.

In a paper prepared for the National Center for Research in Vocational Education, P. V. Delker has summarized this trend and concluded that: "... during the next twenty years ours will be a significantly expanding adult population and a significantly decreasing youth population. Clearly, the educational market of the future lies with adults." Education, of course, occurs in many environments and takes on many forms which may be a factor in underestimating the number of participating older adults. We do have some estimates of the changes occurring in adult education which may be indicators of future trends:

1. By the year 2000, 50 percent of all college students will be twenty-two years of age or older, according to the Carnegie Council, 1980.

2. Students over twenty-five now account for 40 percent of the enrollment in two-year colleges, says the *Higher Education Daily*.

3. The number of women thirty-five and older enrolled in colleges has more than doubled since 1972, according to the Project on the Status and Education of Women, 1981.

4. The average community college student in 1982 was almost thirty years of age states a report in the *Chronicle of Higher Education*.

This summary does not reflect the numbers who are engaging in non-formal, non-institutional learning activities. Thus, while the information summarized is suggestive of changes which are occurring, the probability is high that they underestimate the current revolution in adult education, especially among the older age groups.

Definitions

Perhaps it will be helpful at this point to define the terms *formal*, *non-formal*, and *informal* education, since confusion can arise when such imprecise terms are used in relation to understanding what is involved in an adult education concept. Delker attempted to bring a degree of precision to understanding adult education when he defined it as "any activity or program deliberately designed (by the learner, another or others) to satisfy any learning need or interest that may be experienced at any stage in an adult's life." In arriving at this definition, Delker summarized and adopted the International Council for Educational Development's definitions of formal, non-formal and informal education.

Formal education is defined as ". . . the highly-institutionalized, chronologically graded and hierarchically-structured education system spanning lower primary school and the upper reaches of the university."

Informal education is defined as ". . . the lifelong process by which every person acquires and accumulates knowledge, skills, attitudes, and insights from daily experiences and exposure to the environment—at home, at work, at play." In general, informal education is often unsystematic and unorganized learning from an institutional perspective.

Non-formal education is defined as "any organized, systematic educational activity carried on outside the framework of the formal system to provide selected types of learning to particular sub-groups of the population." In all likelihood a large number of individuals engage in systematic and independent learning activities without benefit of guidance or sanction from formal learning environments. The plethora of self-help how-to-do-it books and their rising popularity would suggest that this form of learning enjoys wide participation throughout all age groups, perhaps more so than any other learning modality as characterized by the above definitions.

Needs

Regardless of the format within which people learn, it is important to note that learning is taking place within all age groups and it is a lifelong process. In her book, *Adults As Learners*, K. P. Cross has pointed out that lifetime learning is a necessity simply to keep pace with the rapidity of change—". . . in the family, on the job, in the community, and in the world-wide society." Cross further summarized three influences which are contributing to all age groups' involvements in life-long learning activities. First are demographic factors. The age group twenty-five to forty-five comprises 31 percent of the population, according to the 1977 report from the United States Bureau of the Census. It is expected that as a group they are highly educated and will continue to be actively involved in learning, a supposition suggested by the evidence previously cited—which pointed out that the more education one has, the more likely that person will be to continue in lifelong educational activities. This group will become the older generation at or about the turn of the century, and they will be demanding recognition of their long-developed skills and knowledges in ways quite different from preceding generations. They will not quietly disappear from an active involvement in our social institutions, especially work, as evidenced by their active involvement in the social change process during the past ten to fifteen years.

A second influencing factor involves social change. Lifestyles are changing, women's roles are undergoing significant alterations, there is more recognition and acknowledgment of everyone's civil rights, rising educational levels are the norm rather than the exception, early retirement from work will be opted for by some, whereas others will wish to continue working long past the traditionally-accepted retirement age; these and a host of other social changes not yet perceived are taking place. What is important is that social change is becoming an accepted way of life and changes are emerging more rapidly than during any previous era. Because of this, ". . . education for adults has become necessary for some, desirable for others, and more acceptable for almost everyone."

A third area which has continued to influence lifelong education concerns technological change and the knowledge/information explosion. Technological change is so rapid and influential today that it can wipe out whole industries and create new ones within a decade. Keeping up with the knowledge explosion and technological change is an enigma confronting most workers. It is these changes which are rendering obsolete the "one-life, one-career" beliefs discussed by Sarasan.

Wirtz estimated that as a result of the knowledge explosion and the rapidity of technological change, more and more specialized occupations come into existence. Traditional occupations are suddenly outdated, requiring workers to change careers three, four or more times during their adult working years. A parallel problem associated with membership in a highly technological society is the need to adapt to new ways of being a producer as well as a consumer. It is the combined impact of these three categories of change which will not only encourage lifelong learning activities, but will mandate that a worker also be a learner in order to succeed in this new environment.

R. N. Butler, author of *Why Survive? Being Old in America*, recognized that continual learning experiences were needed by the elderly when he asserted that "education for the elderly should include":

1. Education for education's sake—inner satisfaction.
2. Education for retirement—instructional, e.g., through pre-retirement seminars.
3. Education for post-retirement—instructional, e.g., through senior centers.
4. Education for societal utilization—special training, job re-training."

At the time Butler was writing, education still was thought to be essentially for young people, even though it was a frequent key to continued employment. What is significant about Butler's comments is that three of the four educational purposes are either directly or indirectly work-related and involve planned formal educational programs. He obviously recognized that not all older people would opt for a retirement from work, and that in order to maintain one's place in the work environment beyond the traditional retirement age, continuing education was a necessity. R. N. Butler alluded to a paradox which has resulted from medical researchers' successful efforts to increase life expectancy by twenty-six years since 1900. This has contributed to unanticipated consequences. Older people are living longer than expected, raising recent uncertainty as to whether they will receive their Social Security. They become more and more dependent upon youth for this continued support, as well as facing significantly longer periods of leisure than earlier generations did. This situation has contributed to encouraging older people to realize their own educational dreams. The potential for realization of the educational dream now raises questions as to the purpose for older people continuing to learn.

Purpose

Adult learners are a diverse group and, as such, seek learning options for a wide variety of reasons. As a group, adult learners typically have had prior educational achievements, come from advantaged backgrounds, and are upwardly mobile from the working class. They include housewives, displaced homemakers, college drop-outs and "stop-outs," lovers of learning, individuals without high school diplomas, career seekers and career changers, and those individuals whose upward mobility depends upon the acquisition of new skills or information. They are generally young adults, though older adults are more and more in evidence. Their reasons for pursuing continued education may be clustered into three categories: job and career related, changing life patterns, and "future shock."

Job and Career Related: In their research study for the College Entrance Examination Board, C. B. Aslanian and H. M. Brickell noted that job or career changes are the most frequent motivators for adults who seek formal educational opportunities. They found that most career transitions fell into three categories: moving into a new job, adapting to a new job, and advancing in a career. An individual's career progression is obviously here. By today's standards, many adults need to learn in order to get their jobs, keep them, and progress in the career hierarchy. This is somewhat consistent with what Cowgill found, however, he assumed education at a younger age level and that adults—especially older adults—would be bypassed in upward job mobility due to lack of education. His model did not allow for lifelong education since he presupposed a linear life progression. This seems to be changing as society more readily accepts the belief that regardless of age, most individuals can and will continue to learn, especially as that learning relates to their work.

Altered Life Patterns: The traditional linear life patterns are giving way to more "blended life plans." Increasingly, people are opting for part-time, part-year working arrangements in order to take advantage of part-time study. More and more older adults are choosing gradual withdrawal from long-term working arrangements rather than abrupt retirement; they are often using their free time to study and learn or develop new skills which can later be used in different or less strenuous working activities, either paid or unpaid. What is important here is that a more blended life plan is not socially imposed upon adults. Rather, it frees adults to experience new and perhaps more satisfying work-leisure-living arrangements in order to improve the quality of their lives and break the traditional "one-life, one-career" imperative and the traditional linear life pattern so much a part of previous generations.

Future Shock: Intermeshed with career issues and altering life patterns is the pervasive phenomenon of rapid change. In a paper compiled for the American Association of Community and Junior Colleges, E. J. Gleaser, Jr. asserted that change is basic to life, it is inexorable, and it is an unmistakable fact and a force with which the individual must deal. The unparalleled and unprecedented changes occurring today ". . . perplexes the public, confounds the authorities, and demands response from education." Alvin Toffler, in his book, *The Third Wave*, concluded that fundamental changes in values, institutions, technologies, and world views have stunned people as the "third wave" rolls in upon them. As people begin to recognize the obsolescence of their personal and technical skills for coping with these changes, they often turn to education for help. This, of course, is what Butler and Yankelovich were referring to when they described the surfacing values and aspirations of the "New Breed" of American Worker.

In summary, we can conclude that adult learning for all

generational groups is upon us, more so for the younger adult than older adult. Their reasons are as diverse as they are themselves and will be seen as more diverse as they get older.

EDUCATION AND THE MARKETPLACE

So long as society continues to experience a recessionary economy and a decline in unskilled jobs, job competition and unemployment will continue. Many older workers who experience job cutbacks, reductions in hours worked, and other unsettling job-related conditions are likely candidates for early retirement, or they seek modified working arrangements. This mode of behavior among older workers—especially those at or near retirement age—has been observed throughout most recessionary cycles. It seems related to a lack of desire to continue the struggle to remain competitive in the labor force, as well as to social forces and attitudes which work to mitigate against their continued employment. Removing workers from the labor force through retirement has had the net effect of reducing competition for existing jobs and has done little to solve unemployment problems.

Economic recession has the effect of convincing some who are at or near retirement age to, indeed, retire rather than remain in the work arena. Others may choose retirement because they perceive themselves as being too old to re-enter the labor force in another capacity or because their belief in the "linear life" concept leads them to drop out and not continue to look for work. Our current education structure does not encourage them to attempt retraining for other jobs or seek changes in their work patterns, which will continue to put strains on existing entitlement programs, i.e., Social Security. Frances Perkins attempted to address these same issues prior to the enactment of the Social Security Act in 1935, but met with little success. The net effect of not encouraging older workers to remain in the labor force results in a potential drop in productivity due to the loss of experienced workers. Drops in productivity and not working can result in reduced incomes due to job layoffs which can adversely affect their future retirement and Social Security incomes and purchasing power. There is then the possibility for a ripple effect in the nation's economy and, in some cases, dissatisfaction among older citizens regarding rewards for life-long productivity. P. K. Ragan and W. J. Davis have indicated in their research exploring the diversity of older voters that the political consequences of this form of discontent are only recently being manifested primarily through senior citizen organizations—such as the Gray Panthers—which are attempting to exert political pressure for senior citizen special interests. These political consequences may in the future become magnified as the ranks of the older population increase with time. Apparently our current education system "... has failed to meet the needs of older persons. It has not helped them anticipate or deal with the stress of human development in the later years of life. It has failed to help both middle-aged and older persons learn new skills or adapt old ones, thereby denying them the opportunity to contribute to society as members of the work force or as skilled volunteers," according to the Department of Health, F⁻·⁻ation, and Welfare, in 1980.

Volunteer programs for senior citizen participation are on the upturn but do little to relieve the economic pressures many of them are experiencing. P. Yuknovage described a number of these senior volunteer programs which are sponsored through the efforts of such groups as VISTA, ACTION and the Peace Corps. The majority of these programs are designed to assist older individuals to cope with the exigencies of living their later years, as well as to bring them an awareness of and access to existing entitlement programs and services. The programs described utilize senior citizens as human resources able to assist other senior citizens, often with no pay and very little reimbursement for costs incurred. Others who wish to participate perhaps cannot economically afford to or may not have learned the requisite skills to participate.

M. H. Morrison, author of *Aging and Income*, has suggested that all our social policies, from which many volunteer programs have evolved, need to be examined in greater depth so that various experiments and new ways to use time can be compared in an effort not to lose the expertise of older workers. He pointed out that the advantages of such procedures as variable work time, split work, divided holidays, early or postponed retirement (in whole or in part), and retraining programs for new jobs or volunteer activities all be examined because of the changing economic environment. In exploring the changing work options for older workers, S. Gray and D. Morse found that two of every five older retirees they surveyed returned to work for pay after retirement either for economic, social or psychological reasons. One-third chose salaried employment, while the remainder chose consulting, self-employment, or some combination. What seems to be spreading is that increased alternatives to how one lives the later years are being opted for in an effort to keep pace with a rapidly changing society and to maintain independent living arrangements.

On the other hand, formal social institutions apparently are not equally keeping pace with what appears to be newly-developing lifestyle changes for the older adult. Evidently older people—in spite of formal social institutions—are seeking and finding new avenues and new forms of living styles which accommodate their better physical health and their economic, social and psychological needs. The frail and vulnerable elderly will always need comprehensive caretaking services similar to those currently in place. Fortunately, the majority of older persons are able to and desire to remain independent which, for some, continued work activity would make possible. They need only be shown how and then be allowed to do so.

Many older people are not aware that there are some jobs available to them, even though there is a growing number of senior employment services. Often they feel they are "too old" to work and that skills mastered during a forty-plus-years work history are no longer applicable or acceptable in the current labor market. Some of them have observed past labor market practices which mitigated against older people's working. Given the trends toward improved health which prolongs the life span, a continuing increase in educational levels among the older population, the recognized diversity of this group, a con-

tinued drift toward early retirement practices, increasing infla-
tionary and economic factors, a highly elevated nationwide
unemployment situation, and the very real possibility of living
ten, twenty, thirty or more years beyond the socially-defined
retirement age, it is conceivable that many older people will
wish or need to seek new or second careers. If such be the case,
then education for re-entry of older workers into the marketplace will become a necessity for some and desirable for others.
New and diversified education-work programs will be needed,
programs which are nationwide in scope and acknowledge that
older workers are able to continue to learn and are not used up
with regard to prolonged productivity in the labor force and are
not to be cast aside. A very real question is whether the marketplace will be ready and willing to accept the re-entry workers
which social custom has conditioned society to believe have no
productive contributions left to make.

Such programs which involve older people in education
and work activities show promise in overcoming the pejorative
view of the older learner-worker, and they are currently in
operation or are being recommended. R. DeCrow has summarized these programs and activities into five principle types:

1. *Skill Banks:* These list old persons' hobbies, avoca-
   tional or vocational talents. Individuals exchange services in lieu of money. These exchange services are
   variously called talent banks, swap-a-job, and ability
   banks.

2. *Community Work Centers:* These centers serve anyone
   interested in "new ways to work."

3. *Community-Based Senior Employment Centers:* They
   operate as free-standing organizations supported by
   local churches, foundations, and employers, or by
   elderly-serving agencies, such as the American Association of Retired Persons.

4. *Educational Brokerage Centers:* These centers
   mediate on behalf of adults seeking educational counseling and referral to appropriate training opportunities in what is often a disconcerting array of providing

agencies. There is much vocational guidance, and many older adult clients use this service.

5. *Women's Centers:* Such centers are active on many campuses, with long experience in individual and group counseling, consciousness-raising, and extremely creative job development. They have many interests congruent with, indeed almost identical to, those of the senior employment centers.

However laudable these services are, they only point the way toward possible nationwide programs and cannot be construed as the answer to all questions. What is lacking with regard to education, work, and aging is a national policy which reflects a more positive view and attitude toward older people—an attitude that education—formal and otherwise—and the business/industrial components in society can and will combine to identify new and innovative ways to involve older people in the productive activities of education and work.

8

WORK, AGING
AND MENTAL HEALTH

In his book, *Work in America,* J. O'Toole asserted that "... the mentally healthy person feels he is leading a rewarding life and esteems himself." The rewarding life and self esteem to which O'Toole refers is related to work satisfaction and a person's perception of his own productivity. In describing the Senior Center in Santa Rosa, California, S. Brown notes that "Retirement is not a blessing for most seniors. It's either an emotional or financial rip-off. They're tired of living in a dependent relationship with bureaucracy and society." These seniors were expressing a desire to be full participants in the society they helped form. One way they perceived doing this was through work. We have learned from developmental psychology that "feeling good" about oneself and knowing that one is contributing to self and society are lifelong processes which help to identify the self in relation to society—one's role in life—and to foster feelings of positive mental health. Society's attitudes on aging, concepts of retirement, social programs designed to do *to* or *for* older people, and society's negative attitudes toward apparently nonproductive persons, may be counter-productive to nurturing the positive mental health of older people. Most find and express their identity through work for which they receive a psychological or financial reward. Finally, R. N. Butler has warned us that "One of the greatest dangers in life is being frozen into rigid roles that limit one's self-development and self-expression." To be old and frozen out of the labor force brings no psychological or financial rewards which had been earned by work and then lost through its denial.

To reach an older age—or to be perceived as being old— is to be locked into a stratified category, with death the only way out. M. E. Wolfgang reminds us that there are differences between "the elderly" and "old age." "Senescence is normal; senility is a disease. Growing old is normal but aging is not ..." Even participants at the 1971 White House Conference on Aging assumed a degree of role stratification of the aged. Without intending to, they stereotyped all older people in the same category. This is evident in the section on Mental Health Care Strategies and Aging. The recommendations contained in the document, "Toward A National Policy on Aging," reflected only mental illness without mentioning or alluding to the mentally healthy older adult. The report leaves the reader with the illusion that all old people are homogeneous with regard to "mental impairments." If the data are correct, one must ask, how did an apparently healthy group of adults suddenly start suffering from mental impairments when they reached an arbitrarily-defined old age?

When moving from a working to a non-working status, many people experience an abrupt shift in living styles, regardless of how prepared they thought they were. As a result, some older people suffer from identity crises which can contribute to many forms of mental dysfunction such as depression, loneliness, neuroses, a sense of isolation, guilt, etc. (This phenomenon—identified as non-normal—generally has been associated with males who permanently leave the labor force. With increases in female labor force participation and increased numbers of female heads of households, this phenomenon may, in time, also become a female characteristic.) Instead of adopting a mental impairment view of aging, society might extend greater efforts toward assisting older people in maintaining their identity through productive work, should they so desire. Society might also see the worth in re-evaluating and re-designing strategies whereby the transition from a work-for-pay mode of living is extended, rewarded and socially esteemed.

Obviously, a "mental impairment" concept is a jaundiced perception of older people. Numerous work- and socially-rewarding living options are needed for older people if a more positive opinion of them is to become a reality. Older people, although of a heterogeneous make-up, are clearly homogeneous in their desires for independence through active participation and contribution to both their society and themselves. They desire to achieve these objectives through a variety of activities, active employment being one such option. Older people can be productive through utilizing various self-help strategies while moving from one life stage to another. Such stages are experienced to a greater or lesser degree throughout the life span. An older individual, for example, may decide to view retirement as a movement from one lifestyle to another, while another may deem it as a terminal event. Apparently the latter is a prevailing societal view. There do seem to be some signs, however, that this view is eroding, at least among older segments of the population. And this seems to be the focus of S. Brown, author of *Taking Senior Citizens Off The Shelf*, in his report on the Senior Skills Center. But pejorative attitudes toward aging and the elderly will prevail until the view that reaching a later life age is a prelude to continued contribution and personal development becomes the norm.

The concern with an aging population's mental well-being as it relates to work has been referred to throughout gerontological literature. When one reviews these works, the psychological well-being of older people is of obvious concern. Most approaches dealing with this issue are primarily concerned with doing *to* or *for* (which assumes an underlying pathology), rather than exploring what can be done in a more healthy and positive way *with* older people. It would seem worthwhile from political, economic, social and psychological vantage points to explore the implications of mental health, aging and work in America.

MENTAL HEALTH/MENTAL ILLNESS: DEFINITIONAL CONFUSION _____

A cursory review of the literature on aging reported in scientific and lay journals leaves the reader with the impression that mental illness among the elderly has reached epidemic proportions and that there are few, if any, mentally-healthy older adults. Certainly, the increased rates of mental health problems among the older population appears to parallel age. It may be argued, however, that the increases in mental dysfunctions among this age group and a rising awareness of their problems are the result of an increased availability of health care and custodial facilities. Some of these are mental hospitals, nursing homes and improved financial aid from public as well as private and individual resources, making treatment economically more feasible. Changing social mores also suggest society's (especially the young's) desire to treat older adults as a homogeneous group, rather than recognizing their heterogeneity. Such acknowledgment would require individual rather than collective attention to their health problems, not to mention a host of other problems which are occurring in today's rapidly-changing society. Another reason for the mental illness focus on the elderly is that identification, the greater visibility of mental dysfunction, and diagnosis of illness require treatment programs and health care interventions and institutions which previously were in short supply or thought not to be needed. Mental wellness demands no similar attention or concern. Yet, even with an increased awareness of the potential for observing these mental abnormalities, R. N. Butler and M. I. Lewis, co-authors of *Aging and Mental Health: Positive Psychological Approaches*, estimated that only 15 percent of the aged need mental health services. Thus, 85 percent may be considered mentally healthy.

Part of the problem of undue attention to mental dysfunction is an apparent lack of clarity as to what is meant by the terms mental health/mental illness and similarly-used language. It is also important to be aware of the medical profession's singular lack of sensitivity to treating older persons' physical problems which, through their myopic use of pharmacological treatment may manifest a psychological problem. Before we can explore related issues, some clarification of terms is necessary.

Mental Health

The etiology of the term *mental health* reveals that it stems from two independent viewpoints. One is the medical/psychiatric view, which generally refers to the chronicity of dysfunctional behavior as a disease, has given rise to elaborate diagnostic procedures and categorization schemas. One of its offshoots is the extended treatment programs which include the use of psychiatric therapeutic interventions, electro-shock, and pharmacology. The second is the mental hygiene view which focuses on mental wellness in terms of one's adjustment and conformity to social values and norms, living styles and socialization processes.

Throughout its etiology, mental health, as a descriptive term, has connoted a concept of illness and has generated considerable confusion as to how it might best be defined. While the term has been used interchangeably to mean both mental dysfunctions as well as positive mental well-being, popular usage has taken on the negative valence of illness when used with certain individuals and groups. Thus, when a person exhibits prolonged and undue sadness or stress as a result of a severe shock to his or her way of living, he or she is said to exhibit a mental dysfunction or have a mental health problem. In reality—and perhaps temporarily—that person does. But by association, the popular view would assume that such behavior is or will be chronic and that it has a pathological basis. It is possible tht some individuals need to exhibit grief longer than others. Recall that among some ethnic groups it was—and in some cases still is—the norm for a widow to wear black clothing for at least a year after the death of a mate or immediate family member; this indicated that they were grieving for a loved one. To communicate the same message, a widower generally wore a black arm band. Also, it was not uncommon to continue this practice until the griever's own death or possibly until she or he remarried. This same practice in today's American society could conceivably be viewed as a pathological dwelling on death.

Remember also the grieving some older workers express when they are forced to retire, when they are terminated or laid off for long periods of time because of their advanced age. Invariably they dwell on their years of work, their successes and achievements to the point where people who hear these stories are bored, and sometimes stop associating with them. An apparent grieving process is being experienced and time is important for the shock to wear off. The point here is that mores, customs and life events change with time. Life for others goes on. New and socially-accepted behaviors are looked upon favorably when a person conforms to them, at least among the young. However, when older people begin exhibiting behaviors which are not in accordance with some capricious or newly-emerging social standard, e.g., retiring from the work place at age sixty-five or before, they are often looked upon as exhibiting "senile" behavior, a sure sign of mental illness.

It would appear that our current social institutions, as well as government legislation, are designed to assist older adults to survive (mental illness) rather than thrive (mental wellness). From our perspective, the fact that the majority of older individuals in American society are psychologically healthy and functioning suggests that to focus undue attention on mental illness is inappropriate and counter-productive in addressing their concerns. Continuing to focus attention predominantly on the mental dysfunctions of older adults (some of whom have been chronically mentally ill throughout their lives) is a disservice to the 85 percent who are mentally functioning in healthy and constructive ways.

Criteria for Mental Health

It will be helpful to establish some bases against which we can examine the relationship of mental health, aging and work in a prevalent context. Author of *The Nature of Mental Health*, H. H. Bowman, has presented eleven criteria by which to evaluate a person's mental health, criteria which are related to our concerns. They are summarized as:

1. The individual works to improve the human condition but also accepts most people and situations as they are. This is especially true in those minor situations which one cannot possibly alter. There are few expectations that events and people will adapt to the individual's convenience.

2. The individual feels himself to be a part of a group or groups and has a feeling of usefulness to the group or groups with which he identifies.

3. The individual is reasonably self-confident and is aware of his or her own strengths and limitations. Life can thus be met realistically without apology for one's limitations.

4. The individual has a sense of self with which he is comfortable.

5. The individual does not evade life's problems and responsibilities, but approaches them realistically and constructively.

6. The individual has a sense of future. He or she does not ignore the past but learns from it in order to achieve future goals.

7. The individual is able to establish positive relationships with others.

8. The individual has a reasonable degree of self-discipline and follows through on his own decisions.

9. The individual appreciates the value of work and derives satisfaction from a job well done.

10. The individual has a mature perspective on sex. He or she appreciates it but is not consumed by it.

11. The individual is capable of living with commitment. He or she is aware that love involves both giving and taking and involves both privilege and responsibility.

These are certainly worthy criteria by which to judge the degree of one's mental well-being. The arenas in which most of these are manifested are work settings and non-work social activities and environments. For the working adult, however, we can assume that work setting predominates. When any or all of these circumstances are denied or are severely limited to older people, then continued mentally healthy growth and development may be severely curtailed. Older individuals who reach out to re-establish themselves as displaying a fulfillment of these criteria may do so in the face of social sanction and may risk being labeled mentally ill. Denying older people outlets (work environment being one of several) through which they can be involved in life's activities contributes to their deterioration; society also loses the services and contributions which older people are uniquely equipped to render. Refusing older people access to a work environment also forces them to be dependent upon society's largess rather than being self-directing and autonomous.

MISINFORMATION AND ATTITUDES _____

Conceptually, three sources of misunderstanding may be defined as being associated with a mental dysfunction view of older adults. They are *physiogenic, psychogenic* and *sociogenic*. Misinformation about and attitudes toward older adults' mental well-being may be said to be the result of the interaction of the physical, psychological and social conditions as observed and interpreted by society and self. Operationally, the terms cannot be perceived to be mutually exclusive. The three conditions are interactive; observed human behavior is in terms of all three.

Physiogenic. The physiogenic basis for interpreting an older person's mental wellness may find its onset when one first experiences disruptions in sensory processes, for example, hearing loss, decline in visual acuity, kinesthetic disruptions, and dulling of the senses of taste and smell. These and other observed physical manifestations of the aging process bring with them a full awareness of a sense of aging. As the human organism attempts to accommodate itself to these changes, previous behavioral modes are modified. Rather than play touch football, one is content to observe others playing. Health problems begin to manifest themselves and may often become chronic, thus forcing the older person to adjust himself to these intrusions. How the older person adapts himself to the physiological changes he experiences often will influence younger society's understanding of being well or not well. Thus, when older people tend to withdraw from social interaction due to physiological problems they are experiencing and with which they do not want others to be bothered or because of which they do not wish to be pitied, they are often adjudged to be isolating themselves, assumed to be senile, withdrawn, or otherwise on a downward slide. Or when an older person is suffering from high blood pressure and his medication is too strong or inappropriate, he or she may manifest severe depressive symptoms which are interpreted as signs of mental impairment or dementia. In any event, regardless of the physical problem, its chronicity and the reactions are often interpreted by the older person and others as signs of physical decline which may also accompany mental decline.

Another source surrounding misinformation on the physical deterioration of older people is the popular media—especially television. While it is conceded that through some benign benevolence the media wish to focus on positive attributes of older people, their efforts may really have a reverse effect, similar to the nineteenth-century romantic writers.

Physical manifestations of the aging process are normal, but sensationalizing the process is not. The recent publicizing of Alzheimer's Disease and other forms of dementia—along with the research associated with uncovering their etiology and diagnoses—and their treatment—perpetuates a continuation of the negative attributes of aging. The point here is that when society focuses on selected attributes of the aging process, an implication is left that all persons will experience these changes. Hence, a negative attitude is projected—a stereotype of old persons being helpless and sick. J. Rodin and E. Langer, writing in *The Journal of Social Issues*, have pointed out that at least 95 percent of older people do not conform to such a representation. Yet, as the negative forces and views about physical aging are popularized and as older people have few positive role models to emulate, the prevailing and sensationalized views become the norm.

Psychogenic. Extensive research in cognitive processes and psychological functioning—while demonstrating slight differences between age groups—strongly suggest there is little decline among older age groups. Both the professional and popular literature, however, continue to extol the pathogenic aspects of mental dysfunction among select age groups, almost to the total exclusion of positive mental attributes. Certainly, the normal everyday well-functioning older person does not make headlines, nor do professional gerontologists or other interested researchers establish professional reputations through studying the healthy older adult. It is more exciting and sensational to uncover the secrets of pathology, since most people seem to have an unspoken fear that they may become the next victim of such pathology. This seems to be true, regardless of the recent shift in the news media and some popular television shows which are beginning to focus on happy, productive, and long-lived independent older people. Somehow this focus seems unconvincing to both younger and older age groups and especially to employers in regard to retaining older employees in the work force.

A medically-oriented view would argue that in order to enhance wellness—physiological or psychological—we need to focus upon and understand the etiology of illness and disease. This position assumes that most mental health problems are disease-based. While this position has merit in some cases and is justification for research in uncovering disease-based mental health problems among the elderly, to sensationalize these efforts to the exclusion of even mentioning mental wellness is to perpetuate an injustice toward the 85 percent of the mentally healthy, active and productive older adults in today's society.

Sociogenic. As more and more people survive longer, society begins to feel economic stresses. In earlier history this was not seen to be a serious problem since the family unit assumed care and responsibility for its older members. The elders maintained a definite position in the social group and were accorded due respect. The indigent, poor and destitute who survived to an older age were shunted off to the "poor farm" or "old age home," which was usually physically removed from the population centers. Society had done its duty. It had provided food and shelter, such as it was, and had assumed no further responsibility for the care and maintenance of the elderly. The costs to society for these provisions were relatively small with the attitude being: "The old geezers and dames won't live too long so we don't have to do anything else. Anyway, they ought to be happy that we are providing food and housing for them." In such an environment it is not unreasonable to assume that those persons who were suffering from what today is collectively termed dementia, acted in bizarre ways. Such behavior helped establish the connotation that to grow old implied going crazy. It also is not unreasonable to assume that paranoid and depressive behaviors were exacerbated by their living conditions. If they became too unmanageable they were removed and sent to the "crazy house."

These observed behaviors were ample proof for the unthinking population to support the notion that to be old was to go crazy and need to be institutionalized. Further, as society began to become more urbanized around the turn of the century fewer families had facilities to care for the elderly. Costs for extra-institutional care were within an affordable economic range, especially with recent governmental subsidies, and our health care programs becoming more commonplace. It became the norm to think in terms of institutionalization of the elderly. These arrangements (today called nursing homes, senior living centers and the like) have now become widespread. Along with these changes there arose the socially-accepted myth that mental illness is a concomitant part of such a placement. Until very recently, one need only visit an average nursing home to see verification of these views. Nursing home personnel—especially those not properly trained—have brought their negative caretaking behavior, reinforced the mental illness myths toward the residents, giving credence to a self-fulfilling prophecy. These same attitudes parallel the idea that to be old is to disengage oneself from society, become ill both mentally and physically, and need to be cared for by others in society. The emergence of social caretaking institutions, which grew out of an industrial society opting for the easy way of dealing with an aged segment of the population, perpetuates the notion of disengagement and the accompanying view of mental illness.

The dangers of such a perpetuation of old age mental illness in today's and, perhaps more importantly tomorrow's society are very real. It is now commonly recognized that the over-sixty-five age group is the fastest growing segment of the population. Demographers project this trend to continue well into the next century. A larger portion of income is being earmarked by government deduction just to maintain the elderly at a level that was previously believed necessary and sufficient. (Note: It is not difficult to see that today's maintenance level of economic support for the elderly is not too different in attitude from that which was associated with the support for the "country poor house" and "old age home" from an earlier era.)

Another aspect to society's focusing on the negatives regarding mental illness and perpetuating this attitude both covertly and overtly is related to role modeling. In today's world, the young are provided with a negative image of what the latter years are like, especially when the mental and physical health focus is on disease rather than good health. They see few, if any, acceptable rewards to becoming old. Thus, at least among some younger individuals, the attitude is one of not worrying about the future.

The myths about aging which have given rise to negative dispositions and misinformation in regard to the elderly's mental health as influenced by physiogenic, psychogenic and sociogenic factors, are pervasive, persistent and insidious. What is true for a few is not true for the vast majority of older people. Physically, different parts of the body grow old at different rates for different people. We can no longer think that sixty-five is old. This is especially true when we accept the concept that the heterogeneity of people becomes greater as people age and that physical decay, in the sense of inability to function, is not an inevitable attribute of all people, at least in early old age.

Perhaps the most insidious myth is the concomitant mental decline associated with aging. While the over-forty age group may exhibit some slowing down in decision-making and the like, as well as having stronger belief systems, they do change their beliefs. Our youth-oriented society, however, sees these changes as not "keeping up," ergo, senility. Older members in society do remain part of the mainstream but in modified ways. It is this type of misinformation, past beliefs, over-emphasizing negatives, and focusing on mental impairment which perpetuates the negative stereotypes of poor mental health among the older population segment and fosters a dependency upon society rather than promoting independence and autonomy.

DEPENDENCE/ INDEPENDENCE

A resurging independence among the elderly in American society would enable them to assert a more positive life role, especially as related to work. Currently, our social institutions, governmental policies, social attitudes and mores mitigate against this view and encourage an increasing dependency attitude among society's older segments and between generational groups. These dependency forces can be found in our economic, political and health-oriented support systems. We also see them at work within family groups concerning caring for older family members, and in society's general disposition toward older people in their everyday activities, such as work settings, public transportation, education, and living environments. Most of these have been geared toward meeting the needs of society's younger groups, with only a passing thought toward their effect on older people.

Perhaps it is erroneous to call for a resurgence of the independent older adult, since today's society is structured in such a way that we are all dependent upon each other. Rather, what is of central concern is preserving the individual's autonomy in decision making and his right to continue exercising associated responsibilities in any environment for as long as possible without socially-imposed restrictions. While no one is truly independent, many work very hard at being "dependent on no one." America's work-oriented society is such that to be independent is "good" but to be dependent is "bad." When older people demand the right to continue to work at being "dependent on no one," social forces become punitive toward them. Earning limitations associated with Social Security entitlements provide a case in point. As people age, they often need many kinds of social and family support mechanisms. When needs begin to emerge, older people—to be eligible for and to receive these support services—usually must relinquish some of their autonomy. R. A. Kalish has provided some examples of supports needed as people age. They are: "Ill health requires help from physicians, nurses and family members; inability to drive requires help from neighbors, friends and relatives; the loss of a spouse brings about the need not only for help in doing certain things, but also for emotional support; increasing difficulty in keeping up with the fast-paced, modern day world may require help in decision-making." These realities are difficult and painful for an older person to accept, especially those who have prided themselves in doing for themselves and who have accepted the social and religious norms which make it degrading and often embarrassing to ask for help.

The concept of autonomy and independence is so pervasive in our culture that help-givers are often patronizing, often punishing, and sometimes angry when such help is asked. While these responses by caregivers are understandable, such behaviors are not conducive to assisting older people in maintaining a degree of self-determination over their lives and to continue to thrive rather than to survive.

The loss of autonomy as one ages is not consistent with the criteria of positive mental health. While it is socially acceptable for children to be dependent upon their parents, it is not so for parents as they grow older to be dependent upon their children or society. There is no obvious future "pay off" for this form of investment. When parental dependency upon children or others becomes excessive, parents may become anxious and depressed. They begin to view themselves as burdens, which is alien to their way of being and to their previously-adhered-to beliefs. And if parents dwell excessively on this necessary dependency (in some cases it is manufactured by children as well as social structures), the accompanying anger, anxiety and depression can become chronic, creating the potential for mental health problems.

Behavioral attributes such as these are often expressed by older people who reside in senior centers and who are partially dependent upon public social services. We can include frustration with the system as well as a sense of impotency on having any meaningful impact on it or control over it, in addition to anxiety, depression and the like. A case illustration:

> A residential senior living center established for middle- and lower-income older people participates in a "meals on wheels" hot lunch program. Each resident pays a small nominal fee, if able, for the hot lunch, which is eaten in a fully-equipped cafeteria at the center. The majority of residents who participate are older women, as one might expect, who live in their own small one-

bedroom apartments. All are physically and psychologically fully functioning. All have modest incomes which pay for their basic needs with little left over for extras. The "meals on wheels" lunch program is nutritious and money-saving, and it also provides socialization opportunities for the residents. Several women desired to set up a cooking program using the center's fully-equipped kitchen. They were unable to afford to because of their meager incomes. They contacted the "meals on wheels" program director to see if the uncooked food could be delivered, then they wanted to prepare the meals on site, using their own pet recipes rather than having the meals prepared by others elsewhere and delivered hot to the center. Such an activity would permit residents to be involved in a group effort, relieve the "meals on wheels" program from having to prepare the food, accommodate the belonging and importance needs of a group, and allow them some freedom and autonomy in preparing and serving their own meals.

Such was not to be. The "meals on wheels" program apparently had no provisions in its mandate to allow for such flexibility. While they could and did prepare and deliver food to these residents, the residents were not allowed to be a part of the process. The residents in turn became angry and frustrated, feeling thwarted in their desire to be meaningful and contributing to each other. A sense of anomie has now settled in over this group regarding collective activities when dealing with external agencies. They attempt to assert their independence and self-determination vocally to anyone who will listen, leaving the casual observer with the impression of garrulous and obstreperous old people.

We found earlier that being meaningful to others is an important characteristic of positive mental health. Meaningfulness is often defined in terms of service to others or productivity in the workplace. Generally, people do not think in terms of meaningfulness to themselves, though each may attempt to develop his or her own capacities and make each one the best person that individual could possibly be. Such is the case of our residents in the above example. Certainly, striving toward such objectives leads one toward self-realization. To become old is the last age at which one can continue working toward the goal of self-actualization. Our culture is structured so that older people are restricted in the options available to them in their continued endeavoring and, as we saw in our example, are often thwarted when they assert themselves in what they perceive to be meaningful activities. They are not permitted to work without socially-imposed economic and psychological penalties. Children no longer need them in ways they did previously. The workplace will not tolerate them beyond a certain age. Physiologically they are slowing down and cannot keep pace with their own earlier standards. Finally, their ways of dealing with and understanding their world are not consistent with prevailing approaches. Their previous expertise is seen as outmoded or irrelevant with the concomitant loss of the power to influence others in today's world.

Older people lose their sense of futurity as the dimensions of autonomy are diminished by age and social pressures to conform to ambiguous or conflicting externally-imposed criteria. Even though the individual may have several more years of good physical and psychological health, what will he be able to do with it? How will he do it? Will he be allowed? Without a sense of independence and social and family supports to encourage such autonomy, the future for older people is bleak and the sense of dependence, the devaluation of being old, and accompanying negative valences are perpetuated.

Thus far we have been discussing the negative aspects of dependence/independence. Is the picture bleak? It probably is, unless we begin to reverse our attitudes and start listening to older people. H. L. Sheppard, in his article in the *Handbook of Aging and Social Sciences*, reported that 55 percent of blue-collar and 76 percent of white-collar workers he interviewed would return to work if they could, regardless of their income level during retirement. This is a strong expression of older workers' desires to use their time in what they perceive to be a productive activity, to regain a sense of meaningfulness in their lives in the arena they value, and to continue to demonstrate their ability to maintain their autonomy. Our social institutions, work environments and social attitudes, however, continue to discourage this form of behavior. An obvious conclusion can be drawn from the following example:

> A sixty-eight-year-old retired city employee (mandatory retirement for his job was sixty-five) who was physically and psychologically healthy found he was having a difficult time sustaining himself and his wife on a combined income from Social Security and a city pension. He had worked thirty-five years for the city, reared five children, bought and paid for a small, modest home (this is his personal savings component of the tripartite retirement plan), sent three children through college, and otherwise lived the "American Dream" in a contributing and responsible manner. He was a proud and independent person, strongly subscribing to traditional family, religious and work ethics. A little additional income was all that was necessary for him to maintain his dignity, autonomy and sense of self-worth—and to retain his home. He secured a night watchman's position which paid him enough to satisfy his needs and to keep up with rising living costs. After one year he found that due to income restrictions associated with his retirement revenue, he was required to pay 50 percent of his additional earnings in the form of taxes, reimbursements and other assessments. In essence, he was working full-time for half-pay in a low-paying job which was important to his employer. He gave up the position. He felt that working for half-pay for full-time work was unjust, and he now has curtailed his lifestyle to a marginal existence, becoming ever more marginal with each rise in inflation. He must rely on his children for any extras. And his children, in turn, are attempting to get their own adult lives started. This is an anathema to his belief system and to the values which sustained him throughout his life.

The only help this man needed was for society to allow

him the freedom to exercise his responsibilities in a work environment in positive and contributing ways, without its systems and laws being punitive toward such actions. Such was not the case. In his eyes, in order for him to realize society's largess (for which he spent a lifetime contributing), he had to choose between relinquishing some personal independence and responsibility via reduced income or being penalized excessively for attempting to maintain himself and his wife according to the rules which had previously governed his life.

This suggests that older people's loss of autonomy is similar to social psychological theories of power. The many problems experienced by older people are the consequences of decreasing power. In our two examples we can see that as power and potency for controlling one's life are eroded, the sense of anomie, of giving up, begins to set in. Surely this is an early sign of the onset of mental decline, withdrawal or forced dependence and is contradictory to the criteria of good mental health. In another context, in a paper presented at a Southwest Psychological Association Meeting, I and colleague R. Garcia reported our findings that nursing home residents who were compared to similarly-aged groups living in their own homes scored higher on a measure of locus of control, suggesting a dependence upon external authority (a giving up of power and autonomy). In essence, successful adaptations to aging—at least by our culture's external standards—imply relinquishing autonomy and power in order to receive the benefits of society's largess.

It is being argued here that *the more independent older people are, the less likely they will be to experience poor mental health*. Notable examples in support of this are prominent elderly represented in the arts, politics and business. The concern is whether society, through its institutions, will allow such independence to flourish for all older people, not for just a few who are well-known or economically well-off.

Work

A special case of the dependence/independence dichotomy as it relates to mental health is found in the concept of work. Throughout this volume the importance of work in an aging society has been championed. It is our belief that no other social activity is more important to continuing positive mental health and the maintenance of power, independence and autonomy for older people. Casual conversations with older individuals invariably turn to their successes and accomplishments during their working years. It seems important for them to convince the listener (usually younger) of their specialness and identity as productive contributors to society. Sarasan reminded us that one way we establish and maintain our identity is through our work. Yet the work activity and the arena in which it takes place are restricted for those who reach an older age. This is true with very few exceptions. Our culture rewards those who work and are perceived as being productive. Society barely tolerates those who do not work. Only the very young are tolerated in their dependency relationships with productive workers. This tolerance of dependent youth is in anticipation of their future productive contributions. Witness how the young are praised and rewarded when they perform a work activity, especially work for financial reward. When older dependent people elect similar behavior, they are criticized as taking work away from those who need it, or are otherwise punished. Older persons who are restricted from the work arena for whatever reason are not accorded the tolerance of their youthful counterparts, even though a lifetime of work and productivity set the stage and established the conditions for future workers' successes.

Health and economic well-being are the two most important attributes for people to experience a successful and satisfactory older age. It can be argued that good health is the single most important characteristic when one is old. Problems of good health appear to be beginning to be less and less a concern for most older people and may in the future become a secondary concern. This is especially true for early old age and, according to Fries, it may become true for most older people at whatever age by the early twenty-first century. As older people believe that good health is a given for them, their concern about it will lessen. Then they will turn much of their attention to their economic needs. These can only be satisfied through paid work, unless society is willing to make a true commitment to economic support of our elderly.

Surely, in order to be a physically and psychologically healthy adult suggests the ability to participate actively in life. This carries with it the need for economic independence, at least for some activities. Senior centers are filling a void for some older people, as are the volunteer activities in which older people engage, activities which demand little economic outlay. Older people, however, do like to go out to dinner, movies, concerts, theaters, enjoy travel and engage in all such pursuits as does any other normal adult group. Such activities cost money. Additionally, our modern society is such that more and more children of the aged are moving away from home in pursuit of their new careers, which often takes them to distant communities, states and countries. This new mobility imposes additional economic burdens on retired and aging parents who desire to maintain close family relationships and contacts. Given current developments in "high-tech" industries, we can expect more and more family dispersements in the future with which upcoming older generations will need to cope. Regardless of published statistics, proximate family living within twenty to twenty-five miles may be a part of history.

A major source of stress for older people will be their having to cope with the active living styles now spreading, especially when they are living on a fixed income, are confronted with rapid and creeping inflation, and are not allowed to continue to work. This stress is similar in intensity to the loss of job, loss of spouse, and forced retirement from work. After all, the older generation has grown up in a society in which work has had greater prestige than play has. We have seen that such a cultural value—while currently being modified—is still very much a part of our society. In his book, *Civilization And Its Discontents*, Sigmund Freud felt that the importance of work to the individual was critical in binding him or her to reality. He also felt that work was necessary if a person was to discharge fundamental human urges that were required for a healthy mentality. Without work or the possibility of work, older people are confronted with a "Catch 22" situation. They are looked down upon if they don't work and are dependent upon society because they have needs. They are criticized if they choose to work for pay beyond the age limits and earning limitations established by social convention and institutions. Such a dilemma is fertile ground for stress-related illness to be manifest.

The stress and stress-related illnesses may be perceived as developmental stress and are insidious to mental health. They are cumulative in nature and will take time, often years, to reach an intensity level calling for clinical intervention. We are not suggesting that stress and stress-related illnesses exhibited by older people are caused by any one factor. Rather, stress—like any psychological disorder—is rooted in internal (self) as well as external (social) factors and is cumulative. In older people, the loss of familiar and supportive social contacts such as may have been developed in their work setting can be very unsettling. Certain areas of life provide social supports, successes, rewards and other benefits. Being prohibited from remaining in or re-entering those arenas—whether by legislation, social sanction, or employer discrimination—can create situations where stress can be both debilitating to an individual and very costly to society. In a sense, we do condition adults during their younger productive years toward an economic preparation for old age, although this never seems to be enough for the average person facing rising inflation. We use enforced savings, such as Social Security and retirement programs, but there are no clear-cut guidelines, role models, or foci on how to prepare to live the fifteen-to-twenty later-life years without the regularity of work. This view is particularly devastating.

PLANNING FOR
INDEPENDENCE

Modern industrial society has efficiently conditioned older people to leave the work force on cue by rationalizing retirement as an inevitable part of and useful to the continued modernization of society as well as solving society's unemployment problems. This has effectively assured older people "that aging means a decline in effectiveness, obsolescence in skills, inability to learn new things, and being a fifth wheel in the midst of younger people doing productive things."

Certainly, the evidence from the past twenty years seriously questions this view. The roots for this rationalization can be found in the influences from the 1930s, when justification for the legislation to restrict large numbers of people from the labor force was institutionalized. Further verification came from the impact of the youth generation's emergence during the 1950s and 1960s, and when post-World War II workers began to be disenchanted with the impersonalization of the work setting, a condition brought about by job fragmentation and increased automation. Certain influences combined to encourage and sanction older workers to move toward retirement. For one thing, veterans were returning to the work force. More income was available and as it accumulated there was a relative ease of living. Income-maintenance programs were also a factor. Business and industry very willingly encouraged and simplified early retirement practices. Leisure was now added to and sanctioned as part of the American Dream.

As that phenomenon unfolded, little thought was devoted initially to how one would use his leisure time. Idleness was not yet considered an American virtue, especially during the immedite post-war era. Idleness has been in the process of becoming a possible life activity ever since the introduction of Social Security in 1935, but it still is suspect as an acceptable lifestyle. Idleness (retirement) still is being "hawked" and promoted through the popular media. Financial planning and preparation is being advocated as part of the idleness activity. Since the number of individuals affected were proportionately few but growing slowly during the 1930s through the 1950s, little attention was devoted to how these new retirees used their time or felt about their newly-found idleness. The young were the focus of the day. There were no role models for the older person to emulate nor idleness traditions to follow other than dependence upon social systems, especially for the urban retiree. It was under these conditions that theories of activity and disengagement began to emerge. These theories were an effort to understand the new phenomenon of retirement from work and to understand the psychology of increasing numbers of longer-lived adults. In all likelihood, the behaviors manifested by post-World War II retirees stimulated research regarding the psychological aspects of aging. These behaviors were really a result of older people's confusion in regard to how to behave in this life stage, how to fill up idle time with activities (this was the age of "how-to-do-its" and "paint-by-numbers"), and a seeking of ways to relieve guilt and associated stress for being alive, healthy, functioning, and not working. The urge to work, however, regardless of age or time in history, is a deeply-rooted aspect of American culture.

The increasing number and visibility of longer-lived adults suggest that the retirement picture is discouraging to the psychological well-being of older people. Our economic support mechanisms for the elderly are currently under severe strain and are being questioned as to their functional utility. The tripartite model of economic support—while theoretically a sound concept—is suffering from intrusions: inflation eroding savings, rising property taxes and energy costs which far exceed retiree's fixed incomes, company failures jeopardizing personal pension plans as well as inappropriate vesting concepts, and the Social Security system seemingly in endangerment or, at best, under rigorous question and strain. Psychologically and behaviorally we are experiencing a rise in suicide and substance abuse by the elderly (increased drug dependence via improper or excessive medication for physical ailments, excessive alcohol use). These factors and their ensuing behavioral manifestations suggest that the anticipated retirement dream is a more fanciful life stage than we imagined. Perhaps the dream is really society's own myth which it has come to believe as truth in order to mollify guilt over how the elderly are being treated. For most people, the current pattern of aging and retiring is not a reinforcement of good mental health compatible with the criteria set forth earlier. Regardless of the reduction of work as "toil" and the accompanying rise in free time, to grow old without work is to grow old with little autonomy, purpose and meaning in life. To deny older people a continued and valued place in the work force under the assumption that they *must* move aside to make room for youth has been demonstrated to be not valid, not cost effective, and not beneficial to society. It makes no sense to forcibly remove healthy, functioning and productive workers from work environments—places where they retain their independence, autonomy and sense of purpose—and force them into a state of idleness. This is contradictory to all moral and ethical values which have given rise to the American Dream.

Reality suggests that something must be done if the retirement stage of life is to have meaning for older people. Older Americans should not be left alone to flounder in their attempts to resolve their problems within a society which imposes restrictions under the benign assumption it is being helpful. Neither should a younger society be left to determine what is right and proper for its elders. What is needed is co-participation in planning. In order to realize the American Retirement Dream, older people need to be *worked with* rather than *acted upon*.

For older people, idleness may not be an important issue. Many others are forced to stop working when there is no need for such action. For them, the readjustment to new routines and lifestyles can be very difficult. There are four sources of need for role realignment and role re-examination in later life when one stops working for any reason. They are:

1. There has been a loss of a work role which may have been the major focus of activity throughout the person's life.
2. Related to the loss of work role is loss of income.
3. Retirement, in many cases, is the result of declining health. However, many persons are automatically retired while they re in good health.
4. The changes in the family cycle, many of which have started in late middle age, are also a major source of need for role realignment.

These realignments and re-examinations will vary for

different segments of the population. Ethnicity, sex, geographical location and lifestyle are examples of such variability. This is consistent with the heterogeneous nature of people which most of our retirement policies are unable to accommodate. Socially-imposed restrictions—either legislated or customary—must be altered in ways to allow older people more degrees of freedom of choice. It should be their option to remain in or leave the labor force. Until this has come to pass, its lack is a reality with which the elderly must deal.

It is being argued that one source of mental health problems among older people stems not from leaving the work force per se, no matter what the reason, but rather from the lack of preparation and planning for such a move. This is especially true when the leave was forced, when the older person has no control over his or her environment. Preparation and planning for life's latter stage without formal working arrangements will need to occur at two levels—personal and societal. These are consistent with the caveat: The individual both acts upon and is acted upon by his environment. Older people, especially those forced to leave work, seem to have little or no impact upon their environment regarding the retirement decision and its ensuing results. With appropriate and early planning for retirement, we can move toward rectifying an imbalance between self and environment; and we can assist older individuals to exercise some control and independence. There are always a few individuals who do plan their future without formal work. They seem to be the group so busy and involved with life that the transition from formal working to informal working is a life stage of anticipation and personal growth and development.

Personal Planning

Pre-retirement preparation takes time, motivation, hard work and individual study. It is not a one-time event; it grows and develops over time. The two cases which follow describe such a process with obvious results. One is successful with regard to a future outlook and the other—which started with the same futuristic outlook—turns out not to be as successful.

An example may be seen in this case:

George Ames (a pseudonym) worked for thirty-three years in a Federal agency. He enjoyed his work, was successful, became a division director, and was well-regarded by his supervisors, peers, and those who worked under his supervision. He enjoyed excellent health and to this day remains a healthy, fully-functioning, active adult. By his twenty-fifth year in his position, George's children were married, involved with their own careers, and otherwise independent from George and his wife. At this point the couple began discussing and exploring the idea of how and where they wanted to live out their remaining years. George was now fifty-six. They began their planning and explorations by reading all the literature they could find concerning retirement. They inventoried their personal assets, began adding to them, and reviewed their individual and combined interests. They spent approximately five years searching for and deciding upon those activities they wanted to continue or to engage in for the first time. What had they put off doing in the past that was really important? They found that travel was important but realized that visiting particular locations was more important that travel itself. They engaged in a study program about those special places and planned trips in detail, since they knew how limited their budget would be. Because helping others was important to her, George's wife wanted to expand her church and volunteer activities and George had always wanted to write short stories and poetry, but he was untrained and he never seemed to have the time to get the necessary training. Upon retirement he began taking courses in creative writing at the local community college; he found that he really did enjoy this activity and that he was good at it. At the time of this writing he had had one essay published in the *Readers' Digest* and several under review by publishers.

George is now sixty-eight and has been retired for five years. He still gets calls from his former agency for special tasks, since his expertise is highly regarded. George is currently planning several special trips; he plans to write a book in which to incorporate the knowledge acquired from previous trip preparations as well as from the trips themselves. George is happy, active, involved with his wife in her volunteer and church activities and is so productively busy he can't be bothered about being old—at least by society's standards. Retirement from one formal work setting was merely a transitory event to move toward another exciting life stage with the promise of a continuing future.

Another illustrative case in point follows:

Alan Johnston is currently seventy-four years old, has been retired from all formal work activity for six years, enjoys moderately good health, and is engaged in almost no activities. As a young adult, Alan worked at many jobs and for many companies related to his specialization. He held his last position for twenty-five years. In this position he experienced job changes both geographically and in terms of assignments. Most of these changes emerged as lateral moves occurring after he became a department head. Alan suffered a mild heart attack at age sixty and with his wife began to plan on an early retirement. They planned to sell their house and move closer to relatives and their children. They wanted their remaining years essentially to consist of involvement with family, since their work life was such that family separation had been extensive.

One year prior to Alan's retirement at age sixty-two, his wife died suddenly. At that point Alan cast aside all retirement plans and elected to remain employed. All planning and talking about retirement ceased. When he reached the age of mandatory retirement, Alan's company asked him to remain in his position on a year-by-year basis until a suitable replacement could be found. Alan was a good employee and did a fine job in his position. He finally left full-time employment at age sixty-eight and has not been called back for special jobs.

Alan's first act after retirement was to take an extended trip for which he and his wife had long planned. Since the trip, Alan has not engaged in any activities other than living at home and making an occasional trip to the supermarket. He is rarely seen by former colleagues but does attend church regularly, a lifelong habit. Alan is considered an alcoholic. Other than a rare visit to one of his children, Alan could have his retirement interpreted as relatively barren.

For both these people, pre-retirement preparation was very different. George spent about eight years at the task, whereas Alan spent at most two years. One has been successful in building a new and independent life for himself; the other has not seemed to have recovered from the death of his wife. Apparently, Alan had few if any personal resources upon which to rely to get over his wife's death and build a new life for himself. George can be said to be living a healthy life, whereas Alan can be questioned regarding his mental well-being. George exemplifies the implementation of our mental health criteria. Alan fails on almost every criterion. If the concept of work is activity-oriented involving productive endeavors, George has only moved the locus of his activity from a formal work setting to the more informal setting of his home. Alan, on the other hand, has left the formal work activity but what he is to do next is unclear. George is "thriving" in his retirement, is productive and a contributing member of society. George expresses a sense of futurity, autonomy and control over his life. Alan appears to be only surviving.

In George's situation, long-term, well-thought-out and researched planning was involved. Such questions as economic information and motivation for realistically fulfilling a future governed George's and his wife's behavior. His recent comment was, "I don't know what would have happened if I hadn't put in all that time planning. No one told me to do it. I just know it was right for me. I wish I could convince everyone to do it and to start very early."

Alan, however, apparently did no real planning until a

crisis occurred (his heart attack). When the next crisis came to pass—his wife's death—there was no previous plan from which to draw strength and direction. Perhaps if Alan had done some long-range planning because of self-motivation or as a result of a company pre-retirement planning program, his life circumstance might be different today.

Societal Influences

The decision to retire is a long-term process and, in order to be accomplished successfully, requires much planning, should be done gradually, and should involve a future orientation and include the significantly affected persons (retiree and spouse). Most of the existing retirement programs, however, are limited and involve little more than information concerning financial and health insurance options.

The phenomenon of retirement planning has had a relatively short history which has paralleled—though lagged behind—the large-scale concept of retirement from work. Adults contemplating retirement need adequate information as well as motivation, since retirement planning is so new. It is thought that early planning and preparation allow for a longer transition period from a working to a non-working-for-pay lifestyle, with the actual retirement event being less traumatic. Such an attitude assumes the retirement from paid work is a social given about which the individual has no choice. Our social systems and organizations have not encouraged such a long-range view, nor do they reinforce the concept that retirement from paid work is the result of lifelong patterns. They ignore the fact that such behavior is a social expectation and that the individual has some choice in the matter. The recent introduction of Individual Retirement Accounts (I.R.A.) and Keogh retirement plans have begun to sensitize some segments of American society to be better prepared economically for a not-working-for-pay life stage option at a much younger age. The long-range effect regarding retirement attitudes associated with these new plans is yet to be determined. Few similar efforts are being instituted to study the long-range psychological effect on retirement.

It is obvious that our social systems and institutions are concerned and are becoming more actively involved in pre-retirement planning programs. The concerns are primarily focused on financial entitlements and procedures to enter into a retirement life stage—also obvious. What is less obvious is the availability of programs that go beyond health insurance, pension plans, and Social Security entitlements; what is also less obvious is the motivation for initiating these programs. Given our society's proclivity to solve employment and unemployment problems in simplistic ways (remove older workers to make room for the young), and given the continued belief in the unlimited supply of human resources, one must question the rationale and motivation for encouraging and promoting organized pre-retirement planning programs which also deal with lifestyle attributes, and personal and social relationships. Expanded efforts are needed which involve time as well as research regarding reasons and motivation for such programs being conducted by social institutions. If pre-retirement planning programs are to become part of the developmental cycle of adult life, then they will need to consider longer-lived and healthier adults who now have an excess of time never previously available to large groups of older people. How to plan for this time utilization and living in such a life stage when an individual's value systems are in conflict are major issues yet to be confronted or adequately addressed. It may very well emerge that our social and work institutions will not assume any pre-retirement planning responsibility beyond the basic information dealing with physical health and income. If such be the case, then planning for retirement—and here we mean lifelong planning—will need to be conducted by individuals themselves.

PLANNING FOR A PRODUCTIVE FUTURE

Maintaining positive attributes of mental health and individual autonomy among the older population is the concern of everyone, not any one particular segment of society. Heretofore, concern for the elderly has been with the maintenance of economic and physical health. There has been little thought regarding their mental health or how other facets of living affect them. This is an understandable but limited view of achieving the quality of life desired, or looking forward to the retirement dream in later years.

The ultimate question relates to how best to assist ourselves to be fully prepared to confront an independent autonomous living style which does not include work. This is of concern to all age groups, since what we put in operation today is really a statement of how we ourselves wish to be treated in the future, where we, too, are denied a place in the work arena. It makes little sense not to use a lifetime of learning to address this question. Certainly, older people have some ideas regarding these solutions. Are we as a society really ready to listen to them? It may be argued that if solutions to the major question can be arrived at, then older people will have a vital role—modeling function—to perform for future generations of elderly. Their continued place in society will be assured and that role will be esteemed. Their meaningfulness to self and others will become obvious and conform to our criteria of good mental health.

What format this planning will take cannot be determined at this time. Most planning programs might be initiated when the worker is in his sixties, near the retirement age, some at a much earlier age.

A possible format for lifelong planning is being tentatively offered. Only time, research, and practice will reveal its merits. If the thesis is tenable and accepted, then the following elements—some of which currently are in place—must surely be included.

Informational Planning. The institution of Social Security assures us a basis for lifelong economic planning since everyone begins to participate at an early age. Increasing numbers of pension programs initiated by companies, governments, and labor unions are continuing to reinforce the early economic planning concept. This is shown to be especially true with heightened interest in pension transferability, entitlements in two-worker households, and pension-vesting issues. The inauguration of I.R.A., Keogh and other individually-initiated long-term retirement savings plans has further assured a movement toward early lifelong economic planning. Whether or not late-life financial sufficiency will be the result in a not-working-for-pay lifestyle is yet to be demonstrated. It is hoped that it will be. Nevertheless, the roots for lifelong economic planning are in place and will need to be extended.

Recently there has been an increasing awareness of the need for lifelong health planning. It suggests that this is now becoming a part of everyday life, evidenced by longer-lived, healthier adults. As we have become more knowledgeable about the long-term health effects, there has come a corresponding rise in urgency in improving physical fitness, dietary planning and practices, and cleaning up our environment. Continued healthy living practices and wider dissemination of related health and economic information are expected. In this regard, institutional pre-retirement planning programs may become superfluous in the short-term future. But such mandatory programs currently in place should be encouraged and expanded to focus on lifelong health planning.

Psychological Planning. It has been only a recent phenomenon that gerontologists—as well as the lay public have become interested in psychological well-being among older people. Life planning, which generally has been limited to career planning, has been of concern mainly due to the past beliefs in the linear life plan and "one-life, one-career" concepts. It has been only since larger numbers of people are seen to survive beyond age sixty-five—people who are also healthy and fully-functioning—that any thought has been devoted to this stage of living. Such concerns having to do with leisure time, volunteerism, and part-time/part-year working arrangements have been of primary interest. There has been little organized thought toward future living with and without work, or living with or without a spouse when in a not-working-for-pay life stage. Attention must be drawn to family relationships, with the reintroduction of multigenerational households, and to areas concerned with those personal aspects which help to make one's life meaningful to self and others.

To maintain positive mental health and lifelong independence without work demands lifelong planning and preparation. This implies learning at an early age to live in mentally healthy ways and to develop new behavior modes to accommodate life changes as one grows older. Psychological lifelong planning takes time and much effort. Good mental health does not just occur; one works at it throughout life. Being able to withstand intrusions in one's life pattern, in addition to altered living and family relationships, is seen in our view as being important and part of lifelong futuristic planning.

Social Planning. Social planning is more complex and more involved than informational and personal-psychological planning. It occurs at two levels: individual, and societal in general. The individual's planning will need to encompass new social relationships and development of interests which may often involve social groups not previously part of one's life, perhaps new and different living environments. Society will need to plan for the dramatic increase in the older population. (Some estimates have suggested this increase as accounting for 20 percent of the population by the year 2000.) Housing, transportation, strains on recreational services and facilities, clothing styles, food preparation, and a host of living aspects which previously have received little consideration must now be dealt with. Little planning has been devoted to long-term effects of altered working arrangements which include older workers. For example, very soon we will be feeling the effects of reduced numbers of new labor force entrants due to the declining birth rates in the 1960s and 1970s. How will this affect society's planning? Will this include older people? If we are moving toward a stationary population as some economists predict, then our concerns may become moot. As one reviews population trends, it seems obvious that birth rates do not always follow economists' predictions. We at least know the population configuration for the next seventy years. Those people are already alive. What is needed is long-term planning to accommodate the altered future living arrangements confronting us all, not just the elderly.

9

WOMEN AS
MINORITIES

We have been concerned thus far with the aging process and the work activity from a historical and broad-issue perspective. Such a view has been influenced predominantly by research and literature concerned with a male-oriented work force. This is understandable, since society's past political, social, and economic systems were predicated on the existence and maintenance of the family unit with a male head of household.

Two previously disenfranchized groups—women and minorities—however, also have begun to make their presence felt in these societal systems; nowhere more so than in the work arena where womens' aging process is being observed and highlighted.

Considering the dramatic social shifts which have been occurring as a result of women and minorities seeking equality in all major societal institutions, it is appropriate to single them out for examination of their impact on the issues of aging and work. It has been only in the last decade that the concerns of these groups have begun to be significantly addressed by researchers and writers.

Those concerned with the development of work and aging theories are only now conceding that past theorizing may not be applicable to the emerging stature of women and minorities. The literature on the subject is relatively sparse, and because of this, the focus here will be on case studies of aging women as related to the issues of human resources, retirement, education and mental health. Such a focus will help bring a measure of understanding to the special problems confronting these groups. It will also provide insight into how they are meeting and coping with their emerging roles in society. In addition, it will consider the ways they are experiencing the aging process.

In an attempt to discuss the special problems of women and minorities confronting aging and work issues, we are faced with definitional and logical problems when placing them in the same category. From one perspective, women are a majority group, since they comprise more than 50 percent of the population. From another perspective, however, they are in the minority with regard to their numbers in the work force. Perlmutter and Hall, who wrote *Adult Development and Aging*, have concluded from their summary of labor force statistics that by 1981, 51.9 percent of white women were in the labor force, compared to 77.9 percent of white males. Non-white females accounted for 53.6 percent of the labor force, compared to 70.6 percent for non-white males. This suggests that regardless of ethnicity, women are a minority when viewed as labor-force participants.

These same statistics suggest that women have increased their labor-force participation rate about 15 percent over what it was in 1960. During the same period male labor force participation rates declined approximately 5 percent. Some of this decline in male participation can be attributed to increasing rates of early retirement. If the trend observed between 1960 and 1980 continues, we can estimate that early in the next century, male and female labor-force participation will be about equal and our assumption of minority status for females will not hold. Today, however, women are still considered a minority in the labor force when compared with men.

When one tries to focus on minorities and their aging while engaged in the work activity, the issue is not as clear as that for women in general. The popular interpretation of minority in the American culture is based upon skin color. From a general perspective this may be appropriate, since skin color is an observed condition which does distinguish some ethnic groups. Such a perspective has an undesirable connotation, though, which can be associated with racism.

Many times when people are classified by race, there is an implication that one racial category is inherently superior to another. The general behavior among the dominant white majority in American society is as if it were superior to other racial categories. If, however, we view minorities from a social stratification perspective, then the hierarchical arrangement of individuals on common grounds such as power, social status, or socioeconomic status is more appropriate than are the criteria of sex, age, and ethnicity. One prominent researcher has suggested there are three distinctions which can be made when defining ethnic groups. They are: "a) peoples distinguished primarily by visible physical criteria; b) peoples distinguished by cultural heritage or language; c) peoples distinguished by conquest. It is obvious that often these physical, cultural, or political conditions are combined in the history of a particular group. And almost always, any of these criteria define 'minority' group status, relative to the broader population."

Women and minorities as distinct units in the work force are numerically in the minority. When we view the two groups in concert, then we must consider that they constitute a significant segment of the existing as well as the potential labor force and as a large group deserve study. A better understanding of these groups has significant relevance also for problems associated with aging and work.

THE HUMAN RESOURCE POTENTIAL

The human resource potential of women and minorities as related to work and aging has been researched little and understood even less. This can be attributable directly to society's traditional view of women's role, as well as the relatively low respect society has accorded the potential contributions of minorities. In this respect, women and minorities suffer the same indignities in the work place, indignities which become exacerbated with age. L. Cohen, in *Small Expectations: Society's Betrayal of Older Women*, has summarized these indignities as applied to older women in Canada. Her summary appears relevant for American women and for minorities. "They (women) expressed bewilderment and dismay at the prejudice, indifference, and alienation they suffer. Many are frightened that if they openly state their anger, they will suffer grave consequences. They are repeatedly told by politicians, by the media, by academics, by gerontologists that they are far better off than their foresisters. 'Far better off' usually translates into surviving considerably below the poverty line. The quality of their lives is generally abysmal, for they are alienated and abandoned, cut off from the mainstream of life. As a society we do not respect or admire our older women. We force them to live financially, emotionally, and intellectually impoverished lives and expect them to be grateful to us."

While Cohen's view is strongly stated and is descriptive of the over-age-forty group of Canadian women and while it does also seem description of American women and, to some extent, minorities, changes *do* seem to be occurring in society which will tend to modify such a view in the future. The black elderly are increasing significantly in numbers. As a result, they represent a major natural resource which has yet to be discovered. The same observation can be made for other minority groups in society. The minority population which will represent their ethnic groups in the 1990s and beyond will be much different in composition, skills, and attitudes than those existing in the past. Women in our society have already begun to demonstrate some of the potential differences.

Mary is getting ready to celebrate her ninety-sixth birthday. She is physically active and lives alone in a modest two-room apartment in a low-income senior center.

Mary suffers from no illness other than an occasional head cold, is intellectually alert, and is a volunteer teacher of a twice-a-week creative writing course for a few residents at her housing center. In the 1950s Mary was forced into mandatory retirement and had to leave her job as a society reporter for a major metropolitan newspaper. Her only income since retirement has been from Social Security. Due to the relatively few years in which she participated in the program as well as the time in history when she retired, it neither was nor is a large amount. Mary left the work force at that point when the "youth cult" dominated society and older people were not accorded any real consideration. Mary had been married, but her husband died of a long illness which drained any cash reserves she and her husband had built up for their retirement years. Mary had no independent financial resource to draw upon. Intellectually and physically, she was willing and able to continue her work as a reporter at the time of her forced retirement. Other than chronological age, there was no evidence that she was unable to be a productive worker. On the contrary, if one reviews the impact of her experiences and how she coped with them it can only be concluded she was a very strong person internally. Continuation in her job probably would have helped her retain a sense of worth and contribution. Instead, she was forced to retire.

So now she is impoverished intellectually, emotionally, and economically and lives below the poverty line. Due to her economic circumstances, she is forced to live in a stifling environment. The majority of the residents in the senior center are generally poorly educated and seem content to sit in the lounge all day with no apparent activity other than talking about their families or watching television. On the other hand, Mary enjoys shopping, attending concerts, and going to the theater, as well as going out to dinner and generally engaging in activities similar to those of energetic younger adults. Due to her circumstances, however, she enjoys these pleasures only occasionally. Mary would like to be more active in her life, but her economic situation is such that more involvement is prohibitive. Recently, a publisher heard through a mutual friend of her past experiences as a reporter, and he has contracted with Mary for her to write a book about her work experiences. It seems that after thirty-five years of relative obscurity, Mary may once again experience a real sense of worth. Since this contact, she has a renewed sparkle and energy. She is much happier now that she sees a purpose in life. No longer is she wondering why she has lived so long. Her big concern is, "Will I live long enough to finish the book?"

Mary's case is exceptional since she herself is an exceptional human being. But what is clear is that women and minorities previously have not been perceived as a natural human resource to be nurtured. Only recently have there been any expressions that they constitute a vast pool of talent which has been ignored. However, the Comprehensive Training and Employment Act (CETA) did provide funds for training and retraining displaced homemakers who were eligible (low income) and who were forty years of age or older. This is exactly what Francis Perkins, Secretary of Labor, was arguing for during the first Roosevelt administration. The CETA legislation has since been diminished to the point where it is relatively ineffective today. There are some programs being initiated in the private sector. The outcome of this interest shown in women and minorities by private initiatives has yet to be revealed.

R. M. Cohn and P. Jaslow, in the *Journal of Gerontology*, both have reported that the work role has been of central importance to male identity in United States culture. A similar view has only recently begun to emerge as applied to women and minorities. Alienation is most evident when viewed in the work context and associated with the large number of unemployed who have never worked or who have stopped looking for work, for whatever reason. Such people will be the older generation in the very near future. Their potential has never been developed, nor does it seem likely it will in the near future.

Salina's case on the other hand illustrates some of the problems facing talented minority women who have been stereotyped by society.

Salina is a fifty-two-year-old Mexican-American who was born into a traditional household in the Rio Grande Valley. Her family was stable in that they were not part of the migrant worker culture. Salina completed the twelfth grade, graduating in the upper 25 percent of her class. This was very unusual for a female from her cultural group at that time. Salina displayed a particular affinity in the arts and contemplated attending a small university not far from where she lived. She wanted to develop a potential talent. The fact that she completed her public school education and did well academically suggests that she perhaps would have experienced some success in college. Family custom, however, dictated that she marry and have a family. World War II had started. Her childhood sweetheart was in the army, and when he was home on leave, they were married. During the next several years, Salina gave birth to five children; by all criteria she was judged to be a successful wife and mother. During this time, family and friends observed that Salina was happy, outgoing, and satisfied with her life. Her husband was a hard worker and earned enough for the family to live modestly.

Salina experienced no real economic deprivation, endemic in that region. Salina appeard to be living the "American Dream." She had never worked at a wage-paying job. Occasionally, she would speculate as to what her life might have been had she developed her interest and talents. But she loved her husband and her children and such thoughts quickly vanished. Her last child left home five years ago, about the same time Salina was experiencing menopause. Her family reports that Salina has begun expressing negative views about life, seems disoriented about events surrounding her, and has expressed no purpose or goal toward which she wants to work. She is alienating herself from her youngest daughter by being very demanding of her time and generally intruding in how she chooses to live her life.

Salina's life has revolved around her mother-and-wife work role. She had found her identity in this role and was rewarded by her family, friends, and community for the success she achieved in this capacity. With her children becoming independent and with low demands placed on her by her husband, Salina is at a loss as to her future. She is experiencing few rewards as a wife only. Her family and husband have encouraged her to go back to school and develop those latent talents displayed during her adolescence. Salina has rejected this idea; she perceives herself as too old, unattractive, worthless, and is apparently terrified at her future prospects.

The lack of the nurturing of Salina's talent looms as a potentially large loss to herself and to her family and society. Salina never learned how to live without the mother-wife responsbility. Life without children in the home requires a new way of living. If she is able to work outside of her home, it would help her to occupy her time productively as well as to provide for a new life meaning and purpose.

The generation of women and minorities between the ages of thirty and forty have, and will have, a strong influence in how these groups are perceived, perceptions which are different from their mothers'. Enough of this group is educated, employed, and politically and socially active to have a major impact on the development of their human resource potential. Baby boomers are the largest population bulge in North America and constitute a tremendous marketing power. In addition, at least for the women of this group, they are not going to allow themselves to be packed up and "put on the shelf," as were their mothers in a prior generation. Salina is apparently allowing herself to be "put on the shelf." Her daughter, on the other hand, is married and currently working on her master's degree. Salina's daughter refuses to consider ever being "put on the shelf." She sees her future in the dual capacity of wife-mother, as well as being productive as a worker. Fortunately, her husband is receptive to this view and is supportive of Salina's daughter's life goals.

Mary and Salina represent two extremes of the human resource potential of women and minorities. What is important is that they both have latent potential which could have been nurtured at a much earlier age for their own benefit and that of society. Their positions in life were largely regulated by the historical period in which they lived. They were expected to step aside, ostensibly to make room for youth, as if they had nothing more worthwhile to offer. Mary's potential has been uncovered or rediscovered and is being given an opportunity to blossom. Salina's may never be uncovered unless some fortuitous circumstance allows her talent to be displayed. In terms of our production-consumption concept presented earlier, Mary is once again on the path to being both a producer and consumer. Whereas for thirty-five years she had essentially been a consumer with no apparent productivity, she is once again in the process of producing. Salina, on the other hand, is a consumer. She had been a producer in the sense that her five children are in the work force in some capacity and are contributing to their own well-being and that of others. Now that Salina's children are independent, Salina has become a consumer only. While this is not bad, since her husband's income appears sufficient to support them both, Salina appears to be unhappy and depressed. These feelings could result in an excessive dependency on family and society at a later point in her life. If, however, she were able to find productive outlets for her talent and energy, she could be helpful to herself and to her society.

Brenda's case is an example of a lifetime of striving for success in the face of social restrictions and personal adversity. Brenda is black and sixty-eight years old. She was one of several children born to a family of sharecroppers. Her childhood and adolescence consisted of picking cotton, attending an all-black school when she could, extreme poverty, and social deprivation, but she experienced a deep sense of family, warmth, and love throughout her formative years. Upon graduation from high school, she married and began having children, five in all. To help her husband financially, Brenda began sewing at home and experienced a modicum of success. Her husband, who worked at odd jobs when they were available, left soon after the fifth child was born. Brenda was stranded with the children, a rundown three-room house, and no financial resources. Her only income was the little she earned from sewing. Brenda entertained no thoughts of breaking up her family. On the contrary, she was determined that regardless of how bad things were, her family would remain as a unit. She accepted a job as a maid in an all-black college to supplement her income from her sewing.

Realizing that she had to do something about her future, since what she was doing barely provided subsistence, she began taking courses at the college where she worked. After ten years of persistence, extreme hardship, deprivation, and often wondering why she was doing this to herself and her children, she earned a bachelor's degree, which qualified her to be a teacher. The only job available was teaching in an all-black high school. (Segregated education was still practiced in the South when she earned her degree.)

Throughout the experience of studying and teaching, Brenda found that she liked working with people, was sensitive to their needs, and, as a result, experienced a sense of personal fulfillment. Regardless of her successes, Brenda found that she still was unable to earn enough to fulfill her ambition to help children financially so they, too, could go to college. She realized that a graduate degree would not only increase her earning capacity, but would qualify her for other positions paying considerably more. With her children's encouragement and some financial assistance through scholarship, Brenda successfully completed her master's degree at a major institution. Brenda went on to a successful second career at age fifty, has achieved her objective of helping all her children complete their college education, and has maintained an intact family.

At age fifty-five, Brenda married a hard-working mason who was stable, and strongly supportive of Brenda in all that she tried to do. Due to mandatory retirement restrictions, Brenda has retired from her professional career, but she has embarked on a new one. She went back to school to learn to be a financial consultant. She is now working in that capacity and plans to continue "Until I drop."

Brenda obviously is not going to be "put on the shelf." She has overcome many odds against her succeeding: her ethnicity, social pressure against keeping her family intact (social welfare attempted to take her children away from her when her first husband left), as well as the general belief at the time that an adult black would be unable to accomplish all that Brenda did. She is an example of an individual developing her human resources potential to the fullest. Had our social system been a little more flexible, Brenda's accomplishments could have come much earlier in life, yielded equal or better results, and could have been less of a financial and emotional strain on her and her children.

THE RETIREMENT QUESTION

A new phenomenon confronting today's women is the retirement question. Whereas women, in an earlier time, were content to live on the wealth amassed by their husbands, today their sense of autonomy decrees that they be financially independent in their retirement years. Recall that Brenda chose not to retire (in the sense of withdrawal from the work force) but has instead embarked on a new career. Since women may start their careers later, they may not be ready to leave the work force and retire as soon as men do. One result of delaying their retirement may be that women will then make a significant contribution toward supporting the rapidly growing over-age-sixty-five population. Difficulties have emerged during the past several years regarding the solvency of the Social Security System. However, the delayed retirement of women may help reduce the financial strain the system is currently experiencing.

In addition to women working in their later years, retirement for minorities may be a luxury they cannot ever afford. Minority membership may be a lottery when it comes to retirement in that the possibility of living long enough to receive Social Security benefits is considerably less, on the average, than it is for whites. This is more true for males than females, just as it is for white males compared with white females. In addition, minorities have had fewer opportunities in the labor force and many have not fared too well in steady employment which, over a protracted period of time, is necessary if the tripartite financial base for retirement is to function. Minorities, who have tended to have erratic work histories due to job discrimination, and women, who have tended to enter the work force later or experience an interrupted work life due to marriage and having children and thus work fewer years, are both at a financial disadvantage when it comes to the retirement decision. They have not had the opportunity to build a solid financial base to support a non-working-for-pay lifestyle: retirement.

Willie's life situation is a case in point of the financial disadvantages which can occur as a result of an erratic and interrupted work history. Willie is a fifty-eight-year-old black woman. She did not complete high school, having become pregnant during her junior year. She did marry at the time and subsequently had two more children. Her husband, who also never completed his public school education, worked occasionally at odd jobs, became an alcoholic, and eventually disappeared, only to return home when he was financially destitute, adding to Willie's burdens. Willie received welfare in order to pay for food and the rent. As soon as she was able, Willie began looking for work since the welfare checks were insufficient to live on, even at a subsistence level. Willie had no help from family, who were equally destitute, a situation which also contributed to her decision to look for work. Willie was a proud woman and was not happy to be on the welfare roles. She believed that she would be able to support herself and her children and still maintain her independence. She perceived herself to be reasonably bright and able; she had been a good student, and was not afraid of hard work.

Job hunting for Willie was a frustrating experience. She had never held a job, consequently, she had no work history. She had not completed her high school education, and therefore was not competitive for the few jobs available. In desperation, Willie accepted a two-day-per-week maid's position. This eventually led to her working for several people in order to earn at least enough to reduce her dependence on welfare and allow her a small measure of financial autonomy.

All the money Willie earned went for living expenses, leaving none for savings. Certainly there was no such thing as a pension plan, since she was an independent worker. The only resource which contributed to her financial base for retirement was the Social Security payments made by the people she worked for. Since her rate of pay was close to the minimum, the amount contributed to her Social Security was also low. Given the situation of low pay and erratic employment (working as a maid does not insure regular employment because most jobs are temporary and blank spots occur during the work week), the best that Willie can expect when she reaches retirement age is the minimum Social Security assurance. (Note: Social Security is an assurance program, not an insurance program.)

Willie's case is not atypical for women of her generation. Her story could be repeated, with minor variations, in almost any community. Women similar to Willie are those who live at or near the poverty line when they get too old to continue working in any capacity. This also may be a reason why women tend to retire from work at a later age than men. They can not afford retirement. It is apparent that the new generation of women will not be content to repeat Willie's experience. Although that does not mean that the Willies of the world will disappear, it does suggest that there may be fewer of them.

EDUCATION

Women, perhaps more than men, have been victims of age and time traps for education and work modes. Giele has suggested that this attitude did not truly change for women until the 1970s, when more were in the work force than were remaining in the home. Whereas during the pre-World War II era men and women both experienced the education-for-youth stage, work for men was in the labor force and women were assumed to marry, have children, and take care of the home. If they did work (we were experiencing a depression at the time and any extra income was a help), women, who became pregnant, were expected to return to the home and rear their children. Their retirement(?) was to be experienced through their husbands. In this view, one can argue that women never had the opportunity to retire because their lifestyle, keeping house, did not differ from what they had always been expected to do. While it was acceptable for women to remain in an educational environment such as college, they were expected to drop that phase of their lives upon marrying. Their expected work task was having children and keeping house. Some women, those who are currently between sixty and seventy-five years of age (mothers of the baby boom generation), experienced an interruption in this cycle when they accepted positions in war industries during World War II. At war's end, these same women went back to their homes and most began producing babies. But by the 1970s, changes were occurring that today seem to be irreversible.

It was from the middle of the 1960s to the beginning of

the 1970 decade that the baby boomers began leaving home to start their own lives. Most women who were in their forties began to realize they were facing at least thirty more years of life without the responsibilities of motherhood and, on the average, would outlive their husbands by as many as ten or fifteen years. With time on their hands, these women began entering the labor force in record numbers. What they found was that their training was either inadequate, outmoded, too general, or irrelevant. Giele feels "They frequently could not find jobs commensurate with their education and intelligence. Relative to their husbands, many of them had fallen behind because of years out of the work force, lack of graduate work, or lack of special professional training." Women during this time period may be viewed as being in a transitional age group. As such, they were particularly disadvantaged, since they had grown up believing the ideals of their mother's generation but were forced to live with a different reality.

> Joan's experience reflects the conflict with which mothers of the baby-boom generation were confronted within the realities of today's changing world. Joan is now fifty-five years of age, has four grown children, and is married to a highly-esteemed professional. Joan is an intellectually bright and able woman who graduated with honors from a prestigious liberal arts college. Her parents were strong believers in education for women and struggled financially for Joan to receive the best available. While in college, Joan met her husband-to-be and married him soon after they both graduated. Following their marriage, her husband, an honor student in undergraduate school, began to work on his Ph.D. Joan became pregnant during the first year of marriage and had her baby. Even though financially Joan and her husband were in desperate circumstances, there was no thought of leaving graduate school until Joan's husband completed his degree. Because the student housing co-op where they lived had a time-sharing system for baby-sitting, Joan accepted a teaching position in order to help

financially. Regardless of their income, Joan and her husband suffered material deprivations similar to those experienced by others in their peer group. They willingly suffered such deprivations in the anticipation of future financial gains and material rewards which would result from a potential increase in earnings consistent with a Ph.D. This was a typical value and belief system prevalent during Joan's parents' lifetime. Both Joan and her husband unquestioningly accepted these beliefs and values. Both had a strong sense of family and welcomed the new infant as an important and enriching addition to their lives.

The inconveniences and deprivations they suffered were acceptable as part of the lifestyle they had chosen. Upon graduation, again with honors, Joan's husband accepted an academic position with a major university and began what has turned out and continues to be an illustrious career. During the next five years, Joan had three more children. By all independent reports from friends, neighbors and family, Joan was (and is) an exceptional mother and an outstanding wife who actively supports her husband's career. Joan spent the next twenty years successfully fulfilling her role of wife and mother.

As Joan's husband began reaping the rewards and accolades for his academic excellence, their children also began completing their education and leaving home to start their careers and their own families. It was at this time that Joan decided to begin looking for a job in her chosen area. She soon realized that her formal education was dated and she was unable to be competitive with younger applicants for similar positions. Since Joan revered education, she began a program of graduate study to upgrade her knowledge and skills which eventually led to her master's degree. Joan worked for a year in a position which utilized her skill and her expertise as a teacher. She found that her work time was restrictive in that she was unable to travel with her husband, who is much in demand as a consultant. What she really wanted was work which allowed her to set her own hours or at least set the days she would or would not work. Ultimately, she has settled for being a substitute teacher. Such a position, while not regular and not necessarily high-paying, does allow her to work and practice her skills as a teacher as well as to use her academic talents. Being a substitute teacher also allows her the freedom to travel with her husband.

Joan is a member of that in-between age group of people who were reared in a generation subscribing to traditional values but, as adults, must confront today's realities. She has now come to an accommodation with both herself and her desires. Joan is outstanding at what she does, whether it is mother, wife, or teacher. She has, however, elected to take advantage of the rewards resulting from the earlier deprivations associated with helping her husband succeed in his career. She has some mixed feelings about this still, since she feels also that her own accomplishments need to be recognized.

Jessie, forty-four, is a forerunner of the baby-boom generation and appears typical of women who are using formal, non-formal and informal education to develop and to enhance their careers. Jessie's pattern is in a sense traditional in that she grew up in a fundamentalist home which taught the basic values of marriage and motherhood roles for females. Her family was not so rigid, however, that they didn't encourage college education for their daughters. Consequently, Jessie attended college and earned a liberal arts degree. Upon graduation, she accepted a position as a secretary in a large insurance firm. While she did not perceive this to be a life career for her, Jessie was content to remain in that job until she decided what she wanted to do for a career or until she married. Within two years she met a young man from her church who subscribed to similar value systems, and they were married.

Jessie terminated her job soon after she became pregnant and devoted her energies to being a wife and mother. Jessie was good in this role; she had an excellent teacher in her mother and was content for the first few years of her marriage. She and her husband decided that three children were enough for them. Eight years after their marriage, their family was complete. While the children were young, Jessie engaged in all the mothering activities she assumed were expected of a middle-class mother: picking her children up from school and taking them to music lessons, Little League, and the like. Her home life was all that she expected; she had a loving husband who was an excellent father and she had well-adjusted, happy, bright children. Her early married life was the American Dream personified. Then the emptiness began to set in.

Jessie had always been a reader, and as her children began to be more and more independent, she found that she had more time to explore those areas of interest which had begun during her undergraduate education. She began a wide-ranging study of how to help people and the more she read, the more interested she became in human relationships. It was at this point that Jessie began contemplating returning to college to earn a graduate degree in one of the people-helping areas. At the same time, she was participating in church activities which sponsored encounter groups and consciousness-raising groups, and she was attending lectures and seminars related to these areas.

About this time, Jessie's husband decided he wanted to go into business for himself which meant that for a period of time the family would need to curtail the lifestyle they had taken for granted. Jessie agreed to this. In order to help, she attended the local community college and took courses in bookkeeping, finance, and similar subjects to be an asset to her husband's business venture. Her participation in the business was an outlet for Jessie, filling the time voids caused by reduced demands made on her by her children.

Jessie worked side-by-side with her husband for five years, during which time he had established his business as a profit-making concern and the family had returned to its former standard of living. Throughout this interlude, Jessie never relinquished her interest in engaging in some form of helping activity. Rather, the experience of working with her husband convinced her that the business world was not for her and she would seek some other way to fulfill her primary interest. Jessie returned to graduate school, earning a master's degree in social work.

Currently, she is engaged in this career and believes the direction she is following is correct for her. She is experiencing a sense of independence which is new to her, but she likes it. She is earning her own money, providing for her own retirement, and for all intents will be independent for the rest of her life.

Jessie's case is exemplary of the new breed of American women. They are using education in all its forms to achieve their personal as well as their professional goals. In the process, they are becoming more independent, pursuing the good life to the extent society allows, and are actively demonstrating that they are not going to be put "on the shelf" after having a family or reaching a certain age. They are demonstrating that regardless of all the stumbling blocks, through judicious use of education, they too can become something other than a "baby machine." Women are learning how to develop a blended life plan. It is through a belief that one can experience multiple careers as well as achieve those career goals through multiple means and through the use of a variety of educational experiences that women and minorities will gain the respect and dignity due them.

MENTAL HEALTH

In an earlier chapter we found that mentally healthy people believe they are leading rewarding lives and enjoy high self-esteem. Such phenomena long were believed to be male oriented. Only recently has such a view been considered significantly important to the self-concept of women. Previously, it was commonly accepted, at least among males, that women gained their personal gratification and self-esteem through motherhood. Presumably, for a woman to feel worthwhile she had only one outlet—having babies. Renewing the species was a reflection of a woman's worth. The more one produces, the more one is esteemed. When we were primarily an agrarian society, producing babies was important. Families who had many children were to be envied; they had a built-in labor force to run the farm. That same attitude in today's world would suggest a pejorative view toward a woman in that people would respond to the immorality of the woman not being able to control herself and she would be accused of overpopulating the world. Women's work, and the gratification which accrued from it, was in the home. To work at a paying job in the labor force was only to supplement the family income, especially during hard times. No thought has been given to how a woman maintains her sense of worth after her children mature and leave home to start their own lives or after other experiences which are intrusive in an orderly life.

J. Z. Giele, in *Women in the Middle Years*, points out that many women need jobs other than housework in order to fulfill their own interests as well as to cope with inflation. She suggests also that jobs for women are important, in some cases, to counter the effects of separation and divorce. We would add only that for some women working is also important if they experience the premature death of their husbands, since this, too, is a form of separation. For an older woman, life without some form of work can be stressful; the likelihood of living for ten or more years after her husband dies is very real. Also, the fact that women tend to marry men older than themselves suggests the very strong possibility of a fairly long life alone. The very fact of growing older is stressful for some women; in American society, being an older woman (often defined as being over age forty) suggests loss of status (no more babies are produced) and the developing feeling of being useless (my children don't need me any more). Such feelings can trigger a psychological state called depression.

Butler and Giele, among others, have argued that being employed can be an antidote to depression. This is especially true when the job provides the woman with options, gives her some leverage against the demands of the nurturant role, and opens up new sources of social contacts. Giele stresses that the type of work which provides adequate earnings, rewards competence and generally reinforces a sense of worth is critically important. She points out also that women who are particularly vulnerable to depression are heads of single-parent families, have poor education, have responsibility for young children—and are working at low wages.

W. Grove and M. Hughes, in *American Sociological Review*, determined that the highest rate of psychiatric and physical symptoms occur in women who have the greatest caretaking responsibilities. We know from our previous examination of mental health issues that as people age, their psychological problems age with them. This is not true in every case. The rewards accruing from work, may act as the antidote also to psychological problems.

Cases peculiar to women can be observed daily. What is important is that when their lives are disrupted, they do not have to sink into the oblivion of mental illness. There is a way out. Certainly, uncovering and nurturing their resources is an important key to recovery. Earlier we referred to the five policy issues for the nurturing of human resources as described by Parnes. The first issue, fullest development of the productive capacities of human beings, is important here. Such development may be too late if one lacks the basic labor-market skills which might speed up the process of recovery.

> Wilma is sixty-one, mother of five children, and has seven grandchildren. Her husband of forty-two years works at the same job and for the same company. He is eligible to retire and receive Social Security, an apparently generous company pension (a program in which he has been vested for over thirty years), and savings

amassed over a lifetime of work. He has chosen to continue working. Their home has no mortgage and their expenses include the usual maintenance costs, utilities, and taxes, as well as daily needs. Wilma and her husband were both lifelong residents of the same rural northeastern community. Wilma's husband dropped out of high school, went into the army, and completed three years of military service during World War II. Wilma completed her high school education but was not distinguished as a student. She was content not to go to college since she planned to marry soon after graduation. For all intents, Wilma and her family represent the ideal, stable American family which one can expect to find almost anywhere in the United States.

Wilma's early married life was occupied with having five children in eight years, being involved with her church, and participating in community activities. With each pregnancy, she experienced a period of depression, which lasted longer with each pregnancy. She recalls that at that time she was asking herself, "Is this all there is to life?" She was feeling that there was more to experience than washing diapers and cleaning house but she really didn't have time to think it through in order to discover what was lacking for her. Wilma was a good wife, a good mother, and a good community member. Being good at these things, however, did not fill the nagging void she experienced. Successive complaints to her physician led to a beginning dependence on prescription drugs to relieve her quasi-depressed feelings. In Butler & Lewis's sense we could conclude that during her early adult years Wilma was surviving but not thriving. Her use of drugs to relieve her undifferentiated mood swings appear to be her attempt at least to survive on a daily basis and also to make an attempt to regain a sense of positive mental health suggested by the definition of thriving.

After all her children were in school, Wilma began seeking outside employment. She felt the need to be

away from the house, at least for part of the day. Wilma
had no specific job skills; she had followed an academic
curriculum when in high school. She did take a typing
course "just in case" she might need such a skill. Wilma
found a part-time job doing general office work such as
answering the telephone, and typing. She accepted the
job in spite of her husband's protestations, but it eventually led to her becoming a bookkeeper-office manager,
skills she had lerned on the job. Within two years, Wilma
began realizing that she was consuming excessive quantities of alcohol and gaining weight. (She had been a
moderate drinker prior to this. Moderate for her was two
or three highballs per week.) The weight gain was acceptable, since she became excessively thin after the
birth of her last child, but the excessive drinking dis-
turbed her. For the next several years, she attempted to
cut back both on her consumption of alcohol and prescription drugs. For a period of time, this worked. Fifteen
years ago she was diagnosed an alcoholic. Even though
she was aware of this, she made no effort to stop drinking
or get help. She did go from physician to physician in
order to continue getting her prescriptions for depression and insomnia. Five years ago, Wilma suffered a life
function problem which led to her near death. At that
point her physician warned her that any more alcohol or
drugs would surely kill her. Wilma had a choice: live or
die.

Throughout the period of extreme alcoholism, Wilma's employer was tolerant of her absences and relapses
during the day. She had become a valued and exceptional worker over the years and he did not want to lose her.
Wilma chose to live. She now attends AA regularly, and
also a drug rehabilitation program. Her employer is
allowing her to work at home since her important work is
keeping the books and paying the company's bills which
can be accomplished as well outside the office. Having
the work responsibility has helped keep Wilma on a
routine, which has also contributed to her recovery. She

is still recovering and could suffer a relapse at any time. The one constant in Wilma's life seems to be the responsibilities of her job. Because of her many years of service, even though much of it has been part-time, she has come to be depended upon and realizes she is an important part of the company's success. Wilma is now truly feeling self-fulfilled in her work. While motherhood was important to Wilma, she didn't seem to esteem the role because it was both expected of her and was what other women were doing. It is to be hoped that Wilma is on the road to thriving, but only time will tell whether she will continue to be creative. Certainly her job is playing an important part in the recovery process.

CONCLUDING COMMENTS OR "SOMETIMES THE DRAGON WINS" _____

The cases we have presented certainly are not representative of all possible cases; but they are, we believe, representative of the aging and work issues upon which we have been focusing. (Human Resources, Retirement, Education, Mental Health) and are indicative of the many problems women as minorities are confronting in the work place. Their stories exemplify the indignities they suffered when trying to cope with their aging as well as trying to participate independently in the work place. Their stories depict the desire of women to be dependent on no one. The stories of these women suggest strongly that they will not be "put on the shelf." Yet, to achieve this goal, they must overcome great odds. Some women, at least, are beginning to be valued in the work place. As women grow older while working and begin displaying signs of age, will they continue to be valued? Or will they, too, be urged into early retirement as men have been?

The cases we presented were selected because they represent the primary focus of each issue. Certainly, as with all life stories, there was considerable overlap with other issues.

Women as minorities who are attempting to experience successes in the work place while they are aging are confronted
with a multitude of problems; so, too, were the women whose
histories we presented. Lilly's history is a case in point and
summarizes problems confronted which are related to all issues
associated with aging and work. It is also a story of a woman
who struggled against severe odds to be "dependent on no one"
and who never accepted the remotest possibility of ever being
"put on the shelf."

> Lilly is eighty-three. She lives alone in a three-room
> apartment in a highrise building catering to older
> people. The building is in a medium-sized metropolitan
> area in the northeast. Lilly has been legally blind for over
> twenty years. She is the second of four children born to
> her immigrant parents during the early part of the cen-
> tury. Lilly remembers her childhood as a struggle for
> family survival. Lilly completed the eighth grade before
> leaving school to get a job to help out at home. Soon after
> she began working as a sales clerk, her father left home.
> Lilly's mother, who was a strong woman in her own
> right, worked at whatever she could to keep the family
> together. Lilly's first twenty-two years were hard work,
> family responsibilities, and struggle.
> At twenty-two, Lilly was beginning to be perceived to
> be an "Old Maid." It was at this point that a marriage was
> arranged for her by her mother, a marriage with which
> Lilly agreed. (Within Lilly's ethnic group, arranged
> marriages were not uncommon at that time.) Lilly gave
> birth to a child within the first year of marriage and had a
> second child three years later. Life was no different for
> her in that she continued to work hard, have major family
> responsibilities, and struggle. Lilly's husband worked at
> a steady factory job but earned only a minimum income.
> As a result, Lilly worked whenever she could to supple-
> ment the family finances. This activity was a source of
> friction and was destined to continue so throughout
> Lilly's marriage, due to the fact her husband was a tradi-

tionalist, believing that a woman's place was in the home. With the onset of the "Great Depression" during the fifth year of Lilly's marriage, the struggle for survival began. Any thoughts of "thriving" were dispelled, due to the need to keep the family together and to continue working. Lilly, throughout those difficult years, never gave up the hope of realizing the "American Dream" that through hard work, life somehow would be better. She accepted any work she could find, whether it was for a day or a few hours. It was at this time she began to realize that she had a talent for sewing and that people were willing to pay her for that talent. With $300 she received from her father's estate and against her husband's protestations, Lilly moved to another city, opened a tailor shop, and began a business career which would span the next twenty-five years.

Lilly realized that her actions could jeopardize her marriage, might cause the breakup of her family, and that she would suffer the disapproval of friends and relatives. (During the 1930s it was unusual for women to go into business for themselves, much less take the initiative to assert their independence as did Lilly. Also, within Lilly's ethnic group, women didn't behave in this manner.) She was willing to risk all because she believed that life could be better than it was and that somehow she was responsible for making something positive happen. She did experience repercussions. Her old friends began to gossip about her and eventually ceased associating with her. Her husband followed her and commuted to his job, since jobs in the new city were virtually non-existent. Regardless of all personal adversity and of the fact that small businesses were failing in record numbers at that time in history, Lilly was determined to succeed. She embarked on a study program to learn all she could about sewing, business management, and the like, while at the same time getting her business underway. When she encountered difficult problems which were beyond her expertise, she sought and received help from others who were in a similar business and whom she perceived to be successful. Lilly, while short on formal education, used her intelligence to train herself to succeed in her business.

With the onset of World War II and after a trial separation from her husband, Lilly sold her business and stayed at home to become a fulltime housewife and mother. Her husband had found a job in a local defense plant and was earning an income high enough so that they were able to save money for the first time in their married life. Lilly made an effort to be a good wife and mother during this period at home. She found, however, that by mid-morning she had completed her housework and had time on her hands. When Lilly was in business, she had become used to working twelve to sixteen hours a day. She was not a back-fence gossiper, nor did she enjoy those usual activities non-working women engaged in at that time. She missed the bustle of business, her work, and the daily contact with her customers. To fill her time, she began sewing at home for some of her longtime customers. After a year of such activity, she still had vacant time. She was becoming despondent and had second thoughts about giving up her business. Lilly, in an effort to help herself, found a job in a local defense plant. Her husband objected but conceded that with the extra income they could save enough to be able to buy a house after the war and begin thinking also of retiring from work someday.

With the war over and defense plants shutting down to convert to peacetime production, Lilly and her husband both were out of work. Lilly decided to use the money she had saved during the war to open a new store. Her children were gone from home and Lilly decided that she was not going to sit around doing nothing. Getting back to doing what she did best was both therapy for her and a way to earn a living. Soon after this decision, Lilly and her husband permanently separated and eventually divorced.

As a result of the disruption in her personal life, which led to long periods of depression and loneliness, Lilly turned to her work in seeking direction in her life. She again worked long hours and turned her business into a success. Her success, coupled with her depression and feelings of loneliness led to her making decisions which led to her losing everything. She began taking in male business partners upon whom she relied to make decisions. She was convinced by them that expansion to more stores was the route to success, and as a result she became financially extended beyond which she could ever hope to repay. After a few years of this, and living with the continual worry of losing her good name (Lilly was known in the financial world as being a good risk), Lilly sold all her business assets to pay creditors. Lilly was now without a business, but free from debt and rid of all business partners. At the same time, Lilly discovered she had a degenerative eye disease which would eventually lead to irrevocable blindness. This was the worst possible news, for her ability to make a living depended upon good eyesight.

Lilly now entered her worst depressive period. She felt self pity, she was despondent, unsure of her future, and was without funds to sustain her the rest of her life. Lilly was adamant that she would remain independent regardless of what happened to her. She began once again to take in sewing to pay for the basic necessities, as well as provide her with time to reflect on what she would do with the rest of her life. Lilly decided to move to a southern state where she planned to work until blindness would interfere. She again started sewing, but this time she was sewing in her home with no thought of opening a store. She eventually bought a modest little home which she always wanted, became active in civic life, and at age seventy when she was blind, she remarried. After ten years of a calm and stable life, her husband died. In time, Lilly moved back to her old community because she decided, "That is where I want to die." She is now living a very full life within her modest means. She has many friends, is still utilizing her sewing skills through teaching others how to knit and crochet, even though she is blind, and is close to her family. Lilly, through a long and difficult route, is still dependent upon no one and has yet to be "put on the shelf."

Lilly represents the core of our issues regarding the aging process and the work activity. She, against all odds and social norms, developed her own talent as a natural resource to survive and live her life. One can only speculate with regard to Lilly's potential contributions had she been encouraged as a young woman to develop her talents instead of having to do this on her own in the face of social pressure and negative perceptions of women who behaved independently. She truly suffered the indignities of the work place to which Cohen referred. Women in Lilly's time in history were believed to be neutral as a potential human resource. As we have seen, Lilly was far from neutral. She found ways to provide for her retirement years through participation in the Social Security Program when she was allowed (it wasn't until the late 1950s that self-employed people could participate in the Social Security System) and through judicious savings. She is still independent and not a drain on society. She educated herself and used that education in highly productive ways. While our social institutions would not accept her education as sufficient for today's required credentials, she has been using her experience and modest education to the fullest. She has experienced mental health problems as well as alienation within her traditional social group, which in today's world might have crippled a lesser person. Lilly found work to be the antidote to her difficulties. In her own way, Lilly is still using work (teaching knitting and crocheting) as a way to cope with life, though not to the extent she did previously. Yet Lilly, in her time and in her world, was and is still a minority.

10

TOWARD A DEFINITION OF OLD

A definition of "old" as related to aging and work is important in order to truly address the issues about aging, in the hope that, in time, we can arrive at satisfactory solutions to the concerns of an increasing number of longer-lived and healthier older adults.

Most concerned people agree that *aging* is a process which is experienced throughout a lifetime. Growing older is a normal developmental process, but there is no agreement as to when one is old. Most people agree the *aged* are individuals who have reached the late stage of a long life and are presumed to be old. *Aged* is considered to be that late period of life prior to death. B. L. Neugarten referred to aged people as the "old old." Others refer to the aged as the "frail elderly." While there seems to be agreement with regard to "aging" and "older," there appears to be little agreement as to the onset of the life stage called old. Real questions are related to the point of when an individual is defined as "old." Frequently—and erroneously—

when people talk about "aging," there is an implicit assumption of "old," as if these two terms are synonymous.

There appear to be many and varied interpretations on how a person is defined as "old." Our view is that until all elements of society can reach agreement regarding when a person is "old," without resorting to idiosyncratic definition to satisfy a particular vested interest, we are left with a high degree of ambiguity. It is such ambiguity and multiplicity of definition which will keep the semantic pot boiling with continued controversy; and discrimination or "agism" against all older people, regardless of their age, will continue.

K. B. Hoyt, author of *Toward a Definition of Career Education*, in another context discussed the importance of definition. He stated:

> Definitions do make a difference in describing and delimiting the basic nature and purpose of any concept. While definitions have limited usefulness in helping one understand *how* a program is to operate, they are of central importance in specifying *what* the concept is intended to accomplish. The words are used and the ways in which words are joined together combine to form the basic rationale and justification for the concept itself.

We can also add that the more precise a definition, the simpler is our communication concerning it. Then qualifiers are no longer needed in order to impart the meaning of the concept. Our use of the term "old" implies that it is both a concept and an attitude. As such it is influenced by time which is not the sole criterion for definition. Virtually all current research and writings in the field of aging are prefaced with definitional qualifiers which create difficulty when trying to compare different views or to communicate within and between interested groups of individuals. By default, chronological age has determined the definition of "old."

Obviously, chronological age is a precise way to define

any age group. According to Hoyt's view, using a specified chronological age as a way to define older people does accomplish what is intended, defining a group on a single agreed-upon quantifiable criterion—date of birth. Governmental policies and resulting programs designed to assist the elderly, along with employers making employment decisions, are prime users of chronological age as a standard of reference. It serves their purpose well. Use of chronology, however, as a single defining variable of who is or is not old conspicuously omits attention to individual differences; though recently there appears to be a modification in Federal legislation and program implementation when using such a definition. *The point of onset of old is an arbitrarily imposed criterion which makes for administrative expediency but does not allow for individual uniqueness.*

Given the prevailing and anticipated future increases in the number of people labeled as "old," based upon the chronological age standard and arbitrary cut-off points, some very fundamental issues will need to be addressed. Overriding these issues is, of course, a moral question. Do we as a society desire to treat older Americans as a homogeneous group to be set aside at a certain date, whose expertise is no longer needed or wanted, or do we need to re-examine this group's potential with regard to its continued productivity both to itself and to society, considering the question of how we will allocate society's resources? Before this moral question and related issues can be addressed adequately, we need to know precisely about whom we are speaking. It may surface that chronological age will be the only measure upon which there is universal agreement, rendering all other views moot. We do not accept this limited assessment. We do accept the uniqueness of the individual. While there is a sameness for a defined group (age), the variability within an age group is such that a single base for defining it is meaningless for most purposes.

The intent of this chapter will be 1) to examine the current and prevailing view that older people may be defined similarly through the use of a chronological age criterion, and

2) to offer an alternative definition which accounts for individual variability and, more precisely, to specify what characteristics in concert define one as old or not old.

CHRONOLOGICAL AGE _____

In the *Annals of the American Academy of Political and Social Sciences*, L. D. Cain traced the historical origins of chronological age in relation to "old" to clarify the use of the chronological age standard of reference within a legal context. He concluded that the chronological age criterion is currently the most widely-accepted and easily-understood definition. He found that the root use of this standard of reference has persisted throughout recorded history. It may be inferred that this was because of the definition's convenience in establishing legal codes, resolving social issues, establishing relationships between generational groups, specifying who may or may not legally be employed in organized industrial societies, as well as for a host of other reasons. In spite of this persistent and continued use, when the purpose is to classify groups of people, it is an efficient and accurate predictor. When used to delimit human functioning, however, such as deciding whether one can continue to work, it has questionable predictive qualities. Use of such a univariate old age predictor influences political, social and economic decisions affecting individuals so defined. From a psychological perspective, continued use of a chronological age criterion serves to perpetuate negative stereotyping of older people to the detriment of the total society. It also gives tacit support for "agism" to be practiced in society.

Certainly, Cowgill's views on society's modernization are relevant in discussing the perpetuation of the use of the chronological age measurement. His view is that when a society moves from a relatively rural and toward a predominantly urban way of life, society's emphases are on efficiency and progress. When this occurs, the entire society is transformed; no part is left untouched. Changes are unidirectional. Resulting changes are always away from the rural traditional form and in the direction of an urbanized and highly differentiated form. Fischer's treatise demonstrated the respect old people had in rural society and the loss of this respect during society's modernization. Paralleling the development of these views was an emerging youth "cult," with a corresponding social value that new and modern is better, more efficient. Anything old or aging was discarded as non-functional or not important. To grow old in such an environment brings with it an aura of being useless and discarded. The result is that ". . . older people are usually relegated to a position in society in which they are no longer judged to be of any use or importance." In a youth-oriented modern society, to be over forty is to be older; to be over sixty-five is to be old. Our social, economic and political institutions have consistently and strongly reinforced this view. The chronological age criterion is a convenient measuring device to defend and justify labeling a person old in order to satisfy society's need for order and to justify replacing the old (?) with the new (?). This view perpetuates the belief in a unidirectional change in society. Yet we are confronted in the 1980s—and can expect to be again in the 1990s—with the fact that our society will change in multiple directional ways. This suggests that relying on chronological age to define groups of people will have less and less relevance.

Current Views

The concept of who is or is not old or aged varies from society to society, age group to age group, and generation to generation. In India the beginning of old age is fifty-five, whereas in the United States it is sixty-five. (Perhaps with the full implementation of the 1978 amendments to the Age Discrimination in Employment Act, age seventy will become the "official" beginning of old age in the United States.) In the Soviet Union the official retirement age (thus the assumption of old) for men is age sixty and for women age fifty-five, whereas in Sweden it is age sixty-seven. During the recent past, American youth talked about not trusting anyone over age thirty. They relegated approximately 50 percent of the population to an arbitrary "old" category. Apparently, the primary purpose for the social use of chronological age to define old is to remove groups of individuals systematically from continued participation in certain of society's activities, essentially the work arena, to make room for a rapidly-growing youth population.

At the upper end of the life span spectrum, most Americans at the age of seventy ". . . continue to describe themselves as middle-aged," and it is not ". . . until they have reached the age of seventy-five that more than half of all Americans describe themselves as *old* or *elderly*." Recall our eighty-eight-year-old man referred to earlier—who at eighty-three began to accept the fact he was getting old. Categorical age differentiations are influenced by historical precedences, social custom, legislative fiat, labor force actions, and attitudes projected by whomever is doing the defining. At best, views as to who is or is not old and how such a definition is applied are becoming more variable. As time progresses, as society continues to experience the numerical increase in longer-lived adults, as the increasing numbers of older adults are also more educated, healthy, economically independent, as they become more vocal, and as society casts aside linear life plans and the "one-life, one-career" imperative, we will experience more and more resistance to being labeled as "old," using a univariate chronological age standard which has been arbitrarily established for some questionable administrative convenience.

Social Custom

In our industrial societies, chronological age has been chosen as the definer of one's functional ability and worth, largely as a result of Bismarck's social legislation concepts set forth in the late 1800s. The United States embraced this idea in 1935, primarily as an attempt to resolve an economic crisis.

The purpose in establishing the arbitrary age of sixty-five as the onset of late life was to: 1) eliminate a population segment from the work force, ostensibly to make room for youth, 2) resolve problems of workers aging and retiring in their jobs without leaving them when industrialists preferred younger and cheaper labor, and 3) define a point in time when individuals would be eligible for socially-supported entitlements. When age sixty-five for social support eligibility was initiated, it was felt not to be economically burdensome on society. Politically that age group was felt to be small enough not to be a problem. These same beliefs in today's world are being severely questioned. Within the next quarter century—or when the World War II babies become society's "old"—we can only speculate as to the hue and cry they will make if we treat them as we currently treat society's older segment.

Chronological age as a definer of "old" has had its uses, but whenever an arbitrary criterion is set forth to define some category or attribute, inadvertent abuses and injustices often emerge, especially when people are involved. Not everyone fits the definition. Not everyone is ready to or desires to conform to a set of presumed behaviors—most notably, to terminate the work activity at a capriciously-designated age.

As noted earlier by Brown and Butler, the chronological age definition is perceived by older individuals to be an "emotional or financial rip-off," one which tends to place older people into specific stratified role categories which they seem powerless to avoid. Harris, et al, also found a similar attitude. Older people generally do not seem to appreciate this form of rigid labeling and encroachment into their lives, regardless of the "condition of functioning." Gerontologists have attempted to be more flexible and moderate in defining "old." They have ". . . divided old age into early old age—sixty-five to seventy-four years—and advanced old age—seventy-five and above." Neugarten labeled the elderly as the "young old" and the "old old." Regardless of these moderating views, gerontologists have fallen into the "time traps" to which Wirtz referred. They have maintained old persons in "age ghettoes" and maintained chronological age as the traditional definition of old.

Legislative Fiat

A brief review of legislation enacted by Congress during the last several years suggests that these policy makers have attempted to make a break with the chronological age syndrome as a basis for social service programs. But their efforts have fallen short. This may be due to the policy recommendations of the 1971 White House Conference on Aging, which outlined the "Stages of Later Life," using age categories to define them. The Conference's statement did come close to recognition of differential aging patterns, but unfortunately relied on chronological age as a delineator of a group characteristic. The intent was laudable; the results were questionable. The conferees were attempting to break the arbitrary old age definition and, in a small way, they succeeded—if only by bringing attention to the issue.

An analysis of the Older American's Act of 1965 (Public Law 89-73) and its various amendments over the years, as well as other selected legislation concerning services and entitlements of older Americans, suggests that policy makers are beginning to recognize that differential criteria are necessary when delineating groups of older people. All older people are not alike, nor do they need or want similar services. For example, the 1965 Older American's Act, Title III, Section 302 (2) under "Allotments," explains that states will receive funding for that portion of the population age sixty-five or older. Under the 1969 amendments to this act (Public Law 91-69) Section 304 (2) and (4) (c), the age sixty-five designation remains as the defintion of old. In these same amendments, Title IV, Part A., "retired Senior Volunteer Programs" and Section 601 (a) (2) and Part B, "Foster Grandparent Program" and Section 611 (a), the recipients of services and opportunities are persons age sixty and over. The "Nutrition Program" enacted under the 1972 amendments is also for age sixty and older (Public Law 20258). The 1973 amendments (Public Law 93-29) Title IX "Community Service Employment for Older Americans" Section 902 (a) uses age fifty-five or older for unemployed low-income persons, thus broadening the chronological age criterion as well as recognizing a differential financial need of some older citizens. (Note: Frances Perkins was arguing for similar easements under Social Security forty years earlier.) While age sixty is specified as the definition for entitlement under the 1973 amendments, it is significant that Section 305 (a) (1) (E) concerning eligibility of states to participate in Community Programs does not specify an age, but mandates that states ". . . provide assurances that preference will be given to providing services to older individuals with the greatest economic or social needs and include proposed methods of carrying out the preference in the state plan." We again see policy makers putting into law the recognition of the differential needs of at least some older individuals. The only drawback is that chronological age is still the overriding criterion upon which eligibility for services and entitlements is predicated.

There does seem to be a slight shift toward recognition among legislatures as to the elderly's differences, especially in terms of economics. This has been more recently evident in the Age Discrimination in Employment Act Amendments of 1978 (Public Law 95-256). These amendments have further expanded and broadened the chronological age definition by extending age limitations. Section 12 (a) states, "The prohibitions in the Act shall be limited to individuals who are at least forty years of age but less than seventy years of age." Through this statement we see that policy makers are beginning to recognize the differential nature of aging as a long-term continuous process and that older people can continue to function in the workplace beyond previously designated ages. They, however, still reinforce the concept of "old" by specifying the age at which persons can be mandatorily retired from the labor force and become eligible for Social Security entitlements.

Social Attitudes

Two apparent sets of conflicting attitudes expressed toward older persons are prevalent in American society, neither of which is necessarily related to chronological age *per se*. The assumption that an over-preoccupation with chronological age, as a terminus to work productivity, acts as a negative attitudinal force against acceptance of older people as part of American society, perhaps has some validity at face value. Even though some people may believe that the work ethic—which has sustained both an agrarian as well as an industrial society, is eroding or changing—apparently there is still a pervasive opinion that if one is not gainfully employed in our society, one has little or no worth. The unemployment of youth in society is usually tolerated in anticipation of their future productivity and contribution to society. The aged enjoy no such tolerance.

Butler has summed up the seemingly conflicting social attitudes of Americans toward older people. He stated:

> We pay lip service to the idealized images of beloved and tranquil grandparents, wise elders, white-haired patriarchs and matriarchs. But the opposite image disparages the elderly, seeing age as decay, decreptitude, a disgusting and undignified dependency. Our national social policies mirror these conflicts. We talk earnestly about our "senior citizens," but do not provide enough for them to eat. We become angry with them for being burdens, yet we take for granted the standard of living that their previous work has made possible for us. Neglect is the treatment of choice, with medicine failing to care for their physical needs, mental health personnel ignoring their emotional problems, communities neglecting to fill their social expectations.

How best to overcome these conflicting attitudes continues to be a major social and moral issue. Apparently, when using chronological age as the primary benchmark to define "old," we only emphasize the negative and foster a dependency relationship of old persons on a social welfare system which fails to meet their needs. Is this is what we, who are chronologically moving toward this life stage, desire for ourselves?

Employment

The age at which a worker should cease active participation in the labor force is a critical point which has yet to be resolved, regardless of the Age Discrimination in Employment Act. It is a question which has surfaced in Western societies ever since they became modernized and workers, consequently, experienced more leisure time. It assumes an arbitrary age when people cease to be productive in the labor force.

By not addressing the real question, the differential nature of aging, industrial society attempts to uniformly move people into and out of the work force. In the application of health and economic entitlements, the "lock step" movement of workers into and out of the labor force becomes a socially and administratively convenient and efficient mechanism. Prior to enactment of retirement legislation, industrialists were unable to or chose not to deal with the retirement problem. So long as the number of non-productive "old" workers were few in number, they constituted an insignificant economic burden. As their numbers increased, due to better health care and the like, industrialists turned to government to resolve their problem. This resulted in various retirement programs. A convenient guideline to decide who would qualify for entitlements under these programs was chronological age. At the time of legislating who would or would not be eligible for retirement entitlements—which also effectively defined who could or could not continue to be employed—human resources were thought to be unlimited. Few people lived to reach—much less live beyond—age sixty-five, so economic costs to society needed to sustain an older segment were minimal. Industrialization was becoming a way of life and demanding more highly-educated and mobile workers. Demand for agricultural workers was declining in importance and people began accepting the "wear and tear" theory popularized by medical researchers and associated with hard physical labor.

It was believed that assuring all workers a supplemental retirement income was a concept that would be acceptable to all. So it was. However, the supplemental income has become the primary income for many retirees today. At the time retirement from work was legislated, attitudes toward older workers began taking on a negative valence. Legislative actions treated older persons as being homogeneous. Forced withdrawal from labor force participation was legitimized. Age sixty-five became synonymous with "old."

Two Views

Perhaps one of the more comprehensive and promising attempts to identify the functional status of older persons has been offered by G. L. Maddox and D. C. Dellinger, in the *Annals of the American Association of Political and Social Sciences*. Their efforts have focused on assessing a person's *Social Resources, Economic Resources, Mental Health, Physical Health,* and *Activities of Daily Living.* They have called these dimensions the SEMPA profile of functioning. SEMPA was developed as a result of a perceived need ". . . to develop information systems which are demonstrably useful for program evaluation, planning, and resource allocation. . ." The structuring of SEMPA concentrated on three elements:

1. A reliable, valid, quantifiable assessment of functional status which could be used to characterize individuals and, cumulatively, defined populations;
2. A systematic procedure for characterizing the types and qualities of services received by individuals in the defined populations;
3. A transition matrix for charting stability and change in functional status of a defined population over time in relation to types and quantities of services received.

Essentially, Maddox and Dellinger's efforts were designed to assess the effects of social services extended to the elderly (age sixty-five and older), to examine the impact of these services over time, and to identify the functional status of those elderly persons receiving social services. The underlying assumption with regard to level of functioning, however, appears to be predicated on the state of impairment being experienced by an individual and on the assumption that social services were a "given" and a "must." The subjects who were tested through the SEMPA program were receiving some form of social services. Those persons age sixty-five and older who were not recipients of social services were excluded from the study.

Additionally, the measures used to assess an individual's level of functioning were those which assumed a degree of face validity based upon the criterion to be measured. This raises a question of instrument reliability and validity, since the researchers admit that there is some concern as to whether these instruments are appropriate for use with an aging population. The researchers report interrater reliability ranging from 0.74 to 0.88 on the characteristics of the five dimensions, however, which suggests a relative degree of acceptability of the measures used.

When Maddox and Dellinger applied their clinical ratings to subjects from two communities, people who were receiving social services provided interesting data. In the two groups they investigated, 58.5 and 56.7 percent respectively demonstrated no functional disorders on the SEMPA profile. When adding in those who manifested at least one functional disorder, the percentages increased to 75.7 and 79.3 respectively. By extrapolation on the basis of the older population who were receiving some form of old-age assistance, one can conclude that approximately 57 percent exhibited no functional disorders as assessed by clinical observers, and approximately 20 percent exhibited only one functional disorder. About 10 percent were identified as functionally debilitated only in the area of *economic resources*. Thus, if the economic difficulties of this 10 percent were alleviated, we would then have approximately 67 percent of an older population who manifest no functional disorders and who need few, if any, social services. They probably could function quite well on their own and could conceivably continue to be productive members of the labor force should they so desire. From a functional definition viewpoint, we can raise the questions: "Is it legitimate to define these persons as old or elderly with all the social sanctions these terms imply? If they desire to enter, re-enter, or not leave the labor force, should they be denied because they have reached some arbitrarily-defined age which presumed their need for social services?"

The GULHEMP Program (G-General physique; U-Upper extremities; L-Lower extremities; H-Hearing; E-Eyesight; M-Mentality; P-Personality) was designed to assess physical health, mental health, and personality of older (age forty and above) individuals. (Due to the problems associated with personality measurement of older persons, these dimensions were eliminated from the GULHEMP Program.) The basic assumption in this program was that regardless of age or disability, an individual can function productively in a job provided its demands are congruent with that person's physical and psychological capacity. The proponents of this program have demonstrated that a person can be employed once an accurate job profile is developed and the person's GULHEMP program is matched to it. The GULHEMP Program is aimed toward a functional approach in assisting older individuals to become active participants in the work force. The process employed involves knowledge about the person, knowledge about the job, and matching the person with the job.

The difference between the GULHEMP Program and the SEMPA Program is that GULHEMP appears to adopt a more humanistic view. That is, the program's focus is doing something "with" the individual. This approach assumes that an individual is capable of controlling his or her own life, and that with a little help that person exerts primary control over external influences such as environment, social milieu, and institutional forces. SEMPA, on the other hand, assumes doing something "to" or "for" an individual. The program's focus assumes that social services are externally-controlled environmental forces and are to be imposed upon a person. This view leads to the development of service delivery systems and definitions of needed social services, based upon the view of the aging person as passive recipient.

If aging is a process we all experience, then how can we justify the arbitrary categorization of people into "age ghettoes," especially those who have lived the longest? It seems that part of our definitional problem is predicated upon humanistic beliefs vs. behavioristic beliefs or self-help approaches vs. social services approaches. This dichotomy is at the core of the philosophical debate surrounding aging issues in the United States, most especially those associated with aging and work.

A DEVELOPMENTAL VIEW _____

Realistically there is no specific point in time when one can be defined as old. This has created problems since society has been primarily concerned with an apparent need to classify old from a chronological perspective in order to implement entitlement programs. *Our view is that aging is a developmental process and, as a result, to be classified as "old" using a chronological criterion creates a misperception which acts to stereotype people to their detriment and perpetuates "agism."* The functional developmental view of aging which we are conceptualizing presupposes four basic assumptions:

1. Aging is not a point-in-time event. It is a developmental process all humans experience.
2. The aging process, which affects everyone, continues throughout a person's life and includes all the physical, psychological and social elements experienced in a person's life.
3. The continuous process of aging is uniquely individual. People do not age similarly or at the same rate. For example, while we all experience slower reflex actions as we grow older, we do not experience this slow-down at the same rate or across an equal span of time.
4. The impact of environmental factors on life span development has a differential affect on aging, depending upon physical health, psychological well-being, economic stability, socialization, life satisfactions, and chance factors.

Based upon the above assumptions, the following functional developmental definition of aging is offered: *The developmental aging process occurs in direct ratio to a slow-down in physical functions, the level of psychological well-being, the degree of economic stability, the degree to which one maintains* social activity, perceived life satisfactions, and chance factors over which the individual has no control, such as economic recession, catastrophes, or rampant inflation. The degree to which an individual perceives or experiences aging and the manner in which he or she accepts aging as part of living are functions of what can be termed an "Aging Index." We can hypothesize that the more harmony one experiences in terms of the elements of this definition, the more uniform and comfortable is the aging process; the more an individual is in control of his or her life, the less need there will be for social services to maintain that person. External assistance and the relinquishing of a degree of autonomy should be required only when an individual experiences significant uncontrolled disruptions in the elements of the aging process.

Questions, however, which are yet to be resolved are: "What is the range of tolerance within which people can independently maintain control of their lives, maintain their independence, and continue to develop productively and thrive while experiencing the aging process?" "At what point is one defined as old?" Our current methods of implementing retirement systems and developing and offering supporting social services when people retire from the workforce would suggest that people reaching age sixty-five or seventy no longer have much tolerance for self-maintenance. They are believed to have atrophied in all aspects of their development. As such, they are expected and often forced to begin the process of dependence on social service systems. They are suddenly perceived by others to be "old" when they reach a socially-imposed age cut-off defining "old." The truth of society's assumptions is yet to be ascertained.

The SEMPA Program of functioning includes several of the elements in the definition presented above, as does the GULHEMP Program. The application of SEMPA to two populations did not include, however, an assessment of the range of tolerance within which one can live and function independently from social services. Nor did it include the assessment of individuals who currently function independently from social services and are sixty-five or older. GULHEMP was basically concerned with matching the functional level of an individual in terms of demands of a given job, and it did omit an assessment of mental health as being too difficult to assess within the age group under consideration. Also, GULHEMP was concerned with a broader age range than was SEMPA. In order to test the assumptions of our proposed definition, it will help to specify an operational definition which has verifiable characteristics, is applicable across a wide range of individuals, and whose attributes are definable at least to some degree. The proposed operational definition can be specified as:

Aging Index (AI) =
> Physical Status (PS) + Psychological Well-Being (PW) +
> Economic Stability (ES) + Socialization (S) +
> Life Satisfaction (LS) + Chance Factors (CF)

> divided by

> Age (A), or

$$AI = \frac{PS + PW + ES + S + LS + CF}{A}$$

where,

1. *Aging Index* (AI) refers to a sum score when combining the six attributes in the equation divided by age.

2. *Physical Status* (PS) refers to bodily function, e.g., strength, reflexes, lung function, blood circulation, liver function, muscular coordination, etc.

3. *Psychological Well-Being* (PW) refers to one's self-perception, usually referred to as self-concept, mental health, and the degree of psychopathology one manifests.

4. *Economic Stability* (ES) refers to level of income necessary to maintain one's financial independence in society.

5. *Socialization* (S) refers to 1) the degree to which an individual continues to actively participate in his or her

environment and 2) the degree to which he or she continues role-modeling consistent with his development.

6. *Life Satisfaction* (LS) refers to how happy one is with his or her life now and what one anticipates in the future.

7. *Chance Factors* (CF) refers to those historical events in one's life space over which he or she has no control—such as war, inflation, economic depression or recession—and which can positively or adversely affect elements two through six.

8. *Age* (A) refers to the number of years one has lived and is the divisor for elements two through seven.

This is not an easy formula to quantify since several of its elements cannot be measured adequately, given their multiple dimensions and our existing assessment tools. This conceptualization suffers from the same measurement shortcomings identified in the SEMPA and GULHEMP Programs. We suffer from a serious deficiency of measuring tools which can accurately assess the dimensions of individual functioning for specific age and work groups. This, however, should not deter us from conceptualizing the problem, articulating those areas where we find deficiencies, and attempting to find solutions.

We can measure *Physical Status*. The measuring tools used by the medical profession are adequate, reliable and quantifiable. What is not clear is which measures are the most appropriate to measure physical status in relation to an individual's functional ability to continue working. Given our earlier finding that 84 percent of all work performed in America does not require high levels of physical stamina, we are left with the question of how much is enough. There have been several studies in recent years attempting to evaluate physiological functioning with age. Generally, they focus on stamina, reflex action, strength, and the like. They do show via cross-sectional studies that there are differences between younger and older workers. With few exceptions, however, these studies do not equate their findings with an inability to function in the workplace due to physiological decline.

Psychological Well-Being is a domain where a considerable body of measurement data exists. L. W. Poon, author of *Aging in the 1980's: Psychological Issues*, has compiled the major relevant research that reflects a clinical pathological perspective on the psychological well-being of older people. Given the focus of more recent gerontological research, one could conclude that the psychological well-being is in rampant deterioration among the older population. This notion is misleading, mainly due to definitional problems with regard to lack of agreement as to who constitutes the older population— the general focus of most gerontological research. We reported earlier that only 5 to 10 percent of the elderly population suffer from mental decline at any given time. This leaves approximately 90 percent who are mentally healthy, which allows for the assumption that they are experiencing continued positive psychological well-being.

Perhaps one of the more efficient measures of psychological well-being is self-report. Clearly a sense of self-esteem, conviction of one's worth as an individual, having a clear sense of identity, having concrete goals and values, feelings of potency and efficacy, having a sense that one's world is stable, a sense of meaning and coherence in one's life, and the belief that one's actions make sense to self and others are all important elements of psychological well-being. Recent literature suggests that bits and pieces of this attribute are being quantified with some degree of accuracy; what has yet to be attempted and demonstrated is an overall measurement. We believe this will occur as we gain in knowledge and understanding of the construct, as well as in measurement sophistication regarding older people.

A third attribute of our model is *Economic Stability*. This is easily quantifiable from one perspective. We can specify the actual amount of income one has at any one time. It is far more difficult to assess the degree of adequacy of that income to provide a stable existence which assures independence and autonomy. Adequacy for those persons on fixed incomes is affected by inflation, recession, etc. When the adequacy question is addressed, we face a moral dilemma. Should we as a society suggest that as we grow older our incomes should be equalized? If so, how best to determine minimum and maximum income ranges? Who will or should determine this? Given our existing entitlement programs, the movement in our society is toward minimum income levels for older people since there are "means tests" associated with certain financial entitlements such as Social Security.

A movement toward minimum income levels for older people negates the preponderance of evidence that as people age their heterogeneity becomes more evident and is reflected in their differing needs and lifestyles. Further, the notion is antithetical to the work ethic which has sustained people throughout their lives. This moral dilemma is deliberately overstated to dramatize the complexity of economic stability for older people. Other than actual income and society's standards for adequacy of that income, we are left with the individual's own perception of adequacy of *economic stability*. If the individual perceives he is able to maintain a satisfactory living standard, then we can assume a reasonably high rating on his or her attribute.

The attribute of *Socialization* is somewhat more elusive to quantify, due to the way this concept has been defined traditionally. Man displays his socialization through various human interactions at home, at play and in the work place. The frequency and quality of such interactions can be observed and quantified essentially through self-report and behavioral observations. Continued socialization is especially important for those who have led active lives. Any dramatic decline in or intrusion on this activity without adequate explanation could be suggestive of poor socialization or some other life dysfunction. Furthermore, socialization is a major mechanism for integrating individuals into social groups commensurate with their ages.

Apparently socialization involves two dimensions—social expectations of behavior and the individual's own expectations. How best to measure these two dimensions will occupy researchers in the future. Part of the socialization process as defined by society relates to learning role behavior from the next older age group. Such activities are "rites of passage" ceremonies (graduation from high school or college, marriage, job promotion, retirement) which typically involve increased responsibility and independence and reflect roles learned by younger age groups. Retirement from work, however, carries with it an implicit loss of responsibility (can't hold a job) and loss of independence (increased dependence on social entitlements). A key element for an individual's own standard for socialization is planning and preparation for living the next life stage.

Life Satisfaction has been intensely researched for the last several decades. Most of this research has focused on a retrospective view of past life and is an attempt to associate the retrospective view with successful aging. In our definition, *life satisfaction* is concerned with the here and now as well as the future, though it recognizes past influences. Researchers have concluded that life satisfaction is a consequence of individual characteristics and that these traits will manifest themselves both now and in the future. A global measure of life satisfaction may be illusionary, since it may be transitory as opposed to stable and affective versus cognitive. One of the more widely-used measures of life satisfaction was developed by B. L. Neugarten, R. J. Havighurst and S. S. Tobin. Their scale attempts to assess the apparent multi-dimensional aspects of the construct. They have included some of the concepts of our definition in addition to life satisfaction.

Our final definitional attribute is *Chance Factors*. This is perhaps the most ambiguous and will be the most difficult dimension to identify and measure. For instance, how would we quantify the impact of a 6 or 7 percent-per-year rise in inflation on the aging process as we have defined it? What historical events contribute to slowing down or speeding up the perception of getting old? During national emergencies, apparently age is not a factor in employability; this was evidenced during World War II. After the war it became fashionable to retire from work at younger and younger ages, with the corresponding connotation of being old. The vagaries of chance factors leaves us with gross judgments and generalizations, both of which can contribute to methodological errors when trying to assess this attribute.

In order to convert the six attributes of functionalism into an *Aging Index* (AI) which can be used to define who is or is not old, and to bring more precision to the definition of old, we need to introduce chronological age (CA) into our equation. One way to do this is to assume an individual's Aging Index is a simple ratio of his functional attributes to age and multiply by a constant such as 100, to eliminate decimals. As a result, our equation becomes AI $= 100$ (FA/CA). For many readers this formula is familiar. Its form is similar to traditional computing of intelligence quotients. For the I.Q., the traditional ratio has been replaced by a deviation I.Q. in order to account for comparability throughout age ranges. It may be that should our Aging Index prove to be a useful definition for "old," similar changes will need to be instituted to account for between-age-group differences. For purposes of our discussion, the simple ratio Aging Index (AI $= 100 \times$ FA/CA) will suffice.

The quantification and measurement problems of assessing the process of aging—which in turn lead us to a definition of "old"—are many and complicated; they are not necessarily impossible. Conceptually, our definition is subject to many questions, one of which is practicality. The primary problem with which we are confronted is that people concerned with aging have not really begun to address the problems and issues associated with this form of assessment and definition. More research needs to be done. Writers and researchers concerned with a population which is growing older will undoubtedly acknowledge this issue in the future. What is abundantly clear is that there is a paucity of research concerned with a practical and useful functional definition of "old." We are still left with chronological age as our criterion for a definition. As a result, there yet remains inferences on functional aging— inferences based upon fuzzy definition reflecting a researcher's idiosyncracies. It is hoped that our proposed theoretical developmental definition of aging will at least stimulate thinking and research designed to clarify the definitional problems associated with issues, problems, policy formulations, service delivery systems, and research concerning an aging American population. Perhaps through validation of our proposed definition (or one similar to it) it may be found that some persons who are chronologically "young" are in fact "old," whereas some persons who are currently considered chronologically "old" are in fact young. Who, then, should be defined as "old?"

THE AGING INDEX: POSSIBLE USES _____

Society's current attitude regarding who is or is not old is predicated on assumptions about the linear life plan, which presumes a chronological concept of growing old. This is depicted in Figure 10-1. An examination of it suggests that from birth to about age twenty-five and from age sixty-five to death, the traditional view of one's functional contribution to society is curvilinear. Both groups are assumed to be dependent upon society, with youth moving toward independence and post-age-sixty-five becoming more dependent. The years of independence (twenty-five to sixty-five) appear also to be curvilinear to age. That is, as one actively participates in productive activities—usually employment in the labor force—he or she functions in the independence range. This middle-range age group is inferred to support the dependent members of society. Lifestyle changes which have occurred since the 1960s—and which are becoming more and more evident—strongly suggest that the traditional linear life view is subject to question and modification. For a growing segment of the population, traditional life-living patterns are no longer required, desired, nor an expected way to behave. For example, education is becoming a more and more important activity throughout the life span and no longer reserved for youth. Changing social forces, changing technology, and more differential proclivities toward life, among other factors, have all contributed toward negating this traditional view. No longer does the vast majority of the population conform to the traditional expectations for functioning both within and between groups. Variability within age groups is almost as pronounced and expected as it is between age groups.

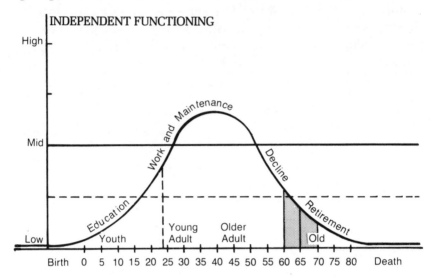

Figure 10-1. The Traditional View of the Aging Process

We are suggesting that the validation of our proposed Aging Index is a more parsimonious way of viewing the aging process than one which is dependent solely on chronological age. Our index allows us to view individuals both within and between age groups to better understand their behavior and more accurately determine who is or is not "old." In this way we may be better able to allocate society's resources to those persons truly in need, rather than to follow our traditional "lockstep" patterns. We are suggesting that in today's—and perhaps more importantly in tomorrow's—world, we will need to view all age groups, not just older age groups, differentially rather than similarly as is the prevailing view.

Figure 10-2 is suggestive of how our Aging Index could begin to differentiate between individuals as well as between and within age groups. As can be seen, people—regardless of age—differentially exhibit a range of functionality. Some individuals will never be able to function in productively-contributory ways by society's standards and will be dependent always. Others will function at marginal levels. The vast majority are functional, however, and will continue to be so long after society's predetermined dates.

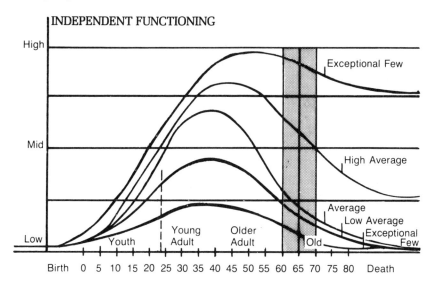

Figure 10-2. Range of Functionality by Age

For all practical purposes, differential functioning attributes begin to display themselves soon after birth. Some children display higher or lower physical or mental attributes which quickly separate them from others in their peer group. This separation, usually on the basis of intellect and academic performance, continues to display itself throughout the life span. Through social selection processes, individuals are productive to a greater or lesser degree from low to high performance levels. Only an exceptional few in the population are either never productive and contributing social members of society or are perceived to function at very high levels throughout the life span. The vast majority of people function somewhere in between. It is argued here that the majority of people can continue to be productive by our definition long after the socially-mandated age cut-offs. The shaded areas in both Figure 10-1 and 10-2 suggest that the majority of older people are either forced or choose to remove themselves from the labor force through retirement while they are still able to function productively. Certainly, society's imposition of chronological age cut-off points have encouraged and fostered forced early retirement.

It may be speculated that an advantage to developing a more functional definition of aging designed to specify more precisely who is or is not old has to do with allocations of various social entitlement programs. We cited earlier that legislative entitlement programs—regardless of apparent modifications—are age-bound. For the most part, to be eligible for the various benefits one must reach a given age and retire from the work force, disregarding functional ability. Distribution of social benefits on the basis of functionality as opposed to chronological age could conceivably lead toward a more equitable distribution of society's resources.

11

AGING AND WORK: IMPLICATIONS AND CONCLUSIONS

POLICY ON AGING _____

For older people to be perceived as thriving, new and creative styles for maintaining them within the mainstream of society will need to be conceptualized. One way is to distinguish them as a vast human resource reservoir whose expertise is desired and utilized.

Prior to any significant changes or any further legislation being enacted, a commitment toward a long-term policy planning must be made. It will need to include:

1. A basic and committed belief that all persons, regardless of age, can continue to be productive members of the labor force, should they be physically or psychologically able and willing to participate.

2. A belief in the heterogeneous nature of the older popu-

lation and a commitment to making options available, without penalty, to participate in paid or unpaid activities in the labor force that reflect this heterogeneity.

3. A recognition that older people can and do function differently, regardless of age, as indicated by our functional developmental aging definition.

4. A recognition that in order to understand the differential participatory nature of older people in the labor force, there needs to be an ongoing program of basic research to guide policy makers. Such research will need to be designed to allow for a high degree of specificity regarding description, explanation, and prediction concerning the group of persons under consideration.

RETIREMENT

Knowing what happens to retirees, who they are, what their specific needs are, etc., would assist us in addressing questions of concern in more precise and systematic ways than have been done in the past. Some representative questions are:

1. What program of social service for older retirees are needed which are not currently available? For how many persons, under what conditions, at what point in time, etc.?

2. What is the impact of the Age Discrimination in Employment Act, 1978 Amendments on retirement practices of older workers, employers? How many people are affected? Who are they? What types of work were/ are they engaged in? Should the age-seventy ceiling be lifted? If so, how many persons would be affected? For those persons who do retire and then go back to work, where do they work, under what conditions, what kinds of jobs do they find, etc.?

3. Are our current Social Security laws and pension pro-

grams punitive? Do they, under threat or loss of financial security, inhibit the desire of older people to work? Should there be revisions in the law making it possible for people to be rewarded for continued productivity and independence while under Social Security support? Again, how many persons would be affected? Who are they? What alternatives are available to individuals who need additional financial support but fear loss of independence and dignity?

MENTAL HEALTH

Much has been written about the mental health problems affecting older people. Visualizations as expressed through the popular media frequently depict older people in distressful psychological and physiological situations. While it is true that older persons do suffer from mental and physical problems, it does not necessarily follow that these problems are the result of the aging process; nor are they the only age group to suffer from these problems. Some researchers and writers in the gerontological field would have us believe that these problems experienced by an aging population are normal and follow a developmental sequence associated with physical deterioration and age (*Toward a National Policy on Aging*, Vol. II, 1971). What a dismal future to look forward to. The psychopathologies associated with aging are often coupled with normal physiological deterioration. Thus, by connotation, to be old in America is to be physically disabled and mentally incompetent. This is how old people are often perceived. Perhaps this pessimistic prospect of aging is one reason why our society has developed a reverence toward being young. The idolization of youth by our adult population could be perceived as resistance to and rejection of growing old. Perhaps, also, adults tend to resist the phenomenon of growing old and all the attending problems because of the relatively recent increase in the numbers of old people, which has made the problems faced by them so visible and, for some, so painful.

Mentally healthy individuals perceive themselves as being of worth and value in society. These perceptions are generally associated with satisfactions experienced in the labor force. Further, older people are resisting being "put out to pasture." They are expressing a desire to be re-integrated into society through paid or unpaid employment. Such work activity, however, needs to be perceived by society as being worthwhile.

Older people seem to be rejecting the "make do" activities currently in vogue. The desire for continued active participation in the labor force seems to be associated with an increasing longevity, a desire to continue to be productive and of worth, and a wish to reassert control over one's life course. Longevity is the result of such things as significant advances in medical technology, lower mortality rates at birth, improved health practices and nutritional programs, and shorter and less arduous lifetime work activities. The less rigorous physical demands from the work setting—due largely to improved technology and electronic computerization—seem to have facilitated increased vigor and health in older people and provided leisure time unparalleled in history. Society must question whether the attitudes expressed by some older people toward continued worthwhile productivity are really manifestations of psychopathology or expressions of positive mental health.

Perhaps those older individuals who attempt to conform to some ambiguous role model which society has vaguely defined would really rather behave in some other way. One could assume that should an older person opt to redefine his or her social role in a manner which conforms to an image that individual chooses, he or she risks being labeled as suffering from mental illness. It would appear that an examination of the psychological well-being of older persons in relation to improved physical health, perceptions of self-worth, being needed, and contributions they make to society through some form of work needs to be undertaken.

Our analysis—along with the data presented from the SEMPA Program—suggests that the relative number of mentally dysfunctional older persons is small. Butler has presented data which indicate that as people age, incidences of mental illness rise. He questions the accuracy of these findings, however, due to poor and inadequate diagnostic procedures used to define mental illness in older people as well as to the "agism" practiced by psychiatrists, social workers, and mental health specialists who work with old people. If, as has been suggested frequently throughout this volume, people gain their identities, maintain their sense of self-worth, and experience their life satisfactions through work, is this any less true for older people whom society has attempted to set aside under the guise that older people have earned a life of leisure after a lifetime of work? Some of the pertinent questions as they relate to mental health can be expressed as follows:

1. What affect will continued participation in the labor force have on reducing the incidences of mental dysfunctions experienced by older people? Who are they, from what work groups, from what occupational groupings?

2. Do older people want or need to work in order to maintain an important place in society? Will working—paid or unpaid—become a therapeutic tool for maintaining mental health among older people, a tool which currently is little understood by most mental health practitioners who work with older people?

3. If work for older people is demonstrated to be therapeutic in reducing incidences of psychopathology, to what degree and for whom? Can we reduce demands for mental health services currently in place through reintroducing work in the lives of older people, thus reducing medical costs.

EDUCATION

The mystique of education and the rewards education provide have been and continue to be a basic value, a belief, and a way of life in American society. In a paper published in the

Monthly Labor Review, W. V. Deutermann reported that in 1940 the mean educational attainment for males (sixteen to sixty-four) was 8.6 years and for women 9.8 years. By 1973, these figures for the same age ranges were 12.0 years for males and 12.1 years for females. Such changes represent one demonstration of increased values about and beliefs in education, resulting in a highly-educated society. During recent years, there has been a rise in educational savings plans, insurance programs for educational assurances for the young, and other forms of investment programs to guarantee a financial capability to assist youth in attaining anticipated educational achievement levels. These private efforts have been combined with such Federal programs as Basic Educational Opportunity Grants (BEOG), increased public and private scholarship funds, and subsidized educational loan programs. Such examples are expressed manifestations of the reverence Americans have for higher education. While planning for future education for their children, adults often assume a four-year collegiate experience. It is not so limited. One merely needs to review the phenomenal enrollment increases in public and private junior and community college programs, as well as the increasingly successful private proprietary schools to witness the fundamental belief that educational attainment is basic for future opportunities for everyone.

Paralleling the rise in the belief in and the importance of education for youth has been a corresponding increase in educational opportunities and options for adults. Adult basic education, special adult classes for personal development learning, and life-long learning concepts are examples which reflect a recent upsurge of interest and activity in adult education. As was noted, adults who are taking advantage of available education and re-education programs are generally in the young-adult category. Older adults are not flocking to these programs. Several reasons for this apparent lack of participation are courses offered at a poor time, restrictive entrance requirements, and lack of transportation, to name a few. It may be that older people themselves believe the myths about aging, especially as the myths relate to learning. Learning, in recent years, has taken on a pragmatic connotation—if one expends a certain amount of mental energy and financial resources, then this should translate to an improved position in the work place and result in economic gain. Older adults who believe in this logic may see education as a luxury they cannot or do not want to afford. They may see education as an expense which will yield little, if any, return. It may be speculated that in the near future attitudes toward lifelong education will change. The "baby boom" generation—which is currently entering mid-life—is the most highly-educated group in history. Continual learning, especially job-related learning, continues to be part of their lifestyle. This has been necessary in order for them to be competitive in a tight job market. There is no reason to assume that they will not continue the learning process when they reach the retirement age, if they choose to retire.

What most people fail to take into consideration is that learning takes place—to a greater extent than realized—in non-formal or non-structured environments. How to implement a multiple-style learning concept and make it an acceptable option for people in later life becomes a very real national problem which has yet to be fully addressed by educators and policy makers. Yet, if we accept the notion that people are an untapped resource whose potential has yet to be realized in our society, then we must reassess our educational system and values to maximize such potential.

Another aspect of the adult learning boom involves demands on workers to continually up-grade their skills and knowledges to keep pace with the technological changes in business and industry. Most employers tend to encourage the younger employees to take advantage of educational opportunities under the assumption that an investment in education (be it time or money or both, to which employers are frequent contributors) will produce a longer period of high productivity from their employees. Employer contributions seem to be a sound economic business practice. And with the changes in mandatory retirement coupled with a rapid movement toward informational and service-based industries—rather than product-based industries which require strenuous physical output—

this attitude toward education and re-education for young-adults-only may need reassessment to include all adult age groups.

With the new learning/work styles presently emerging which have been described by N. D. Kurland, it is reasonable to assume there will be a greater mobility in the labor force, with a corresponding emergence of multiple learning/work styles and patterns. We may speculate that as a result there will be a greater need for a pool of skilled and knowledgeable workers who are amenable to change and short-term job-specific retraining as technological and informational changes spread within the work arena. It seems reasonable to assume that older workers are prime candidates for these retraining programs, supposing that educators as well as employers and older people themselves can get over the myth that older persons cannot learn. What we do know is that older persons *can* learn new ways of behaving, new skills, new knowledge, but they learn in a mode different from that which educators are trained to deliver.

Currently, vocational education programs, community colleges, proprietary schools and, earlier, the Comprehensive Education and Training Act (CETA) Programs (now replaced by the Job Training Partnership ACT [JTPA]), come closest to having the resources, skills, and available teaching technology to offer the kinds of retraining programs which would assist older workers to continue to learn and upgrade their skills in order to continue in the work force as productive and contributing members. It is questionable, however, that the advocates of these programs are mentally attuned to the notion of providing such programs, utilizing their current resources, for older workers. CETA was designed to assist in training and retraining of disadvantaged unemployed, as in JTPA. Certainly, the vast majority of older people meet this criterion. Vocational education originally was designed to provide technical education at the secondary school level for prospective new job entrants. Vocational education is now addressing itself to post-secondary vocational training activities as well. But vocational education essentially still focuses its resources on the first-time job entrant or the young job entrant who has left the formal educational environment and has returned for specific job training after having worked for a short while. Community colleges have been designed to meet the educational needs of a given community. They, too, seem to gear their educational efforts to the young adult aspiring to upgrade his or her skills in order to be more competitive in the job market. It would seem that if we advocate that all human beings are a natural resource, then all our post-secondary educational efforts will need to provide programs which will include older workers who also desire educational upgrading in order to remain in or re-enter the labor force.

Community and senior colleges, in addition to other formal educational programs, will need to begin to rethink their educational missions with regard to the place of older learners. Those older people who want or need to work will, in all probability, need to be retrained in order to participate actively in the labor force or engage in other productive activities. Are our multiple and diverse educational systems geared up to assist this group? We think not. Our current educational systems are still designed to accommodate the "linear life" concept and presume that education is designed to reinforce the "one-life, one-career" imperative. They are not ready for nor are they gearing up for the multiple living, learning, and working styles being demanded, advocated, and implemented by citizens of all ages.

Numerous work options such as split shift, flex time, shared jobs, job rotation, and contract work are coming into vogue and appear to be becoming part of the employment picture. Many of these new work structures and arrangements are ideal for utilizing older people as workers in the labor force. Older people have the time, the hours are right for them, and they are willing to be active participants. In fact, many older workers are already in the labor force—many surreptitiously. What we do not know is how many older people are working full-time, part-time, or engaged in volunteer activities. Who are they, what work do they do, for whom, under what conditions? Systematic organization and gathering of data would facilitate interpreting the results in order to suggest appropriate education programs to meet the different needs of this potentially vast and untapped human resource.

RESEARCH

Research in the realm of aging and work is potentially a rich domain for exploration. A description listing our lack of knowledge related to aging and work would probably be greater than our knowledge. One can begin at almost any point to raise pertinent and important questions which would have implications for policy formation and program development, suggest practical application, and open avenues for future research. We have raised a host of researchable inquiries throughout this volume which are suggestive of several research dimensions. The verification of the many researchable questions and the proposed functional definition of aging we have proposed are important in terms of the knowledge base they would contribute to our understanding of the relationship of the aging process and the work activity.

It is appropriate to call for at least two dimensions of research related to aging and work, and labeled as "basic" and "applied"; and a program of basic research concerned with theory building is necessary in order to propose an aging policy which has national significance. Emanating from such theory building will be programs and practices to assist an aging population, which can be evaluated in terms of cost effectiveness, utility, and long-term need. Basic research of the kind we are suggesting would provide baseline information about those persons whom society perceives as "old," as well as those who are moving into the upper ranges of their life spans. Basic research would help build support for some of our assumptions about the nature of age and help to identify more accurately those who comprise the population now identified as "old." Current information and knowledge about our older population suggests huge deficits which essentially have been filled by myths, pseudo-inferences, hunches, and emotionalism. On such flimsy and unsubstantiated evidence, it is very difficult to suggest—much less plan—effective long-term policy with regard to aging in America at any governmental level. We do have available demographic data, some of which we have reported. But these statistics fall short in terms of specific descriptive characteristics, since they assume homogeneity of the group under consideration. Instead, these data do serve to perpetuate our aging myths and provide justification for us to continue to practice "agism." Time and again responsible writers who address issues of aging in America have pointed out the heterogeneity of older people. Yet policy planners and deliverers of services persist in presupposing that all older people are alike. How can we justify continuing in this manner when we have yet to accurately define who is or is not old?

When is a person old? How do we recognize this condition? These seem to be very basic and fundamental questions which have never been adequately answered as they relate to a changing "high-tech" society. Social custom—not research—has arbitrarily made the distinctions. The functional developmental definition of aging, which needs to be tested and verified, could help identify those parameters which collectively would define what we mean by "old." Can people, defined as old, function productively as active participants in the labor force should they so desire? We have assumed they can. But due to individual differences in the aging process, we also assume that different individuals under different conditions and ages are productive at varying times and ages. How valid are these assumptions? A program of basic research could be designed to support or refute these postulates. It would seem that if American society has a desire to reverse its attitude toward our older citizenry and extend to them the right to continue to pursue their Constitutional freedoms, basic and fundamental questions need to be resolved. A program of primary research which is longitudinal in scope would greatly assist in obliterating myths on aging. Such a research program will need to be basic in order to effect an attitudinal shift in society concerning the aging process and the aging person's value to self and society.

A corresponding program of applied research is also necessary. Real people have real problems and need help now.

250 Golden Goals, Rusted Realities

But because of immediate need we should not be deterred from asking fundamental questions having to do with the quality and effectiveness of services and service delivery systems. What kinds of self-help programs are operating, for whom, and how many persons are affected? If "old" people work, where do they work, for whom, for how long, and under what conditions? Why do they work? How are other facets of their lives affected by their employment or lack of employment? Are these second careers for those who elect to be employed or are they extensions of their primary careers? The list can go on. Answers to these and other queries, however, form the basis for program action and policy development predicated upon knowledge rather than myth, someone's intuition, or emotion. Data resulting from seeking answers to these and similar questions would be helpful in our finding a resolution to some of the more theoretical and fundamental questions raised earlier.

It was not the intent of this volume to suggest that work was *the* sole therapeutic medium by which to solve the problems society is facing now and will face in the future with regard to our aging population. What was intended—and perhaps overstated at times—is that work and its relationship to aging is an important domain, one which is little understood or explored as a means to help older people thrive rather than survive during the latter stages of their life span. Apparently, there are no available guidelines to suggest what path to follow or what agencies or groups should take the lead, other than to remove older people from the labor force at a capriciously-designated age.

Historically, removal of older people from the labor force has not solved any of society's problems. In fact, it can be argued that such action has created more problems which have been and continue to be of major social concern. It is proposed that research is one path to problem understanding and resolution. Such a conceptualization is intended to help clarify through description, analysis, and identification a strategy whereby older citizens can continue to participate as full and autonomous partners in our society in ways not recently perceived as possible. An acceptable avenue for re-entry to this participation is through work, either paid or unpaid.

REFERENCES

Achenbaum, W. A. (1978) *Old age in the new land: The American Experience since 1790.* Baltimore: Johns Hopkins University Press.

Anastasi, A. (1974) Individual differences in aging. In W. C. Bier (Ed.) *Aging.* New York: Fordham University Press. 84-95.

Anderson, Jr., A. (1978) Old is not a four-letter word. *Across the board. 15,* 20-27.

Annual report to the president - 1977. (1977) Washington, D.C.: Federal Council on Aging.

Aslanian, C. B. & Brickell, H. M. (1980) *Americans in transition: Life changes as reasons for adult learning.* New York: College Entrance Examination Board.

Atchley, R. C. (1983) *Aging: Continuity and change.* Belmont, Calif.: Wadsworth Pub. co.

Barrow, G. M. & Smith, P.A. (1979) *Aging, agism and society.* St. Paul, Minn.: West Pub. Co.

Bengtson, V. L. (1979) Ethnicity and aging: Problems and issues in current social service inquiry. In D. E. Gelford & A. J. Kutsik (Eds.) *Ethnicity and aging: Theory, research, and policy.* New York: Springer Pub. Co. 9-31.

Bennett, C. E. (1962) *History of manual and industrial education to 1870, Vol. 1.* Peoria, Ill.: Charles A. Bennett Co., Inc.

Borow, H. (1973) *Career guidance for a new age.* Boston: Houghton Mifflin Co.

Bowman, H. H. (1975) *The nature of mental health.* Austin, Texas: The Hogg Foundation for Mental Health.

Brown, S. (1977) Taking senior citizens off the shelf. *Worklife, 2,* 14-19.

Butler, R. N. (1970) Looking forward to what? *American behavioral scientist, 14,* 121-128.

Butler, R. N. (1975) *Why survive? Being old in America.* New York: Harper & Row, Pub.

Butler, R. N. & Lewis, M. I. (1973) *Aging and mental health: Positive psychosocial approaches.* Saint Louis: C. V. Mosby Co.

Butler, R. N. & Lewis, M. I. (1977) *Aging and mental health.* Saint Louis: C. V. Mosby Co.

Cain, L. D. (1974) *Political factors in the emerging legal age status of the elderly. The annals of the American academy of political and social sciences, 415*, 79-99.
Calhoun, R. B. (1978) *In search of the new old.* New York: Elsevier.
Carnegie Council on Policy Studies in Higher Education (1980) *Three thousand futures: The next twenty years for higher education.* San Francisco: Jossey-Bass.
Clark, R. L. (1979) Age structure changes and intergenerational transfer of income. In J. Kreps (Ed.). *Economics of a stationary population: Implications for older Americans.* Washington, D.C.: U.S. Government Printing Office, 65-78.
Cohen, L. (1984) *Small expectations: Society's betrayal of older women.* Toronto: McClelland & Stewart Ltd.
Cohn, R. M. (1979) Age and satisfaction from work. *Journal of gerontology, 34*, 264-272.
Comfort, A. (1976) *A good age.* New York: Crown Pub.
Cowgill, D. O. (1974) The aging of populations and societies. In F. R. Eisele (Ed.) Political Consequences of aging. *The annals of the American academy of political and social sciences, 415*, 1-18.
Cowgill, D. O. (1974) Aging and modernization: A revision of the theory. In J. F. Gubrium (Ed.) *Late life: Communities and environmental policies.* Springfield, Ill.: C. C. Thomas, Pub. 123-146.
Cowgill, D. O. & Holmes, L. D. (Eds.) (1972) *Aging and modernization.* New York: Appleton-Century-Crofts.
Cross, K. P. (1978) *The missing link: Connecting adult learners to learning resources.* New York: College Entrance Examination Board.
Cross, K. P. (1981) *Adults as learners.* San Francisco: Jossey-Bass Pub.
DeCrow, R. (1978) *Older Americans: New uses of mature ability.* Washington, D.C.: American Association of Community and Junior Colleges.
Delker, P. V. (1979) *Adult education - 1980 and beyond: Implications for research and development.* Columbus, Ohio: The National Center for Research in Vocational Education.
Department of Health, Education, and Welfare. (1978) *Lifelong

learning and public policy. Washington, D.C.: U.S. Government Printing Office.

Deutermann, W. V. (1974) Educational attainment of workers, March 1973. *Monthly labor review.* p. 58.

Drucker, P. (1975-1976) Pension fund socialism. *The public interest, 46,* 3-46.

Dunn, J. D. (1981) *Reappraising social security: Toward an alternative system.* Austin, Texas: LBJ School of Public Affairs, The University of Texas at Austin.

Eisele, F. R. (1974) Preface. *The annals of the American academy of political and social sciences, 415,* ix.

Erickson, E. H. (1963) *Childhood and society (2nd. ed.).* New York: W. W. Norton.

Erickson, E. H. (1968) *Identity: Youth and crises.* New York: W. W. Norton.

ERISA, Public Law 93-406, 29 U. S. C.

Fischer, D. H. (1977) *Growing old in America.* New York: Oxford University Press.

Freud, S. (1939) *Civilization and its discontents.* J. Strachey (Ed.). London: Hogarth Press.

Fries, J. F. (1980) Aging, natural death, and the compression of morbidity. *The New England journal of medicine, 303,* 130-135.

Gatz, M. (1980) Introduction. In L. W. Poon (Ed.). *Aging in the 1980s.* Washington, D.C.: American Psychological Association. 3-4.

Giele, J. Z. (Ed.) (1982) *Women in the middle yers.* New York: John Wiley & Sons.

Gleaser, Jr., E. J. (1980) *The community colleges: Values, visions, and vitality.* Washington, D.C.: American Association of Community and Junior Colleges.

Graebner, W. (1980) *A history of retirement.* New Haven: Yale University Press.

Gray, S. & Morse, D. (1980) Retirement and pre-retirement: Changing work options for older workers. *Aging and work, 3,* 2, 103-111.

Grove, W. & Hughes, M. (1979) Possible causes of the apparent sex difference in physical health. *American sociological review, 44,* 126-146.

Gurland, B. J. (1976) The comparative frequency of depression in various adult age groups. *Journal of gerontology, 31,* 283-292.

Haber, P. A. (1978) *Our future selves: A research plan toward understanding aging.* Washington, D.C.: National Advisory Council on Aging, pub. #78-1443.

Harris, L., & Associates. (1975) *The myth and reality of aging in America.* Washington, D.C.: National Council on Aging.

Havighurst, R. J. (1953) *Human development and education.* New York: Longman's, Green & Co.

Havighurst, R. J. (1972) *Developmental tasks and education (3rd ed.).* New York: McKay.

Havighurst, R. J. (1980) Life-span developmental psychology and education. *Educational researcher, 9,* 3-8.

Hendricks, J. & Hendricks, C. D. (1977) *Aging in mass society.* Cambridge, Mass.: Winthrop Pub., Inc.

Higher education daily, March 25, 1980, p. 1.

Hoyt, K. B. (1973) Toward a definition of career education. In J. H. Magisos (Ed.). *Career education.* Washington, D.C.: American Vocational Association. 15-29.

Jaslow, P. (1976) Employment, retirement, and moral among older women. *Journal of gerontology, 31,* 212-218.

Kalish, R. A. (1977) Social values and the elderly. In R. A. Kalish (Ed.) *The later years: Social applications of gerontology.* Monterey, Calif.: Brooks/Cole Pub. Co. 64-69.

Kazanas, H. C., Baker, G. E., Miller, F.M., & Hannah, L. D. (1973) *The meaning and value of work.* Columbus, Ohio: The National Center for Vocational and Technical Education.

King, F. P. (1978) The future of private and public employee pensions. In H. B. Herzon (Ed.). *Aging and income.* New York: Human Services Press. 195-219.

Kreps, J. M., Spengler, J. J., Herren, R. S., Clark, R. L., & Maddox, G. L. (1977) *Economics of a stationary population: Implications for older Americans.* Washington, D.C.: U.S. Government Printing Office, (NSF/RA-770024).

Kubler-Ross, E. (1969) *On death and dying.* New York: The Macmillan Co.

Kurland, N. D. (1978) A national strategy for lifelong learning. *Phi Delta Kappan, 59,* 385-389.

Maddox, G. L. & Dellinger, D.C. (1978) Assessment of functional status in a program evaluation resource allocation model. *The annals of the American association of political and social science, 438,* 59-70.

Morrison, M. H. (1978) Flexible distribution of work, leisure, and education. In H. B. Herzog, (Ed.). *Aging and income.* New York: Human Services Press. 95-127.

Mowsesian, R. & Garcia, R. (1982) Personality correlates and daydreaming patterns among the elderly. Paper presented at the Southwest Psychological Association Meeting, Dallas, Texas, April, 1982.

Neugarten, B. L. (1974) Age groups in American society and the rise of the young-old. *The annals of the American academy of political and social science, 415,* 187-198.

Neugarten, B. L. (1974) Successful aging in 1970 and 1990. In E. Pfeiffer (Ed.) *Successful aging: A conference report.* Durham, North Carolina: Center for the Study of Aging and Human Development.

Neugarten, B. L. (1977) Personality and aging. In J. E. Birren & K. W. Schaie (Eds.). *Handbook of the psychology of aging.* New York: Van Nostrand Reinhold.

Neugarten, B. L., Havighurst, R. J., & Tobin, S. S. (1961) Measurement of life satisfaction. *Journal of gerontology, 16,* 134-143.

Neugarten, B. L., et al. (1964) *Personality in middle and late life.* New York: Atherton.

O'Toole, J. (1973) *Work in America.* Cambridge, Mass.: MIT Press.

O'Toole, J. (1977) *Work, learning and the American future.* San Francisco: Jossey-Bass.

Our future selves. (1977) Washington, D.C.: National Council on Aging, #77-1096.

Palmore, E. & Whittington, F. (1971) Trends in the relative status of the aged. *Social forces, 50,* 84-91.

Parnes, H. S. (1975) A conceptual framework for human resource policy: Implications for vocational education reserch and development. *Occasional paper no. 14.* Columbus, Ohio: The Center for Vocational Education. 1-5.

Parnes, H. S. (1980) Middle-aged and older men in the labor force. *Aging*, 313-314, Nov.-Dec. pp. 25-29.

Perlmutter, M. & Hall, E. (1985) *Adult development and aging.* New York: John Wiley & Sons.

Piven, F. F. & Cloward, R. A. (1971) *Regulating the poor: The functions of public welfare.* New York: Pantheon.

Poon, L. W. (Ed.) (1980) *Aging in the 1980s: Psychological issues.* Washington, D.C.: American Psychological Association.

Pratt, H. J. (1978) Symbolic politics and the White House Conference on Aging. *Society*, 15, 67-72.

Press, I. & McKool, Jr., M. (1972) Social status of the aged: Toward some valid cross-cultural generalizations. *Aging and human development*, 3, 297-306.

Project on the status and education of women. (1981) *Re-entry women: Relevant statistics.* Washington, D.C.: Association of American Colleges.

Public Law 89-73. (1965) *Older Americans act of 1965.* 91st Congress, H. R. 3709, July 14, 1965.

Public Law 91-69 (1969) *Older Americans act amendments of 1965.* 91st Congress, H. R. 11235, September 17, 1969.

Public Law 92-258 (1972) *Older Americans amendments of 1965.* 92nd Congress, S. 1153, March 22, 1972.

Public Law 93-29 (1973) *Older Americans comprehensive services amendments of 1973.* 93rd Congress, S. 50, May 3, 1973.

Public Law 95-256 (1978) *Age discrimination in employment act amendments of 1978.* 95th Congress, H. R. 5383, April 6, 1978.

Public Law 95-478 (1978) *Comprehensive older Americans act amendments of 1978.* 95th Congress, H. R. 12255, October 18, 1978.

Ragan, P. K. & Davis, W. J. (1978) The diversity of older voters. *Society*, 15, Whole No. 115.

Rodin, J. & Langer, E. (1980) Aging labels: The decline of control and the fall of self-esteem. *Journal of social issues*, 36, 12-29.

Rosow, I. (1974) *Socialization to old age.* Berkeley, Calif.: University of California Press.

Rukyser, L. (1981) Social security tax could bring "age war." *Austin-American Statesman*, January 11, 1981, p. C9.

Sarasan, S. B. (1977) *Work, aging, and social change.* New York: The Free Press.

Sheppard, H. L. (1976) Work and retirement. In R. Binstock & E. Shanas (Eds.). *Handbook of aging and the social sciences.* New York: Van Nostrand-Reinhold. 286-309.

Simmons, L. W. (1960) Aging in preindustrial societies. In C. Tibbitts (Ed.). *Handbook of social gerontology.* Chicago: University of Chicago Press.

Spengler, J. J. (1979) Stationary population changes in age structure: Implications for the economic security of the aged. In J. Kreps (Ed.). *Economics of a stationary population: Implications for older Americans.* Washington, D.C.: U.S. Government Printing Office. 11-40.

Stern, B. & Best, F. (1977) Cyclic life patterns. In D. W. Vermilye (Ed.). *Relating work and education.* San Francisco: Jossey-Bass. 250-267.

Streib, G. F. (1977) Changing roles in the later years. In R. A. Kalish (Ed.) *The later years: Social applications to gerontology.* Monterey, Calif.: Brooks/Cole Pub. Co. 69-77.

Tilgher, A. (1958) *HomoFaber: Work through the ages.* Translated by Dorothy C. Fisher. Chicago: Henry Regnery Co.

Toffler, A. (1970) *Future shock.* New York: Bantam Books.

Toffler, A. (1980) *The third wave.* New York: Bantam Books.

Toward a national policy on aging, Vol. I & Vol. II. (1971) Final Report. Washington, D.C.: 1971 White House Conference on Aging.

U.S. Bureau of the Census. (1975) *Statistical abstracts of the United States: 1975,* (96th ed.). Washington, D.C.: U.S. Government Printing Office.

Wantz, M. S. & Gay, J. E. (1980) *The aging process: A health perspective.* Cambridge, Mass.: Winthrop Pub., Inc.

Ward, R. A. (1979) *The aging experience.* New York: J. B. Lippincott Co.

Wiebe, R. H. (1967) *The search for order: 1877-1920.* New York: Hill & Wang.

Wirtz, W. (1975) *The boundless resource.* Washington, D.C.: The New Republic Book Co., Inc.

Wolfgang, M. E. (1978) Preface. *The annals of the American academy of political and social science, 438,* vii.

Wrenn, C. G. (1964) Human values and work in American life. In H. Borow (Ed.). *Man in a world at work.* Boston: Houghton Mifflin Co. 24-44.

Yankelovich, D. (1974) The meaning of work. In J. M. Rosow (Ed.) *The worker and the job.* Englewood Cliffs, N.J.: Prentice-Hall, Inc. 19-47.

Yankelovich, D. (1979) Work, values, and the new breed. In C. Kerr & J. M. Rosow (Eds.). *Work in America: The decade ahead.* New York: Van Nostrand Reinhold Co. 3-26.

Youry, M. (1975) GULHEMP: What workers can do. *Manpower, 7,* 4-9.

Yuknovage, P. (1980) Senior volunteers bring experience and expertise to action. *Aging, 307-308.* 12-15.

INDEX